SUNSHINE and DANIEL

Seeking Grace in Lost Motherhood

KIM PARIS UPSHAW

Spirit and Grace Publishing
christian literature to grow

SUNSHINE and DANIEL
Seeking Grace in Lost Motherhood

Published by Spirit and Grace Publishing
Elkins Park, PA 19027
Copyright ©2017 Kim Paris Upshaw

First Printing, 2018

Library of Congress Control Number: 2017912404
ISBN 978-0-9992683-0-8 (paperback)
ISBN 978-0-9992683-1-5 (ebook)

Internet addresses (websites, blogs, etc.) referenced in this book are offered as a resource to you. They are not intended in any way to be or imply an endorsement on the part of the publisher, nor do we vouch for their content.

All scripture quotations, unless otherwise noted, are taken from the Holy Bible, King James Version, KJV. Public Domain.

Scripture quotations marked (NIV) are taken from the Holy Bible, New International Version®, NIV®. Copyright © 1973, 1978, 1984, 2011 by Biblica, Inc.™ Used by permission of Zondervan. All rights reserved worldwide. www.zondervan.com. The "NIV" and "New International Version" are trademarks registered in the United States Patent and Trademark Officer by Biblica, Inc.™

Scripture quotations marked (NLT) are taken from the Holy Bible, New Living Translation, copyright © 1996, 2004, 2007 by Tyndale House Foundation. Used by permission of Tyndale House Publishers, Inc., Carol Stream, Illinois 60188. All rights reserved.

Scripture quotations marked (GNT) are from the Good News Translation in Today's English Version- Second Edition Copyright © 1992 by American Bible Society. Used by Permission.

Scripture quotations taken from the Amplified® Bible (AMP), Copyright © 2015 by The Lockman Foundation Used by permission. www.Lockman.org.

Scriptures marked (TLB) are taken from the THE LIVING BIBLE (TLB): Scripture taken from THE LIVING BIBLE Copyright © 1971. Used by permission of Tyndale House Publishers, Inc., Carol Stream, Illinois 60188. All rights reserved.

Scripture quotations marked WEB, are taken from the Holy Bible, World English Bible. Public Domain.

Scripture taken from the New King James Version®. Copyright © 1982 by Thomas Nelson. Used by permission. All rights reserved.

This book includes a compilation of personal stories. It reflects various experiences over time. Events, locales and conversations are noted from the author's memory and notes from those interviewed. While the stories are true, some places, names, occupations and other identifying characteristics have been changed or recreated to maintain the privacy of those involved.

Contents

Pursuing Grace and Hope

*"At one time we too were foolish, disobedient, deceived and
enslaved by all kinds of passions and pleasures. We lived
in malice and envy, being hated and hating one another.
But when the kindness and love of God our Savior
appeared, he saved us, not because of righteous things we
had done, but because of his mercy. He saved us through
the washing of rebirth and renewal by the Holy Spirit,
whom he poured out on us generously through Jesus Christ
our Savior, so that, having been justified by his grace, we
might become heirs having the hope of eternal life."*
(Titus 3:3-7 NIV)

Nurturing. Sacrificing. Tending. Mending. Rearing. Encouraging.
Loving. That's innately a mother. It's what she does. It's who she is.

Unless her child dies.

In this book, I share the story of the loss of my two children. I
lament my heartache, deep sorrow, and confusion. At my lowest point,
not knowing where else to turn, I sought refuge and found myself
searching the pages of the Bible.

To my surprise, I read my own story there. I heard my sisters of
old wail my contemporary tears. They understood me. Their lives

were lived for me. They breathed, moved, and felt just like me. They spoke to me and in the sharing of their stories, they soothed me. Only, however, when I allowed them to do so.

As I became confident enough to talk about my ordeal and healing, the women I live with, worship with, and work with shared their stories of lost motherhood with me. Revealing to me that many sisters living today need to know they are not alone. Their experiences of loss are not strange or abnormal. It became clear that they too needed to be enlightened by understanding that as far back as the beginning of time, women have suffered, survived, and thrived after child loss.

I wanted to tell all my sisters who have experienced this sorrow that I've learned that loss means gain in God's economy. By His grace, what may seem to be gone forever has actually fueled the will and strength within me to live and love again. Though life has been lost and hope challenged, new life, renewed hope, and limitless love is available through the grace given by Jesus Christ, our Lord.

And I have found something wonderful lives on—motherhood.

Before We Begin

Admittedly, Bible stories can be difficult to comprehend. It's why so many of us don't read them or even believe they are relevant today. I ask you to let go of those thoughts. Allow the stories of both the modern and ancient women shared in the pages of this book to comfort and liberate you from hurt, shame, despair, and sadness. Get lost in their stories. Place yourself in your sisters' shoes. Feel with her. Cry when she cries. Beg when she begs. Hurt when she hurts. Most importantly, receive forgiveness when she is forgiven. Have faith when she is faithful. Celebrate when she experiences joy.

Become the mother of humanity who lost her son; the young woman whose health blocked her motherhood; the woman caught in the humiliation of her choices; the teenager disgraced in her youth; the working woman whose greatest desire slipped through her fingers; and the woman whose motherhood was restored after she watched her child's life slip away. Reflect on how her story helps you.

Why?

Because she is you.

You may say, "I lost joy years ago. If I ever had it, I don't know if it can ever return. My child should have lived. I cannot thrive and love again. Besides, love is fleeting and cannot be attained."

My sister, abandon those notions. Grace is available if you know where to seek it. Hope is accessible. Joy is around the corner. Are you willing to reach out for it? Come on this journey with me. Let your sisters of old, today, and me, become your beacons of light and your guides out of the den of despair and into the light of love.

This book is a culmination of more than twenty years of grace seeking and confidence building in my journey toward full obedience to God's call to tell my story. By exposing the details of my life, I hope my testimony will help the countless women who have felt the despair of child loss due to abortion, termination, miscarriage, premature labor, stillbirth, medical error, homicide, and illness with little empathy or lasting sympathy. I pray my outpouring of compassion will sustain and offer hope to all whose plans and dreams for motherhood will never be realized.

The mental, emotional, and psychological tricks the Evil One launches at us is real. I pray you will find the courage to believe you are as strong as your sisters who "defeated him [the Evil One] by the blood of the Lamb and by their testimony. And they did not love their lives so much that they were afraid to die" (Revelation 12:11 NLT).

The sisters whose testimonies you encounter in the pages of this book dared to live even though death loomed around them. Are you willing to live fully right now? As you read though the following chapters, a contemporary woman and a biblical woman will meet you in your zone of need. At the end of every chapter, reflection questions are posed to guide your journey of application and growth. I ask you to take this time seriously and consider the questions and your responses slowly. Resist the urge to move on to the next chapter without a time of mindful deliberation.

Sometimes, the journey will be emotionally difficult, but it is valuable. Pray to God for help. Pray out loud making the words your own, adding your own words. Believe that God hears you, because He wants to bless you, His daughter.

I would be remiss if I did not mention how you can become a child of God if you are not already in relationship with God through Jesus Christ.

You are God's child if you accept His Son, Jesus Christ, as Lord and Savior of your life. It might sound cheesy to say, but it is true. Just as there is a process to becoming a child of an earthly parent, there is a process to become a child of the Heavenly Father. The process is simple: First, admit you are a sinner. You have tried to live a good life, but your good is just not good enough. You are not alone. No one is good enough. Only Jesus Christ, the man who lived and never sinned is. Therefore, secondly, believe that Jesus Christ is the Son of God who left heaven to come to earth to become the sacrifice for your missing the mark. Jesus died a painful death on the cross. He was buried in a tomb and three days later, He rose with power over sin, the grave, and death. Finally, confess with the words of your mouth that Jesus Christ is Lord and your Savior. Tell someone that you took these steps— that you believe in Jesus Christ, that you know He died for you, and that you prayed that God would accept you as His child and save you. Find a church that believes in the Bible and salvation through Jesus Christ, so God may give you more and more grace and peace as you grow in your knowledge of God and Jesus our Lord.

Congratulations! You are a child of God. The promises in the Bible are available to you.

Acknowledgements

To my children, Sunshine and Daniel: I will never forget. You are my constant bright lights! And to my Lord and Savior Jesus Christ: I am desperate for You. Your grace is all I need!

1
..

Seeking Grace in Loss

"And God is able to make all grace abound toward you,
that you, always having all sufficiency in all things, may
have an abundance for every good work."
(2 Corinthians 9:8 NKJV)

The two lines on the strip of the home pregnancy test confirm what I suspect. I'm pregnant. My tears are filled with fear, confusion and the worry that I can never care for my baby and myself.

In the 1980s, at eighteen-years old, naive, and pregnant, my life takes a drastic change. As a little girl, I dreamed of motherhood, of course, but not this soon.

Weeks later, I terminate the pregnancy. I don't speak about the abortion publicly. A lady doesn't talk about this sort of thing, you know. I hurt in silence, harboring the turmoil of my decision in my mind like an unwanted fugitive. Socially, I can't grieve the end of my child's life or consider the abortion a form of *child loss*. Though I desperately need the comfort and support of friends and community, I hide my pain. It's better to pretend that my life is all right.

Abortion is legal, but controversial. With the candidacy of Geraldine Ferraro, the first woman nominated for Vice President of the United States, the issue of abortion reaches a national high.[1] Conservatives and Catholics dispute the morality of abortion against the pro-choice stance of the first female candidate. None of them appreciate or accept the long-term emotional effects of abortion on the mother. Therefore, I assume the role that society assigns to me—a disgraced young woman who committed a murderous act.

Almost twenty years later, I have another chance at motherhood. Though not married, I am excited for the opportunity to have another child growing in my womb and to give birth. Just months after the confirmation of my pregnancy, despite bed rest, diagnostic testing, innovative preventative procedures, hospitalization, and a lot of prayer, my body goes into premature labor. Delivery proceeds. My son dies of a preterm birth a few hours later.

As if two lost children are not enough, a couple years later, I'm advised that I'll never bare another child. The biblically correct term for my status is *barren*. I don't know which hurt more, the death of my two children or the death of my dream to become a mother. All I know is the residue of agony lingers.

I have never told the full story of these life changing events. As the daughter of upstanding, God-fearing parents, long-felt embarrassment about my youth-inspired first pregnancy would not allow it. Later, as a self-sufficient adult, intermediate-level Christian and leader in my church, my second failed pregnancy left me dispirited. In combination, the evolution of my pregnancies was simultaneously exciting, psychologically draining, intellectually confusing, yet ultimately depressing. On one hand, there was the pregnancy I'd been prohibited from mourning, and the other I could more openly grieve. There's the lost child that should not be spoken of, while the loss of the other should be quietly endured. One loss to be considered immoral, and the other sadly unfortunate.

In my heart, I've been a mother for only twenty-eight weeks of my entire life. The twinge of new life grew inside me along with the common expectation of being inadequate and undeserving of such tremendous gifts. The hope of a full future, including first steps, bike rides, kindergarten classes, graduations, weddings, and grandchildren twice flashed before my eyes. Happy thoughts filled my core instantaneously. Just as quickly, the reality of not being blessed to feed, change, or burp my children destroyed my remaining dreams of motherhood. Learning I would not see two lines on the strip again obliterated all hope. The extremes of joy and pain are a contradiction few people understand, and even fewer want to.

If you understand what's been described, then it's likely that you and I have something in common. You might have experienced loss through means other than abortion or premature labor. No matter the source, this most love-destroying loss is devastating. There's no way to describe all of the feelings a mother experiences at the loss of her child. Yet my story, our story, is not new, unique, or an isolated occurrence. More women than you know have lost their chance to be that child's mother. In fact, lost motherhood is timeless.

Our Loss Is Widespread

After joining an abortion recovery meeting, I stay behind one evening to speak with the facilitator. She shares that she's encouraged that brave women attended the meeting. This strikes me as odd since only three or four women participated. She says it's great to have multiple women willing to break through the shame of their decisions. She continues to teach me about grace and Christian love.

"It's when you offer a safe place that people come. But they won't know it's safe if you don't offer and let them find you," she instructs.

Prudent words. It makes me wish I'd kept making myself available years earlier when I offered a mothers healing meeting. A friend had opened her Christian counseling offices for the meeting in which she would coach me in counseling with mothers like me. No one joined our recovery mission. We eventually scrapped the idea. In my heart, I knew God wanted me to complete this mission. How to do it was not so clear.

Knowing how hard it is to step forward to talk about lost motherhood is a high hurdle for such a ministry to clear. Mothers like me are reluctant to share their stories, because we either feel like a failure, a sinner, or are so miserable that we don't want to participate in a group with other women. After all, we think none of those women will understand our story. We think our individual story is the worst of all. It's different than other stories. It's embarrassing. It's not something that a group of women can help with.

But, it is exactly what we need!

We need to hear the stories of other women who have been through what we are going through. We need to know we are not strange or evil. There are women who identify with our experiences, and with whom we can find encouragement. They are our sisters in the struggle with lost motherhood.

We're More Alike Than Different

The biggest lie that the enemy tells us is that we are different. It's generally believed that a woman who suffered a miscarriage cannot counsel a woman whose child was murdered. I've personally been told that women who've experienced stillbirth don't want to talk about child loss with women who've aborted their children, because their losses are not the same. It's a fake distinction within our ranks. It causes us to turn away from each other when what we need is to turn toward each other. The thing we have in common, lost motherhood, is the tie that must bind us together to encourage one another and build each other up.

Think about it this way. Have you ever been in the presence of a group of new mothers? Bear with me for a moment. I'm going somewhere with this example. New mothers talk about everything from the age of their children in months, how to cure colic, the best diapers to use, whether they breastfeed or not, when they plan to return to work, to what new thing their baby did this week. Do you know they even talk about their birth experiences? One mother describes her difficult cesarean section, another her prolonged labor and epidural, still another her smooth natural childbirth with no drugs at all. Despite their different birth experiences and means of giving birth, do you know what they inevitably do? They always return to a discussion about what they have in common—motherhood. They share tips, tricks, cool websites, phone numbers, and stories. There are always stories. When one mother thinks her experience is strange, another new mom will join in and share her odd story. In this way, they develop a rapport that builds up a resolve in each of them to be the best mother they can be. It's a wonderful community of sisterhood.

We can learn a lot from them.

My sister, you see, if motherhood binds their sisterhood, despite their different means of childbirth, why can't lost motherhood bind our sisterhood, despite our different means of child loss?

One of the strongest mothers I met while writing this book is a mother who lost her adopted child. Her openness and strong faith continues to inspire me to never again close the doors of my ministry. She inspired me to turn back to a biblical sister I had resented. My own bias turned my affections away from this ancient mother because she had given her child away. I had no compassion for her. How foolish of me! This woman obeyed God and lost her child. Who was I to judge her? It could not have been easy for her to lose her child that way. No easier than my losses have been for me.

Don't let this happen to you.

Too many of us permit the hurt of the loss of our motherhood cloud our vision of the hope contained in the future. We let our pain convince us that we will be rejected by other women. We decline the opportunity to allow the stories of other women, our sisters, propel us into becoming all we were created to be. We must stop this! Not just because it is isolating, but because it is limiting.

Praise and Comfort

"All praise to God, the Father of our Lord Jesus Christ. God is our merciful Father and the source of all comfort. He comforts us in all our troubles so that we can comfort others. When they are troubled, we will be able to give them the same comfort God has given us." (2 Corinthians 1:3-4 NLT)

The reason I wrote this book is to do my part in offering you comfort. I cannot do it alone. My sisters are here to help me. Some of them lived thousands of years ago. Some live today. Some travelled by foot. Some drive cars and fly in airplanes. Some wore fig leaves and animal skins, others wear the finest designer silks and cashmere. Our differences span time, nations, and language, but what remains is profoundly ours. We are women. Our femininity exposes us to the horrors of life that only we understand. Only we can speak to. Only we can help to conquer.

That's why we must listen to and learn from each other. Together, we have the ability to turn the most unbearable of female troubles into an opportunity for growth and love. The passage from pregnancy to *motherhood lost* is one that is best avoided. Let's be honest. None of us would have chosen this haunting loss for ourselves. We would make other choices if we could. Yet, what we've survived is teachable. What happened is valuable. How we've managed to get through it is admirable. The comfort that another sister will experience from the sharing of our stories is charitable. In the midst of all of this, we learn to give God praise!

The Gift of Motherhood

Let's get started on our excursion together by exploring the story of the first woman to live, conceive, give birth to, and lose a child. Her name is Eve. Yes, the one who talked to the serpent, ate a piece of fruit, gave it to her husband, and caused all hell to break loose.

Right, that Eve.

Did you realize that she is like us? Remarkable, isn't it? I never thought about her life that way before, but it is true. Though old as time, Eve's story is as compelling today as it was long ago. When I read it now, Eve prominently emerges as a woman who lost her child. A mother who wanted to make amends for her loss. A mother who felt the loss in indescribable ways. A mother whose heart hurt for her child.

Before we get to her loss, however, we have to understand Eve, the woman. We have a little glimpse into her character from Genesis 2.

Eve is the only woman who did not have a mother. Her existence originates from a man. Not her father, but her husband, Adam. For her, there are no examples of human female nursing or nurturing. Sure, the many animals that surround her care for their young, but as her husband learned, the animals are not a suitable substitute for human instruction and the soul-to-soul caring a mother supplies her daughter. Lest we feel too sorry for Eve, she does have something many of us don't.

Eve has Adam. A man who loves her, thinks the world of her, and marvels at the uniqueness of her womanhood. Eve sees herself though Adam's eyes. She observed his dream-filled gaze when he first saw her. The original "love at first sight" story. Eve heard Adam's awestruck proclamation of "you complete me" before "you complete me" was a Jerry Maguire[2] kind of scripted thing. He tells all the world that she's his woman. Listen to his words:

"At last!" the man exclaimed. "This one is bone from my bone, and flesh from my flesh! She will be called 'woman,' because she was taken from 'man'" (Genesis 2:23 NLT).

Adam cannot hold back his excitement about Eve. She's a looker! She is the one he's been waiting for all his life. He looks at her and says, "Animals, what animals?"

Good for you, Eve!

Of course, Adam has no competition for Eve's affections, but you get the point. Eve walks shamelessly in her natural nakedness under her man's watchful glee as he beholds her matchless beauty. With a man who is that into you, wouldn't you be inclined to walk around with your head up, shoulders back, and that ever so feminine sway, too? Not only is she the apple of his eye (pun intended), but she lives with him in unity and bliss. From his wonderment and support, Eve develops her own courage and curiosity.

And now, direct from central casting, slithers in the serpent for scene 1 of Genesis 3.

Feeling inspired and inquisitive, Eve speaks with the serpent. I wonder if any of the other animals regularly spoke with her and that's why she engages in a seemingly normal conversation with a serpent. We'll never know. What we do know is that this one conversation changes her life (and ours) forever. While Adam continues to gawk at naked Eve, she eyes the forbidden tree of the knowledge of good and evil. The keen serpent takes notice. Somehow, the slimy Evil One convinces giddy Eve to disregard God, and Adam for that matter, by eating the fruit of the tree. Of course, she generously offers some to Adam as he stands by, watching.

Upon eating the fruit, Eve begins to see what she hadn't before. Her nakedness now means something it hadn't before—shame. I imagine she looks down at her hips and thighs and knows they need extra leaves. Seriously though, Eve now knows she has sinned. She also knows that hereafter when God shows up, it might be a good time to be quiet and let Adam do some talking.

However, Eve cannot escape God's view nor His justice.

After she and Adam sin, God addresses them separately. God knows their individual hearts and their individual reasons for eating the fruit. While Eve ate out of curiosity and a desire to gain greater knowledge, it is God's knowledge of her humanity that's on display.

"Unto the woman he said, I will greatly multiply thy sorrow and thy conception; in sorrow thou shalt bring forth children, ... "
(Genesis 3:16)

When we read that, we immediately see the wrathful punishment of pain that is placed upon Eve. Call me crazy, but when I read that verse, I find God's words comforting and loving. Though Eve didn't yet know what sorrow and conception would mean for her, I know it all too well. At least, I know well what the sorrow of labor described in this verse has meant for me. Despite that, I see more of what God did not say to Eve, than what He did say.

What do I mean? Well, God did not say Eve would not bear children. In fact, this is the first mention of human childbirth in the Bible. Before this, in the bliss of the Garden of Eden, Eve did not bear children. But in this passage, God gave Eve the gift of children. Think about that for a minute. In response to her sin, God first gives Eve a gift—the ability to conceive and bear children. Is that not just like God? Even in delivering His punishment, He is gracious, giving what we do not deserve. Yet, because God is holy, He must address Eve's sin. There's still a penalty for her sin. The penalty given to Eve, however, is that the marvel of conception and childbirth would include hardship and toil, or work.

Hmm. Don't we know it!

A Child is Born and Lost

"And Adam knew Eve his wife; and she conceived, and bare Cain, and said, I have gotten a man from the LORD. And she again bare his brother Abel. And Abel was a keeper of sheep, but Cain was a tiller of the ground." (Genesis 4:1-2)

Isn't it fascinating that it's not until after sin and judgment that Eve and Adam consummate their relationship? That is what it means when the Bible says that "Adam knew Eve." It tells us that unity between Eve and Adam occurred before they were sexually active. That's an order we should always remember. The other order we should remember is that Eve conceived after being known by the man with whom she has sex. Before sex with her, the man established an angelic appreciation for Eve's special complimentary purpose in his life. This is the proper order of things.

Unfortunately, I did not follow this order. None of it. In my life, sex with my children's fathers occurred before unity. Neither man's comprehension of me created in him that irresistible need to make me his wife for life. Neither of them had yet come to appreciate my uniqueness, specialness, suitability, or what makes me essentially Kim. It's acceptable they did not see me that way. Not every man should. And it's not really their fault that I fell into the improper order of things. Like Eve, a thirst for knowledge of the forbidden got the best of me. Let's see how that manifests in Eve's life.

Eve's response to the birth of Cain rings true for every mother. When a child is born, a mother is amazed that this wonder came from her body. Months of growth inside her builds into the tremendous anticipation of meeting this little miracle. And the mother exclaims as Eve, "Look at what God let me do! We created a child."

Can't you just hear her words, her glee, her gratefulness, and her exhaustion? Whether she felt far from God before this or not, at the birthing moment, for Eve and mothers since, it is clear that only God could have brought this about.

Despite her recent epic failure, Eve knows that this thing, this birth, is monumental. She names the small person whose anatomy looks like his father's, Cain, or *Qayin* in the Hebrew.[3] This is the child that is her own possession. Her own little man. The one that came from God. And what do you know, soon after she has another little man. This one is Abel, or *Hebel*.[4] This child takes her breath away. He is a double portion of the miracle of God. Eve has it all—two boys and a husband who loves her. She's the only woman in the house. The object of their protection. For Eve, it seems that life with knowledge is not so bad after all.

Or maybe it is.

"And Cain talked with Abel his brother: and it came to pass, when they were in the field, that Cain rose up against Abel his brother, and slew him." (Genesis 4:8)

Well, knowledge was good for Eve. Until now.

Her oldest child, Cain kills his younger brother, Abel. How tragic is that? Imagine Eve's reaction. Her breath is literally sucked from her.

Not only does she lose a son, but his death is at the hands of his own brother. That has to be unbearable! The boys she bore in multiplied sorrow are now both destroyed.

Her home is not the same without Abel. This son, who gave his best to God would indubitably have given gratefully to his mother, too.

Cain, however, remains. Her thoughts concerning Cain are a painful mixture of sadness with hatred. She understands the forgiveness she's received from God, but can she forgive this son for killing her other son? Does this murder destroy the bond of a mother with her first offspring? Or does this tenuous relationship between Eve and her Cain establish the unbreakable bond of mother to child that not even death can't erase?

She must have asked under her breath, "Why did my son have to die?" It's the question every mother like us asks at some point and on some level.

Only God knows the answer to Eve's *why question* and my *why question*. In my case, could it be because of my disobedience to the God-fearing standards and order my parents taught me? Perhaps that's the reason, but this is not an unyielding principle. The logic that sin always leads to the loss of a child falls apart when I consider my friends who had healthy babies born out of wedlock or even from one-night stands. And what does this thinking say to the woman who conceived as a result of being raped? On the other hand, what does this point of view say to the wife whose child was stillborn?

The point of the account of Eve's loss is not to communicate that every single act of sin will result in the immediate or direct death of a child. Instead, it is to help us understand that child loss has been a part of the female experience since the beginning of time. It teaches us that though our sinful nature deserves repayment with justifiable death, it moreover carries with it the occasion for God's amazing grace.

Yes, we have a sense that God will take care of us. Though we cannot really see how this will happen, we know that it is possible to get through this, but who will take care of the lost child?

> *"And he said, What hast thou done? the voice of thy brother's blood crieth unto me from the ground." (Genesis 4:10)*

God speaks to this very point. Despite Cain's best efforts to conceal what he's done, Abel's death is too distinct to be cast off as a trite event. It demands the attention of Abel's *heavenly* Father—God.

Speaking to Cain, God communicates the deeply personal affect Abel's murder has on Him. Though He allows Abel's death, God feels it so specifically that the shed blood of innocent Abel takes on the power of human attributes. And not just any attribute. The evidence of Abel's death speaks and cries to the ever-attentive God of compassion. There is only one reason for this—Abel's death matters to God.

Psalm 116:15 confirms this when it instructs us that, "Precious in the sight of the Lord is the death of his faithful servants" (NIV). In the short span of his life, Abel proved to be a faithful servant of God.

Yet this is little comfort to you if your child died in utero or while still an infant or toddler. There was no time for your child to faithfully serve God. How can you or I ever move past the emptiness left by our loss and be sure that our child's death is precious to God? For just one moment, I need to turn to another biblical woman who lost her child.

Her name is Bathsheba. She's a woman who committed adultery with a married man and became pregnant. This man then murdered Bathsheba's husband and took her as his own, additional wife. Though her thoughts about all of this are not recorded, I think it's safe to conclude that Bathsheba anticipated the birth of her child.

Oh, yeah. I forgot to mention that the father of her child, the adulterer and murderer, was the king of Israel, King David, and he's a big deal.

At this point in time, Bathsheba is living in David's palace. She knows her unborn child will have it all, including the kingdom one day. But God has another plan. In God's plan, the baby is born terminally ill. When the infant dies, it's King David who instructs us by saying, "But why should I fast when he is dead? Can I bring him back again? I will go to him one day, but he cannot return to me" (2 Samuel 12:23 NLT).

Sure, these are a man's words. Words that prove that men don't really get it, do they? Well, actually, this man does. He's brutally honest, as men can be at the most inopportune times. Certainly, this is not at the time when Bathsheba would have wanted to hear David's words, but he clearly states the obvious—the child will not come back. While any mother wants to bring the child back, love them, and hold them forever in her arms, she understands that she cannot. But the logic of a grieving mother's deep desire for her lost child defies the real possibility of that child's return.

Beyond the evident fact of death, David understands God's heart for his child. He cognizes that God immediately retrieved this young child and brought the child into heaven with Him. David thus declares the hope of being reunited with his child one day when David goes to where the child now resides, in the bosom of God. We have to assume, by her stunning silence, that Bathsheba shares her husband's hope.

Certainly, Bathsheba's child is not afforded this privilege alone. Your child and my children are there, too. And, if you are a child of God through belief in His Son, Jesus Christ, you will be reunited with your child in heaven one day, too.

Before we get to heaven, there is still hope.

Another Chance

"And Adam knew his wife again; and she bare a son, and called his name Seth: For God, said she, hath appointed me another seed instead of Abel, whom Cain slew."
(Genesis 4:25)

Abel's Avenger, God, becomes Eve's Comforter. Her words in this verse confirm that she has suffered since Abel died. Adam is again silent, but I suspect his love for Eve remains strong. He holds her and comforts her as much as he can. But he cannot speak to her loss. Not the way God does. Despite Eve's infectious sin that spread from her to her offspring, God gives her what her heart needs—another chance at motherhood. She does not squander the opportunity. She readily places the glory for this new motherhood where it belongs, in God alone. No longer does she believe that she helped God in the matter. No. Now she sees that she is merely a vessel through which God's gracious gift of life is delivered. She is likewise a vessel through which His plan is carried out.

Through Abel's death and the later birth of Seth, Eve finally exercises the wisdom she so wanted since the beginning. Eve is not so naive as to think that Seth will take away her grief for Abel. Seth is not Abel reincarnated. He does not have the same personality, skills, and innate gifts that Abel possessed. What Seth provides, however is another chance for Eve to exercise the motherhood that still exists in her. He is her underserved child. And that's not all. The Bible tells us that, "[a]fter Seth was born, Adam lived 800 years and had other sons and daughters" (Genesis 5:4 NIV). I presume Adam had these children through Eve.

All Grace Abounds Toward You

I can hear some of you wanting to throw this book at me right now. You lost your child and you did not have another child.

Neither did I. Yet Eve is still my example. Like with her, God has given me another chance to exercise my mothering instincts. My Seth is not a child from my own body, yet my Seth is as much another opportunity as any child I could have birthed. I'll tell you more about my Seth and his siblings later. Just know that Seth comes to us in many ways. You only need to look for who the Lord assigns to your life for your care and rearing. Seth may be in your life for a season or a lifetime. Seth may even be an adult when he comes to you. What is remarkable about this Seth is that he comes at a time when you need him (or her) most. When the weight of your despair for your Abel seems all consuming, Seth is evidence of God's love for you. God is not only near to your Abel, He is near to you, too. He loves you.

Feeling loss is a normal process of grief. And while that loss will always be a part of you, the Holy Spirit promises to fill us with His everlasting love and grace.

Let's reflect on that now.

Reflection

Think about your lost child or the loss of a child that impacts you.

Delineate between feeling the loss and feeling lost. Feel those feelings you hide and never talk about. Write down your emotions without fear or shame.

Prayer

Dear Lord,

You are God. You are sovereign and all-knowing. There is nothing that happens in my life without Your knowledge. I do not understand why You would allow this loss. A child is precious. A child is hope. My hope was lost with the death of my child. I want to believe that there is purpose in my loss, but I cannot find it. I am seeking You. Help me to accept this. Hear me, please. As I relive my pain and feel what I have avoided for days, weeks, months, and years, step in this with me. Be what I cannot be to myself, God. You promised You would never leave me nor forsake me, so right now, I am begging You to be here with me. Be in this with me. Help me break through my sadness and fear. God, pull me out of it all so that I can love a child— mine or someone else's child—again.

I choose to believe that You can do this God. Please do not let me down.

In the name of Jesus, Amen.

2
...

Seeking Grace in Brokenness

*"Now our Lord Jesus Christ himself, and God, even our
Father, which hath loved us, and hath given us everlasting
consolation and good hope through grace, comfort your
hearts, and stablish you in every good word and work."*
(2 Thessalonians 2:16-17)

Plans May Fail

Nancy is a vibrant woman who can't slow down. Everything she does she does with ease and to perfection. On her job, she is known as a go-getter and a rising star. She is the youngest junior partner of the start-up high tech firm that specializes in cutting-edge ransomware detection software. As the only woman in management, she doesn't let the men use their gender to slow her down. No, Nancy is strong and gregarious. Navigating the board room is as easy for her as patching a virus vulnerable server. From one moment to the next, her energy level never slows. Most of her co-workers wonder how she does it.

To Nancy, her job is no big deal. Sure, she loves it and she's grateful she has such a promising career, but it's only a means to an end. She works hard because she can, but she plans to slow down one day. Her ideal life is building homes for the indigenous people of Taos, in the remote mountains of New Mexico. Since childhood, she and her family travelled on missions trips throughout the world. Her father's passion to bring the Word of God to people living in mostly untouched and unvisited parts of the world where the Bible has not yet been preached and whose native languages have not yet been written is now her passion. Nancy's father would take the family, consisting of his daughter, Nancy, plus his wife and two sons, wherever the non-denominational foreign missions foundation directed. Known as a missionary savant, and serving as the executive secretary of the foundation, Nancy's father has consulted, advised, and formed missions groups since he was fifteen years old. Nancy and her mother often joked that the Great Commission was her father's direct marching orders.

"You were born two millennia too late," her mother would say. "You should have walked with Jesus!" Nancy thinks her mother was right. Besides those dusty old sandals her dad insisted on wearing, his good old-fashioned desire to "go ye therefore into all the world" would take him and the family into some scary locations.

Thanks to his amenable demeanor that surpassed any cultural barrier, people gravitated towards her dad who was gifted to understand languages with no training. That ability to understand people made him a brother to everyone he met. Though most little girls want to be just like mom, Nancy wants to walk in her father's footsteps. The money she makes and saves from her job will fund the life she plans. A life of service with few encumbrances. A life that would make her dad proud.

It's Something Else

Nancy's been feeling a bit sluggish lately. She brushes it off as nothing much. She just turned thirty and figures old age is creeping in. She'll take another look at the energy drink she consumes for breakfast and give her morning routine a revamping. But, nothing that will include actually eating a meal at breakfast. That takes too long for on-the-go Nancy. Every minute of every day is scheduled for her for the next ten years.

That sluggishness isn't going away today. Nancy cannot imagine what's wrong with her. She's gotten a flu shot. She's had a physical. Her teeth are clean. Being sick is not an option for Nancy. She hasn't had even a cold in the past five years and she is not about to succumb to anything now. Since the office nurse is not in today, Nancy uses her lunch break to visit the urgent care down the street. As expected, they draw blood. She'll check back next week.

Three days after her visit, the phone rings. "Nancy, this is Dr. Schneider. I'd like to talk to you about your results. Can you come into my office today?"

Nancy rushes to finish the memo she's writing to her boss, proposing a new application for RanSomeOne (RSO), the software she created. If he approves this, Nancy will be eligible for her third Employee of the Month award this year. That will make her a shoo-in for Executive of the Year. The attached $10,000 bonus will be sufficient down-payment on the land she plans to buy and build in Taos. Everything in her life is going exactly as she's planned. Nancy is grateful.

"Thank you for coming in today, Nancy."

The office feels stale and cold. Her heart skips a beat. "What do the labs reveal? Am I going to die?" Nancy nervously laughs.

Dr. Schneider does not. "Nancy, your lab results are concerning. I noticed you checked that your father had heart disease. Do you know how his heart disease manifested in his health?"

"He had cardiomyopathy and died from it. Are you telling me I about to die, Dr. Schneider?"

"Now, calm down. Let's take first things first. Cardiomyopathy can be inherited.[1] Have you noticed feeling fatigued during exercise?"

"Yes." Nancy inhales deeply trying to calm her nerves.

"I want to send you to a specialist who will run more tests and treat you," Dr. Schneider replies. "There's some important steps to be taken here. The good news is that you've been healthy and you've taken good care of yourself. I have a good friend who is the top cardiologist in the region. His name is Dr. Harvey. Go to see him as soon as possible. I'll give him a call and see if he can get you in today."

Nancy sits at her desk not sure what just happened. Heart. Disease. Father. Death. The words keep repeating in her mind like that song you hate but you just can't get out of your head. She can't tell her mom the news. Not yet. She'll have to research this, again. It's been five years since the last time she thought about that disease. Yet the word flowed from her lips with ease when Dr. Schneider asked about her dad. Cardiomyopathy. The thought of it makes Nancy sick to her stomach. She wonders if this is why her stomach has felt queasy. In addition to the fatigue, the upset stomach and nausea that's been her companion for several days may now be explained. She's not sure why she didn't mention that to Dr. Schneider. She'll mention it to Dr. Harvey.

Later that day, Nancy enters yet another medical office where a nurse takes her vitals and blood. She wonders how much blood she has left after all the tests of the last few days. The cardiologist's office is state of the art. It's run like a well-oiled machine. Each station has its purpose. As Nancy is ushered into the red waiting room, the heart waiting room, she is immediately met by Dr. Harvey's nurse.

Nancy is not used to being taken off guard. This whole experience has her a bit on edge. So much so that she can't eat without wanting to vomit. Saltine crackers and an uncanny appetite for sardines reminds her of days on the mission fields with her dad. She wishes he were here right now. He'd know what to say. He'd know what to do. He'd know how to make her queasy stomach relax. Some creative concoction would sound disgusting but would work pronto. "Why can't I remember any of them now?"

Dr. Harvey enters the examination room. He's flipping through a file. "Well, Nancy, we have a couple of things to address."

She rubs her clammy hands together. "A couple?"

Dr. Harvey sits on a stool. "You have pretty advanced heart disease. I understand you are familiar with the term cardiomyopathy?"

"That's right. But what's the couple of things?"

"I'd say that cardiomyopathy is something we should talk about, isn't it?"

"Yes, but what else?"

"Why don't you let me be the doctor for a minute? I want to treat your heart disease. It seems it's been lurking for a while. I want to do more testing, but we may need to surgically correct your disease. It appears you have what is known as hypertrophic cardiomyopathy.[2] Right now your heart is enlarged. We believe you may have inherited this, but since you have been an accomplished athlete for much of your life, we are not entirely sure. What I am sure about is that we are glad we caught it now. You are very in tune with your body. That's good."

"Dr. Harvey. I hate to interrupt you, but you are scaring me. Am I going to die?" Nancy asks sternly.

"Well, no. I am not concerned about your life, because we can certainly correct the problematic left ventricle wall thickening with surgery. But I am more immediately concerned about the life of your baby."

"Excuse me? My who? What?" Nancy is incredulous.

"Your baby? Nancy, your child may not be able to handle the surgery. We need to perform some further testing."

"Is this some kind of joke? This is really not funny!" Nancy screams. She jumps off the exam table. "I'm leaving! You're a quack, sir! A quack!"

"Nancy, calm down. Please have a seat. I'm sorry. Let's start this discussion again. Please?" Dr. Harvey gently touches Nancy's arm. He guides her back to the table. She resists at first, but the queasiness in her stomach returns. She asks to sit in the chair instead.

"Listen, Nancy," Dr. Harvey starts, "this isn't easy. You have two serious health concerns we need to address. Your heart is not functioning as it should. We can repair it, but the repair will be complicated by the fact that you are pregnant. I suspect you did not know about the pregnancy. We'll need to bring in a cardiac obstetrician to guide your care. This is a lot to take in, I know. But I'm encouraged because in many women, the disease does not present itself until further into their pregnancy.[3] Fortunately for you, we are early enough into your pregnancy that we have some choices to make about continuing with the pregnancy or not."

"Choices about my pregnancy?" Nancy asks. "What exactly does that mean?"

"Okay, we're getting ahead of ourselves. We'll slow down and discuss this in real detail," replies Dr. Harvey.

Thank God Nancy's mom has been through this before. Unknown to Nancy, her mom lost Nancy's oldest sibling, a sister, early in her marriage to Nancy's dad. They never talked about it, but now, with Nancy's condition, her mother becomes an understanding tower of strength. Knowing exactly what to ask the doctors, Nancy is grateful that her mom never questions her about the pregnancy. There's little time for that now. Saving Nancy's life is their main concern. That's why Nancy's decision to terminate her pregnancy does not offend her pious mother. Abortion goes against everything they believe. It is immoral.

"Life begins at conception," is what her mom always says. "How a woman could ever kill her own baby just baffles me." Nancy keeps hearing her mother's words in her mind. She's heard them most of her life. Today, they apply to her. Today, those words sound insensitive. Today, she wonders what her mother is thinking as she sits in the clinic with her only living daughter, Nancy. Neither of them ever imagined they would be in this position. All of the advice they received in the three weeks leading to this day said that in order to save Nancy's life, the pregnancy would need to end. Nancy is morally, spiritually, biblically, and unequivocally opposed to abortion. It's is inconceivable. Even when the mother's life is in jeopardy.

Until now. There is no scripture she knows that makes abortion acceptable. Yet, this is her life. This is different. This is not like those other women.

Or is it?

"It's a good thing Daddy is not here for this." Nancy breaks the silence. Her mother looks up. Her eyes are red. She's been crying.

"Sweetheart, he would understand. He would want you to live. Do you remember the story I told you as a child? About Rachel when she gave birth to Benjamin?"

Nancy's heart warms. She needs to hear that story the way her mother, the Sunday School teacher, tells it. "Please remind me."

"Of course, sweetheart. You see, Rachel was loved by her husband, Jacob. She wanted desperately to give him another child. So, she became pregnant. While she was close to her due date, she travelled with her family from Bethel to Ephrath. Though she probably should not have made that journey, she went anyway because she was strong and determined. Just like you, my Nancy. Before they reach Ephrath, or Bethlehem, Rachel went into labor. Her labor was troublesome. Yet with her last breath, she passed her own life into the life of her child. And in childbirth, Rachel died.[4] You know, Nancy, I used to end that story telling you how brave Rachel was for giving her own life for her child. I told you she was like Christ, giving up her own life to save others. Today, my dear Nancy, I think we should see this story from God's perspective. Today, I see that sometimes, the child must die in order to save others. Today, you must live!"

With that, Nancy and her mother pray together. It's awkward at first. Nancy hasn't prayed with her mother since the last time she heard the Rachel story, when she was a teenager. At this moment, a mother's prayer is what she needs. Oddly, she prays, too. For her baby.

Prayer for the Unborn

"Can You hear me, God?" Nancy asks. "Knowing what is about to happen, will You hear my love for my baby? Don't You understand that I do not want this, God? How can You make me choose between my own life or my child's? This is unfair God. This is so unfair! Can You understand this choice? Can You feel what I am feeling? Losing my own child? Who will ever understand that I did not abort this baby, but I had to terminate this pregnancy to save my own life. There is a difference God. Right? There is a difference!"

Nancy's mother holds her tight as they sob together. Nancy feels her own mother's heart. It's beating so strongly. She wonders if her child can hear her heart and its struggle to pump blood through the still thickened ventricle wall. Her own child who has no idea what is about to happen to her or him. This child Nancy has no time to get to know.

"How could I have been pregnant for twenty-two weeks and not know? Some kind of mother I would be. I didn't even know my baby existed. Maybe terminating this pregnancy is better for you, little baby. I'm not fit to be your mother. You deserve better. You deserve to be loved. Go now to be with God, my sweet little baby," Nancy prays.

After the termination, Nancy doesn't return to work. She resigns her position and takes time to reassess her life. Her beliefs. Her purpose. She never tells her best friend, Tony, the baby's father, about what happened. She never tells anyone. Neither does her mother. Without making a pact, neither of them ever speaks of this moment again.

Thankfully, Nancy's open-heart surgery is a success. Her recovery takes the full eight weeks as anticipated. Dr. Harvey calls her a "stellar patient." She jokes with him, but her repaired heart is not happy. It's broken. Though she tried not to become attached to the baby she knew she would have to lose, she misses him, or her. She can't explain her feelings, because the conflict in her soul is consuming. What will settle her thoughts?

Nancy could remain in her brokenness. Wallowing. Sinking deeper into despair. She decides to pick up her Bible again. She won't read Genesis 35. She cannot bear to read about Rachel's bravery. Not when she did what she did. If there is really hope in the Bible, she wonders what God could possibly say to heal her crushingly broken spirit.

To her surprise, Nancy opens her old Bible to her favorite Psalm. She loves the reassurance is gives her to know that she is never outside of God's presence. Normally, she only meditates on Psalm 139:7, which tells her to slow down and stop running long enough to commune with God. But right now, this Psalm speaks to God's affection for her lost child.

The Hidden Opportunity

Pregnancy and child birth aren't always easy. Some of us come into it without knowing or understanding how our own health will affect the baby, or how the baby will affect our health. In too many cases, the choice between our lives and the life of our child is one we have to make. Frankly, that sucks. No mother should have to make that choice. But it happens more often than we talk or think about. Unless it has happened to you.

The truth is, sometimes our loss and brokenness results from hurtful events beyond our control.

Nothing that's happened is hidden from God.

That fact may be daunting, but in this case, it is comforting to know that the timing of your pregnancy is not a mistake. Neither is it or your illness punishment. They are simply the things that happen in this fallen world. Illness, sorrow, and death come. They happen to the good and the not so good. They happen to you and me. The reassuring, undeniable consolation is that there's purpose in everything God allows. He is intimately involved in the goings-on of our lives, including the creation that is planted and grows inside us. The tiny unformed body and soul of the would-be child that we've been honored to support is one not unknown to Him. As King David intimates in Psalm 139, no matter the circumstances of the clandestine formation of your baby, whether produced by positive or negative circumstance, or the horror of your child's untimely demise, God, the Great Overseer, watches over every step in the process. Not merely to observe with no intervention or care, but with a grace-filled hand that guides your little one and you.

It is curious that God wove you together with this child. He used you as the avenue in which the child would get to Him. How did He know that you could endure? Like the pieces to a jigsaw puzzle, He majestically touched your womb to bring that child to you. He knows you in a way you do not. He knows that you, as the mother of this child, the mother with this illness and condition, are the best advertisement of His unequalled power.

"Thine eyes did see my substance, yet being unperfect; and in thy book all my members were written, which in continuance were fashioned, when as yet there was none of them."
(Psalm 139:16)

My sister, you stand today as a testament to the grace that exists in the "unperfect."

There is an intimacy between God and the child of your womb that is even closer than the interweaving of your heart with your child. The child you did not hold is held. The child you did not feed is fed. Though your body couldn't keep and protect your child, God can!

At no time is your child away from God. Every part of your child is confirmed in God's book. What does that mean? Think back to when you were in school. You either read a book, wrote in a book, or both. The things written in your book were so significant that they were memorialized on those pages. The intent of the writing was to refer to them again, to prove that they happened, and that they mattered. This is the same here. Of course, God does not need to refer to a book because He does not forget. But, as a memorial, even God writes in His book for every life that is created. Mere conception makes a life significant enough for God to create a separate book in honor and memoriam of that particular life.

> *"How precious also are thy thoughts unto me, O God! how great is the sum of them! If I should count them, they are more in number than the sand: when I awake, I am still with thee. (Psalm 139:17-18)*

So, it is with your child. His or her materialization is meticulously specified in God's own notebook. Where the pages had been blank, His thoughts of your child are inscribed. Every bit of your child is precious to Him and noted. This child is not restricted to knowledge of his or her post-birth self. Though your child's days may have been few, God's thoughts of him or her are many. And they do not cease. They continue from the time in your womb to their forever time with God now.

Marvelously Covered

> *"For thou hast possessed my reins: thou hast covered me in my mother's womb." (Psalm 139:13)*

Here's where a bit of a Sunday School lesson is order as we move backward in this Psalm. If Nancy's mother could teach us she might start by reminding us about Cain. Remember when Cain was born that Eve said that she "acquired" a man from the Lord? That word for acquired is the same one that David uses here. When he states that God "possessed" him, he declares and confirms that his existence, from the beginning at conception in the womb of his mother was divinely directed. The Hebrew word used here, *qanah*, means originated,[5] but it also implies something more. It suggests a redemption of the conceived one. It tells us that from inception, every fetus is subject to God. He orders the child's steps even before their feet and legs are functionally formed. Through redemption God gains hold of the child and compensates for all that is to come in that child's life, including those things that are outside of the child's control, like the ending of their life in the womb. It is because even in the womb, God covers the child with His superseding custody. Before the formation of human thought or will, the child belongs to God.

Not only that, He possesses the child's "reins" or the very essence of who that child is, even before the child is recognizable to us. It is here, in the unshapen, burgeoning state of becoming identifiably human that God wraps the child, your child, my child, in His loving arms of protection and ultimate care.

As mothers, we tend to think our bodies are the conduit of everything that is life-sustaining for our babies. We are lured into believing we give life to our children. We beat ourselves up when our bodies are not able to stay healthy while still feed the growing, dependent child within us. But our bodies are only vessels.

In the truest reality, God is the sustainer of our children's lives. For the period of time our children rest in our wombs—whether days, weeks, or months—God is the One who borders the child inside of us. He alone determines the future for that child. Lest we believe the decisions we make about our bodies or our babies override God's plan, this verse puts it all back into proper perspective for us.

When I think about how God covers the child in the womb, I think about when I lay in my bed at night. I like to pull the covers up over my head as I rest in the warmth of the sheets. Feeling them gently touching my body from head to toe, I am cradled by the serenity of the fabric. On a good night, I get to dawdle under the covers for a full eight hours. I sleep and dream there. It's wonderful when I can get a full night's sleep. But I am not always afforded that luxury. Sometimes, sleep lasts only a few hours. Other times, I can only nap for twenty minutes. No matter the amount of time there, the covers serve their purpose of soothing me while I sleep.

God is that shelter for our babies. No matter the amount time the child lays in the womb, they are quieted there. It's such a wonderful blessing to be used in God's covering of my precious babies for their brief time within me. To think that God trusted me with that responsibility, if even for just a few weeks.

Well Made

"I will praise thee; for I am fearfully and wonderfully made: marvellous are thy works; and that my soul knoweth right well. (Psalm 139:14)

Would it seem crazy to praise God right now for your child? Yes, the child that you had to terminate. The child you lost.

Whenever this scripture is referenced, we tend to focus on our "made-ness" in terms of who we are right now. We focus on how we are thriving and surviving in our lives despite our circumstances or challenges. We recite it to encourage ourselves. We say it to others to remind them that their lives matter. But what if this is really the praise we, mothers of lost babies, should recite instead?

After all, David said this after he focused his mind on the remarkable nature of his relationship with God from inside his mother's womb. It is from that position that he praises God and grasps the fearful and wonderful nature of God's work of human creation. This is an inside the womb praise. It is an acknowledgement that God's work in conception is worthy of thanksgiving and cannot be ignored.

In many ways, it is beyond our understanding. That may be why this notion is hard to intellectualize and accept. We believe this is not God's will. A baby should not have to die to save their own mother's life. There is no purpose in that. Or so we rationalize. But God is not subject to our rationalizations. His ways are as much outside our intellectual parameters as is your understanding of the timing of the illness that led to this undesired result. Neither change the fact that your child is a miracle. Though we refuse to allow our minds to make that alright, deep in our souls, we know it's true. And that it is right.

*"My substance was not hid from thee, when I was made in
secret, and curiously wrought in the lowest parts of the earth."
(Psalm 139:15)*

We would do well to catch up our thoughts with the Lord's
thoughts concerning our children. We need to think of our children
as real and allow those thoughts to be prized in our spirits. Recalling
the wonderfulness of their existence is good for a mother's soul.

Good Hope Through Grace

It's how my friend Nancy refocuses herself. Grateful that God did
not allow her life to end like Rachel's in Genesis 35, Nancy lives a
heart-healthy lifestyle filled with meditation, exercise, and wise meal
choices. In honor to God, Nancy names the little girl she lost to her
heart condition. She gives her daughter a name that is reminiscent of
the splendor and hope represented in her short life. And Nancy now
follows her ministry calling, too. She moves to Taos where she serves
the town as the children's Bible teacher. Nancy's Beautiful Thoughts
Mission extends her parent's legacy by attending to all the children of
the village. As she starts each day, Nancy declares the words of Christ
in Matthew 19:14, "Let the little children come to me, and do not hinder them, for the kingdom of heaven belongs to such as these" (NIV).

Brokenness did not become her identity. Grace did.

Reflection

Are you ready to release the guilt you feel regarding of your decision to terminate your pregnancy?

In what ways has your loss uncovered God's grace in your life?

Can you write a poem or story of remembrance for your child?

Prayer

Dear Lord,

For years, I have been upset with myself and my body for making me choose between myself and my child. I've felt selfish and ashamed that I chose me. No one knows how disappointing it is that my child suffered. It's not what I wanted. I always thought I needed to be brave enough to have continued the pregnancy so that my child could live. But I see now that You love my baby and they are with You now. Lord, please let my baby know that I love them. I have not forgotten them. They are still my child and I am still their mother. Until I am able to be with them again, Lord, hold and love them as only You can.

In the name of Jesus, Amen.

3

...

Seeking Grace in Silence

"Therefore, since we have been justified through faith,
we have peace with God through our Lord Jesus Christ,
through whom we have gained access by faith into this
grace in which we now stand. And we boast in the hope
of the glory of God. Not only so, but we also glory in
our sufferings, because we know that suffering produces
perseverance; perseverance, character; and character, hope.
And hope does not put us to shame, because God's love has
been poured out into our hearts through the Holy Spirit,
who has been given to us."
(Romans 5:1-5 NIV)

When Naive Means Vulnerable

My life takes an expected turn in the mid-1980s. As many people my age, I embark on the beginning of my future with excitement and anticipation.

The opportunity to leave home and learn about myself in the world takes me farther than the 140-mile car ride indicates. It causes me to confront things never permitted at home. Things like my first away-from-home encounter with the young man who would become my first real boyfriend.

To call it an encounter is to give it more status than it actually deserves. That day, on an elevator, he notices me and vice versa. The people around notice us both. We are awkwardly introduced. Then we say nothing.

Bing!

The elevator chirps. The doors open. I run off, not sure which way to go. Of course, the ultimate embarrassment is I run the wrong way.

Though my preference is for that to be our last encounter, of course, it is not. Our paths cross again, and again. Soon, he begins to look for me—the girl on the elevator. In time, he does his homework and learns about me through our mutual acquaintances. Then, quite innocently he starts to woo me with presents like teddy bears, flowers, candy, gold bracelets, and rings. He sends cute messages. He writes notes. With X's and O's, he uses squiggly lines to highlight his signature and his name, Gary. I read that name once, twice and again. Gary. It's starting to sound nice.

Then, he asks me out. Me!

He tells our friends that he wants me to be his girl. Gary's girl. Wow!

Gary is charming. He's attentive. And, he likes me. Then he does, it. Just what our friends said he would do. He asks me to be his girl. I'm afraid to say, "yes" because being some guy's girl is sort of new to me. Especially when the guy is not some high school boy, but an adult man. This is a man who is interested in me. Despite my fear, I give in. I become Gary's girl.

Being his girl has its perks. Gary protects me. He introduces me to his friends and family. He makes his friends look out for me. He takes me places where I've never been. With him, people treat me like I'm important. But, being his girl also has its consequences. He keeps tabs on me. He follows me. His friends follow me.

And he pressures me to sleep with him. He wants to be my first. Fear seizes me. I'm not ready for that no matter what everyone else thinks about it. My friends and co-workers try to advise me. They all have experience with this sort of thing. They tell me to let him be my first. I don't want to do it but being a party-pooper for acting like a baby about it is no fun either. They all say it's not that big a deal. At my age, who's still a virgin? If they were me, they wouldn't hesitate to "do it" with Gary.

"He's the kind of guy you should want to do it with. He's going places, you know," they tell me. "You should get yourself in with him now. If you're smart, you'd do it. What are you saving it for anyway? Are all the girls old-school-prudes where you come from? Guys like Gary don't come along every day. Do you not know how many other girls would love to be in your shoes? Don't lose him by being a baby, Kim. Why not make him your first? Why not?"

More pressure.

After a while, their questions start to become my questions. "What am I waiting for? What do I have to lose?" says the voice in my head. I know I won't get pregnant because Gary told me he can't have children. Of course, the fact that he already has a little boy doesn't raise any concerns for me. He says his little namesake was a surprise and a one-time miracle. Naive and inexperienced, but curious and not wanting to be the last living virgin, I yield to his request agreeing to have sex with him.

After the first time, I wonder if this is what everyone's been telling me about. Although my friends said sex with him would be great, it's not. It makes me feel dirty. It's not enjoyable at all.

"Why isn't this as great as everyone said it would be?" I wonder. "Is something wrong with me?" It doesn't make me feel like a woman, but more like a little girl performing a woman's inconveniencies. I don't care to do again. But Gary's not persuaded to feel the same way.

Silence is Not Always Golden

One night, Gary asks me to come to his new apartment. He's so proud to have his own place. I'm happy for him and excited to see it. He picks me up and we drive to the other side of town. His apartment is small, but nice. Surprisingly, he has furniture. It's odd to see lamps, a couch and chairs, but I don't ask any questions. He takes me on the quick tour of the place. The last room he wants to show me is the bedroom. I'm reluctant, but I figure, why not see it anyway. It's obvious that the bed is too big for the room, but Gary's a pretty big guy. He needs a big bed. As I quickly turn to leave the bedroom to go back to the living room area, he stops me.

"Wait," he says.

He tries to kiss me, but I pull away near the dresser. It's also too big for the room. He turns to get something in his closet. This feels like my best chance to try to leave the bedroom again. This time, however, he grabs me from behind. He pushes me against the oversized dresser and shoves something against my temple. It starts to feel uncomfortable. Not sure what he's trying to do to me, my mind searches to imagine what is this thing against my head. Straining my eyes, I manage to look up into the dresser mirror. I see it. The silver barrel of a pistol he has rested against the side of my head.

"What are you doing?" I ask, as he lowers the gun to the dresser.

"Nothing. I was just playing with you."

"Playing? Don't play with me like that."

I'm not scared, yet. I've seen guns before. If he thinks this is going to make me cower to him he needs to do more than that to scare me. Nothing some boy does can scare me. But Gary's no boy.

"Get on the bed," his tone changes as he shoves me down.

"What are you doing? Let me go!" I demand, trying to move. His grip intensifies.

"No. Get undressed," he orders, picking up the gun.

"I don't want to. Stop it. And put that gun away."

"No. I'm not playing this time. Get undressed or I'll do it for you!"

He pushes me onto the bed, mounting me. The gun is now on the bed, next to my head where I can see it just out of the corner of my eyes. It's placed strategically where he can grab it. A wee bit out of my reach. He undresses me. Despite my attempt to resist, and my repeated efforts to convince him that if he does this he is going to get me pregnant, he ignores me. He then undresses himself while sitting on me.

I keep talking not sure what to say or why I keep mentioning getting pregnant. I never said that before. In fact, I never said anything before.

Unlike our sexual encounters in the past, this time, he doesn't speak either. This time he's angry. This time, he's not wearing a condom. And, of course, I'm not on the pill. That's another thing I never did before—think about needing contraception. After all, he can't have children, right? Yet, my mouth keeps saying, "I'm going to get pregnant. I'm going to get pregnant." He tells me to shut up. I stop talking.

Then, he rapes me.

That gun near my head reminds me of my two options: fight and die or endure and live. Words escape me as does the desire to fight. The latter becomes the choice. My thoughts go dark almost immediately. Shock, disbelief, and humiliation take over. My brain directs me to halt everything. "Go numb, feel nothing, don't allow your body to respond, then he will stop." I don't know it at the time, but I'm in the grips of "Rape Trauma Syndrome (RTS)," a condition first introduced in 1974 by psychiatrist Ann Wolbert Burgess and sociologist Lynda Lytle Holstrom, to describe the two-phase, life changing reaction to forcible rape.[1] In RTS, victims display distinctive acute and long-term reactions to the trauma of rape. I'm an unwittingly normal victim.

Like many sexual assault victims, my demeanor is calm and seemingly unaffected by the events of this evening. Thoughts of kicking and screaming never enter my mind. Instead, I'm involuntarily immobile. Researcher and Harvard Medical School psychology instructor, Dr. James W. Hopper, PhD, calls this "toxic immobility" whereby my "body is literally paralyzed by fear - [making me] unable to move, speak, or cry out."[2] It's why I don't call the police, or tell anyone about what happened at Gary's apartment.

In the 1980s this kind of sexual assault, known as "date rape" or "acquaintance rape"[3] is not a new concept, but it is not yet a well-recognized thing either. A girl who claims to be raped by the boyfriend with whom she is sexually active is only covering up her fast and loose deportment. If he forces her into sexual activity, it's not his immoral behavior that's viewed as problematic. It's her promiscuity that's ridiculed. She should expect this result. She's only getting what she's been asking for. This societal attitude is the reason why no one ever learns about my visit to Gary's apartment that night. Only my internal condemnation haunts me. That's enough. Visiting his apartment, expecting he wouldn't want to have sex is silly immaturity. It's all my fault. It has to be. Right?

This Can't Be Happening

Weeks later, nausea propels me out of bed into the bathroom. After throwing up, I conclude it must have been something I ate. No one learns about this either. The next day, the same thing happens. This continues for days until I realize that my faithful "Aunt Flow" hasn't visited this month. She's never late. It concerns me so much that I finally tell my friend, Julie about it. She asks if I'm pregnant.

"No! How can I be pregnant?" I sincerely and naively ask.

"Kim," Julie says, "aren't you sleeping with Gary?"

"Yes, but he can't have kids."

"Who told you that?"

"He did."

"Are you kidding? Of course, he can have kids. What twenty-year old guy can't have kids? Doesn't he already have a son?"

"But . . . " The realization that he lied was just sinking in when a million questions came at me like a rocket.

"Kim, you are pregnant!"

"No, no, no! I can't be!" I reason with myself. "What will I do? What will my parents do? Oh, no! Did he lie to me? No. That can't be true. He wouldn't lie to me. Is it true? I can't be pregnant. How can I be pregnant? I am only eighteen-years old. What am I going to do with a baby?"

"Kim. Kim."

"What?" I scream. Now, I can finally scream again.

"What are you going to do?" Julie questions, holding my hand.

"I don't know." It's starting to become real to me that I might be pregnant.

"You have to get a pregnancy test." Julie commands, "You have to tell Gary."

My internal monologue intensifies. "What is she talking about? I have to tell him? Tell him what? 'Um, remember when you made me have sex with you and I told you I was going to get pregnant? Well, I'm pregnant!' What will he say? What will he do? Will he be happy? Will he hate me? He's going to be mad. How could I have let this happen?" The words flood my mind too fast to keep track of them all.

I don't tell him.

After the drug store pregnancy test reveals two lines, disbelief forces me to go to the clinic for a blood test. Just to be sure. On the city bus, it's astonishing that everyone stinks. Underarms, breath, feet, scalps, you name it, it all burns my nose. Amid the stench, my starving appetite craves a can of beef ravioli in spite of my normal vegetarian diet. A little boy is crying. He cries louder and louder. His young mother seems not to hear him. "Why can't she hear him? Why won't she make him stop crying?" As my bus stop approaches, I pull the cord. The bus stops. I escape out the back doors.

The clinic is dingy and cold. The hard chairs are uncomfortable. The staff is uncaring. No one smiles. No one says, "Hello." The girl at the front desk slides open the glass and asks, "What are you here for?"

"A pregnancy test?"

"You pregnant?"

"I think I am. I'm not sure."

"When was your last period?"

I wonder, "Do I really have to answer this in the middle of the waiting room?" Instead of answering, I shrug my shoulders.

"Sign in. Have a seat," she shuts the glass.

A few minutes later, a small woman calls my name. She asks me to come to the back. Once there, she tells me her name, asks a couple questions, and draws my blood.

"Come back in about two weeks for the results," she says. She's offering me no further explanation. Accordingly, I don't ask for one.

Two weeks later, the clinic calls me. They ask me to come in for my results. Back in the clinic with the same small woman, she gives me the results. She confirms what I already know in my heart. I'm pregnant. Six weeks pregnant. The clinic woman tells me what to do next, but her words are as clear to me as those of Charlie Brown's school teacher.

On the bus ride back to my place, a very pregnant woman sits across from me. I watch her and wonder what I'm going to do. "How will I look with a belly like that? What will I name my child? How will I afford to feed a child? What will his father do when I tell him?" Then, I realize, I have to tell Gary that I am, in fact, pregnant. He'll have to be there for me and help me. For the first time, I'm officially feeling scared.

When I call Gary, I can't stop crying. I'm not prepared what happens next.

"I'm busy. What do you want?" Gary asked.

"I'm pregnant."

"What do you want me to do about that?"

"Help me."

"For what? It's not mine. How do I even know it's my baby?"

Is he serious? How can it not be his? What is he talking about, 'It's not mine?'

"I do not know why you are telling me this," he says. "What do you want me to do? Do you know how many girls told me they're pregnant this week? I'm gonna tell you like I told them. It's not mine and I am not helping you with this."

My mind can't compute what my ears are hearing. I want to yell at him, "What? Who do you think you're talking to? This is Kim. Remember? I'm not like that!"

"Forget it," I say instead. "I don't want you to do anything. I'll handle it myself. Don't ever call me again. In fact, forget you ever knew me. Good bye." I slam the princess phone down as hard as I can, with no idea how I'm going to handle raising a baby by myself.

This can't be my life. I'm not supposed to be pregnant at eighteen. For months, this boyfriend of mine insisted that he cannot get me pregnant. Because of that, it never occurred to me that I would actually get pregnant. Counting back the weeks, it's clear that I conceived the night he pulled that gun on me. It had to be that night, because we didn't have sex again after that. Now that I know when it happened, I'll just call him back and tell him. Then, he'll remember.

Of course, he remembers, but what he remembers is different than what I remember. He remembers joking with me. He remembers toys and games. He remembers me being a cry baby. He remembers that he had to take me home earlier than he wanted to and he could not sleep all night. He also remembers that he is not claiming this child. Then, he adds a new memory. He tells me to call that other guy I've been sleeping with and stop trying to pin this on him. He's not going to help me and I should leave him alone. That turns out to be a good idea.

Strangely, though embarrassed, confused, and scared about this pregnancy, I'm falling in love with this life inside of me. I'm not sure that is the proper response. I need someone to help me with this, so I tell Julie and our other friends. Surely, my friends who previously encouraged me to have sex with him will have solutions for my current situation. One of them has a baby of her own. Undoubtedly, she'll help me. Except when I tell her, she offers no help. None of them help. Sure, they're sad for me. They're even scared for me. Mostly, they're glad they aren't poor me.

If I could have it any other way, I'd never tell my parents about my pregnancy. But, I have to. The news surprises and disappoints them. It doesn't however, deter them from caring for me. Thankfully, they take me to see a gynecologist for proper care. He happens to be the same doctor who delivered me when I was born. That's a little unnerving for me. But, the doctor is not deterred as he presents my choices. He doesn't judge me. He advises me. My immaturity causes me to rely on the doctor's data for the answer to my pregnancy dilemma. Though I'm eighteen-years old, my own childishness keeps me from speaking up for my child. I covertly walk into a total independence from God without taking even one moment to ask Him into my life or my decision. Hence, abortion is the option selected. It's what's best for my future which this child will only derail.

So, why can't I get away from the feeling that abortion doesn't seem ethical?

In my home state, what I am about to do is defined in the law, under the title dedicated to "Crimes and Offenses." It's interesting that abortion has its own section.

'Abortion.' The use of any means to terminate the clinically diagnosable pregnancy of a woman with knowledge that the termination by those means will, with reasonable likelihood, cause the death of the unborn child except that, for the purposes of this chapter, abortion shall not mean the use of an intrauterine device or birth control pill to inhibit or prevent ovulation, fertilization or the implantation of a fertilized ovum within the uterus.[4]

My doctor explains that the abortion he will perform for me is not as legally offensive as the Pennsylvania Code describes. He tells me that it is a surgical procedure called a "Dilation and Curettage," otherwise known as a D&C. He'll perform the procedure in his office. During the D&C, my cervix will be dilated. He will insert an instrument inside of me that he'll use to remove my baby from my uterus.[5] In less than half hour, my baby will be gone and my life will return to normal. After a few days of bed rest, and some pain, he says I will forget it ever happened.

On the way to the doctor's office, on that day in May, my hands hold and rub my belly again and again. The sun is shining through the cracks in the doctor's office window glass blocks. In my heart, however there is an indescribable darkness. After the D&C is finished, I'm still touching my stomach with secret cries. No one talks about this "surgery" again. Least of all, me. My shame is overwhelming. Unbearable even. I cry for my baby often. But, I'm not comfortable crying for him. Or her. Or it. "It" is what I've come to call the child, because "it" is the shame I have to bear quietly, secretly. I will eventually name my child, Sunshine, but I'm not ready to do that just yet.

Though the abortion procedure is over, the pain is not. The pain of the rape. The pain of the abortion. The pain of lost motherhood. The pain of secret grief. The pain that lives, sitting in my heart, just under the surface of my emotions.

For decades.

In silence.

The Virtuous Sister

In my desperation to disentangle from the lingering web of emotions associated with my disturbing conception and offensive loss, I begin to drown my sorrow in other men, alcohol, risky behavior, and the unwise advice of so-called friends. Decades of dead ends finally lead me to seek refuge in the Bible. The many stories of women in assorted circumstances caused me to wonder if any experienced what I had. I start to read stories I never read or heard before. There are so many women in the Bible. Women who have something to say to me. Women who speak to my heart. Women like me.

One woman captured my solidarity. You may be familiar with her story, but I was not. When I first read it, I stopped in my tracks. Her story is so close to mine, I wondered if I was reading the Bible or looking through a mirror in book form. Optimistically, her story tells me what happened to me is not outside the view of God.

This story is about Tamar, the daughter of King David of Israel. She's a virgin. And, she's so beautiful that her own half-brother takes a creepy liking to her. This is not some harmless boyhood crush. It's a criminal lust that causes her brother to use a self-imposed illness to deceive their father, convincing the King to send his unsuspecting daughter into her brother's dangerous arms. The mentally demented brother who does the disgusting to Tamar.

But let's talk about Tamar. You may know by now that names in the Bible have significance. In her case, Tamar's name is no different. Her name means, "palm tree," signifying that her parents intended her to be productive or fertile.[6]

Many people who read her story believe that it tells how her natural fruitfulness is stolen from her. I suggest that they didn't look closely enough at her. Tamar's influence over my life and any woman who dares to scratch beyond the surface of her story epitomizes the regal character implicit in her name. Like a palm tree, this story of Tamar's beauty, flexibility and righteousness ultimately yield fruitfulness and triumph.[7]

Dangerous Flexibility

"And Amnon said unto Tamar, Bring the meat into the chamber, that I may eat of thine hand. And Tamar took the cakes which she had made, and brought them into the chamber to Amnon her brother." (2 Samuel 13:10)

Amnon is the name of Tamar's half-brother. He is her oldest brother, the first-born son of the king.[8] Despite this honorable position, Amnon devises a plan to get Tamar close to him. As the plan goes, if she cooks for him and delivers the food to him directly, then his mysterious illness will vanish. He will surely feel better eating from her hand. That's what he tells his father. In reality, Amnon intends to be cured of this self-imposed illness not by receiving the food his sister offers, but by taking what she would never present. Thus, after dismissing all witnesses, Amnon asks Tamar to bring the food into his bedroom where he and she can be alone. Though virgin princesses are highly protected from male suitors by the king and his court, Tamar is presented to Amnon. Both the servants and Tamar innocently accommodate this request.

"And when she had brought them unto him to eat, he took hold of her, and said unto her, Come lie with me, my sister."
(2 Samuel 13:11)

Instead of appreciating Tamar's kindness by simply eating the food she brought to him, Amnon grabs Tamar to make a vile, incestuous demand. Incest is explicitly prohibited in Israel. "Do not have sexual relations with your sister, either your father's daughter or your mother's daughter, whether she was born in the same home or elsewhere" (Leviticus 18:9 NIV). The Bible further advises, "Cursed is anyone who sleeps with his sister, the daughter of his father or the daughter of his mother" (Deuteronomy 27:22 NIV).

As a member of the governing family, surely Amnon knew this kingdom-wide ban. That he would ignore it tells us his character is severely flawed. The notion of his supposed love for Tamar is challenged by his words and deeds. Usually, we see that when a man loves a woman, he seeks to marry and care for her. The man's desire to have sexual relations with the object of his love is only as an outward expression of his internal compassion. Grabbing her for sex is neither an altruistic nor romantic gesture. As we will see, Amnon's purported love for her is selfishly lustful without any intent to honor or cherish her. Like Gary in my story, Amnon is lustfully obsessed.

"And she answered him, Nay, my brother, do not force me; for no such thing ought to be done in Israel: do not thou this folly." (2 Samuel 13:12)

We always hear how women in the Bible have no voice. Especially, in the Old Testament where this story appears. Expecting that Tamar would fit that mold, her boldness is striking. She is not a silent, submissive participant in her brother's scheme. Tamar speaks up for herself while hoping to appeal to Amnon's sense of decency. She obviously thought that as a man of Israel, he'd want to do God's will like his father, who is known as "a man after God's heart."[9] Surely, he doesn't want this silly, immature lapse in judgment to stain his reputation. Worse yet, a counter-cultural act like this would not just bring disgrace to Amnon and his family, but to the entire nation and throne of Israel. Tamar advises Amnon against it.

The wayward prince doesn't care about honor or dignity. He set up this impossible situation for Tamar. Yet, this princess, this palm tree, is forward thinking in her commitment to doing what is right. Refusing to be forced into submission, she faithfully pleads with her brother in belief that the law of God will protect her from the foolishness of incest. And if not the law, common sense. I wonder if she thought about pregnancy like I did.

"And I, whither shall I cause my shame to go? and as for thee, thou shalt be as one of the fools in Israel. Now therefore, I pray thee, speak unto the king; for he will not withhold me from thee." (2 Samuel 13:13)

What happened? How did Tamar's resistance take this drastic turn? Looks like she's intimating a surrender. Only not to God, but to Amnon.

Not so fast, my sister. Tamar hasn't abandoned the movement. In reality, she's only extending the reach of her bold righteousness. Her argument moves from the spiritual, where Tamar dwells, to the natural, where Amnon insists on taking up residence. They both know she cannot physically restrain him. Thus, if he moves forward with his advances, then three things are certain to occur. First, Tamar would never be able to hide her shame. Second, Amnon would never hide his wickedness. Third, neither would maintain the stature of their nobility. Rather than condone any of this, Tamar offers marriage. That's outrageous, isn't it?

Maybe not. Consider that marriage is a commitment. It requires an ongoing relationship between a man and a woman of which sexual intimacy is only a part. By suggesting marriage, Tamar calls into consciousness a sense of wisdom and honor. If Amnon agrees to marry Tamar, his immediate, natural desire will not be satisfied. He will have to wait.

I hear what you're thinking. How can a marriage between a brother and sister be honored or pure? Well, this is where the rightness of Tamar's wisdom emerges. Surely, she is aware that "If a man marries his sister, the daughter of either his father or his mother, and they have sexual relations, it is a disgrace. They are to be publicly removed from their people. He has dishonored his sister and will be held responsible" (Leviticus 20:17 NIV). Though it seems she's offering herself to Amnon or offering to violate the law, she's essentially doing the opposite. By suggesting he seek permission from their father to marry her, she's not submitting to his advances, she's staging her escape. If he falls for her plan, his depravity will be exposed to King David, and she will get away. Her plan is ingenious. I wish I could have been that clever.

On Being Fruitful

"Howbeit he would not hearken unto her voice: but, being stronger than she, forced her, and lay with her. Then Amnon hated her exceedingly; so that the hatred wherewith he hated her was greater than the love wherewith he had loved her. And Amnon said unto her, Arise, be gone."
(2 Samuel 13:14-15)

Oh, no! It didn't work.

Amnon's imprudence is impenetrable. He refuses to heed her warning, because "fools think their own way is right, but the wise listen to others" (Proverbs 12:15 NLT). Instead of wisely accepting her offer, he foolishly rapes her. Her plan fails.

SUNSHINE and DANIEL

Of course, Tamar believes she has no recourse against Amnon. She cannot go to the police station to file rape charges against the king's son. Besides, Tamar cannot publicly expose this family embarrassment. Since no one is in the room with them, it's not likely that anyone will believe her story.

Like me, Tamar does not report the rape. I wonder if she became paralyzed. Unable to speak of it. Unable to gather the details in her mind and sort them chronologically. Unable to make sense of it all. If the secrecy of the rape is not bad enough, Amnon's character declines from unable to resist her to unwilling to favor her. He's downright rude to his own sister. He treats her like a common whore. As if she asked for his wicked advances, he has no further use for her.

He hates her. How can he now hate her? It's odd how quickly ill-formed emotions drastically swing from one end of the pendulum to the other. His hatred is not your run-of-the-mill dislike but exceedingly great revulsion. What did she do to bring this about? Nothing! She could not completely resist him. Nor could she refuse him. It's not her that's the problem. It's his sick mind that's the problem.

Unfortunately, Tamar is subject to his psychosis. Thus, he dismisses her. Once again, he acts against her will. She's treated as if she's the evil wrongdoer.[10] I wish I could talk to her and tell her that she's not the blame for any of this. She has been victimized. Attacked. Violated. Wronged.

"And Tamar put ashes on her head, and rent her garment of divers colours that was on her, and laid her hand on her head, and went on crying. And Absalom her brother said unto her, Hath Amnon thy brother been with thee? but hold now thy peace, my sister: he is thy brother; regard not this thing. So Tamar remained desolate in her brother Absalom's house."
(2 Samuel 13:19-20)

Tamar is vulnerable. In response to her situation, her other brother, her full brother, Absalom, advises against her own revenge. He takes his only sister into his home where it's believed she lives out the rest of her life in shame. It seems that her predictions of disgrace have come true. After tearing off her princess clothing, she assumes a posture of isolation and forsakenness.

Or does she?

Scripture tells us that Absalom instructed her to not speak of the incident. Then, it says that she "remained desolate in her brother Absalom's house." That may seem like a sad existence, but it actually means that she did as her brother instructed. She remained quiet regarding the rape and never spoke of it again. It does not mean that she lived a lonely existence. She lived in Absalom's house with his family.

Admittedly, living with your brother's family is not exactly the independent girl of today's dream life. Based on experience, I don't advise suppressing the rape story. That's what abusers want us to do. They don't want their sin exposed. And too often, it's what many people advise victims to do. "Just forget it. Don't dwell on it," they say. In Tamar's time, and in my time in the 1980s, speaking up and speaking out about male-on-female sexual abuse was not appropriate. Thankfully, today things are different. More women speak up. Still many of us don't. We wish this would all just go away. We wish it never happened. We certainly do not want to rehash it over again. Re-exposing old wounds. Even if there's healing in the telling, silence is unnervingly comfortable.

In remarkable strength, though, we go on with our lives. Just as Tamar did.

You see, she is a champion, because she did not shrivel up and merely exist. The enduring value of Tamar's life is tucked away in 2 Samuel 14:27. There we learn a noteworthy fact about Tamar's life in Absalom's home. It turns out that Absalom's home is filled with four children, including a daughter. That is, a niece who's deliberately named. Can you guess what Absalom and his wife name Tamar's niece? You guessed it. They name her, Tamar. I'd like to call her "Little T."

Why do you suppose they would do this? Obviously, because they value this child's live-in aunt's presence in their family. The Bible informs us that Little T inherits more than just her aunt's first name. She also inherits her aunt's beauty. In my mind, it's not inconceivable to imagine that Little T inherited her aunt's character, too. Traits of righteous perseverance, character, and hope that Little T would imitate under careful tutelage at the nurturing feet of her namesake aunt. What a marvelous legacy of triumph for Tamar!

Into This Grace in Which We Now Stand

Your situation may be like mine or Tamar's. You have not spoken about it to anyone. You're ashamed and believe that you are to blame. Stop thinking that way. You are not to blame for being victimized. You are as beautiful today as you were before this happened. Your life has meaning. Sure, your abuser intended to deter your future. In reality, your future is still bright. You still have life to live and love to give.

Speak to your abuser right now. Wherever you are. Don't call, text, or reach out to him on social media. Don't invite him into your space, but open your mouth and speak to him now, through the atmosphere. Tell him what he did to you. Tell him what he took from you. Now, tell him that his time is up. He can no longer have access to you. Then, forgive him and leave it there. Do not carry this in your head or heart any longer. Speak out loud. Scream if you have to. Let it go. Now. Finally. Tell him, "You intended to harm me, but God intended it all for good. He brought me to this position, so I could save the lives of many people." (paraphrase of Genesis 50:20 NLT)

Now, go live the best rest of your life! You have things to do!

Reflection

Was what happened to you because of someone else's foolishness?

Will you declare in your heart now that you refuse to live in isolation and loneliness any longer, but will seek to create a legacy of righteousness?

Prayer

Dear Lord,

I know You are the God who sits high yet looks low. You are the God who watches over His own children as a loving Father. Yet, God, I do not understand why You allowed these things to happen in my life. Sure, I know that people are flawed, dangerous, foolish, and sometimes they hurt us for no good reason. I purposely look to You for help and protection. When I cry out, and no one else is in the room, please hear me. Please comfort me. God, keep me.

For me, the story of Tamar is my story. I was mistreated and misused. I was lured and taken advantage of by brothers, fathers, uncles, boyfriends, and friends who committed foolish acts against me. They left me to deal with the aftermath of their depravity alone. Though my mouth has been silent, God my life is not. God, I ask You to make me strong, like Tamar, to positively influence other young women. Teach me that You have not forsaken me. Allow me to live in the strength of Your promised presence in my life. Make Yourself known as that strong, tangible palm tree through me, God.

In the name of Jesus, Amen.

4
...

Seeking Grace in Bitterness

*"See to it that no one falls short of the grace of God and
that no bitter root grows up to cause trouble and defile
many." (Hebrews 12:15 NIV)*

Godmother, Not Mother

Events of the 1990s make me realize my abortion will be a part of
my life forever. In one year, I become a godmother. Twice.

When my friend Tina becomes pregnant, she admits to me that
she does not want to keep the child. She already has three children.
As a woman in her early twenties, Tina doesn't want another child
just yet. She asks me to take her to the clinic to end her pregnancy.

What? Is she serious? Me?

I tell her I cannot do it because of my Sunshine. For the first time,
I share the unfiltered details of the soreness of my abortion with Tina.
Telling her how much it still hurts me, now several years later, is uncomfortable. Explaining that it's not worth the future heartache to
abort her child simply because she doesn't wish to be inconvenienced
by the child's life is therapeutic for me. Tina cannot justify her sexual
activity by aborting this child, no more than I could. Especially since
she has what I did not have—the acceptance and support of the child's
father. What she doesn't know is how much she needs him to remain
present. She doesn't want to be in the position I found myself when

Gary left me to fend for myself. While I'm willing to stand with her in this time of need, my help won't include assisting in the abortion of her child. Gratefully, she doesn't go through with it. Months later, she gives birth to a healthy, baby girl. To my surprise, jealousy over Tina's successful pregnancy does not engulf my emotions. Love overtakes me instead. And my awe of her endurance encourages me. In return, I humbly accept her request to become her daughter's godmother.

Within months of my goddaughter's birth, comes the day scheduled for my godson's introduction to the world. He's a baby that we want. "We" means my best friend Renee, her husband, and me. Since learning she was pregnant, we knew her child will be like my child, too. A bit reluctantly however, I respect the fact that her husband should be the one in the delivery room at his son's birth instead of me. My special time with her son would come just a couple days later, but still at the hospital when it's my distinct pleasure to meet my godson to take him home. That's also when it becomes clear that I don't know what to do with a newborn baby. My experience of changing, dressing, and cuddling my little nieces has not prepared me for handling this tiny, brand spanking new baby boy. What are we to do with him?

Seizing the opportunity to take charge, I decide to lead in putting him in the child seat for his first car ride. I gingerly place him in the infant car seat and fasten the hook. Feeling proud of myself, I'm astonished when the little boy lets out a yell that's just not possible for a child of that size. He sounds like he's three years old instead of three days old. He's crying real tears, too.

"What's wrong with him?" I ask.

Renee doesn't know. I don't know. The helpless little guy can't tell us. It's then we realize that I clasped his leg into the car seat hook. Ouch! Oh, my God! I hurt him. I hurt him! Oh no! Maybe this innate incompetence of mine is why God impressed upon me the need to abort my own baby. I cannot possibly handle caring for a baby. I'm such a nincompoop.

"I am so sorry!"

"It's okay. He'll be okay," my best friend says.

My stomach is in knots. Inside I'm screaming at myself. "How can you say that? I just hurt your infant son. How could she ever trust me to touch him again? Every child should fear injury or worst at my hands. It's a good thing I did not have my baby. I'm a baby killer."

Thoughts like this flood my mind for a couple years. They cause me sorrow. My heart becomes increasingly hostile towards women who can have children. I am convinced that I'm doomed. I will forever be without a child to mother, just because eighteen-year-old me did such a stupid thing. I'm determined to never concern myself with motherhood again.

It Never Goes Away

A television commercial airs that brings back every nurturing emotion not fully reconciled in my heart. It catches me completely off guard because I've insincerely told myself that my discomfort with my abortion, what it means about me as a person, and my worth as a woman is settled. The commercial shows a woman staring out on a cloudy dock as a little boy runs towards the water. With each step, the little boy slowly fades away.[1] Involuntarily, I start to cry. The people in this commercial are immediately apparent to me. I know them because I've seen this scene in my mind. Somehow, I'm watching the slow-motion movie that only exists secretly on my internal television screen. I know that any other woman watching this commercial knows what I know about the woman on the dock, the little boy and his fading image. In this political climate of heightened abortion rhetoric in America, the commercial strikingly depicts the lingering torture of abortion that never goes away.

Many nights, I see my baby as a child. What would he be like? How tall would he be? What would he like to do? What would his voice sound like? How exuberant of a personality would he display? Would it be hard to raise him and love him? How would life be different for me? Each time those thoughts and visions come to mind, I allow myself to feel them, for a moment, then I try to think of something else. Frequently, there are nights when I'm all alone in my room, weeping. Desperate to catch my child before he disappears again. Desperate to be his mother. Wishing for a do over. Wishing to be eighteen again.

Youth and the Young

It is about this time that I learn of two teens. Amy Grossberg is eighteen in 1996.[2] Melissa Wexler is eighteen in 1997.[3] They both face the same predicament I had in the prior decade. Like me, they're eighteen and pregnant. Eighteen and scared. Eighteen and immature. Eighteen and about to make the worst decision of their lives.

Amy Grossberg is an affluent girl who hides her pregnancy, gives birth to a baby boy in a cheap motel room, kills the baby, then throws his lifeless body into a dirty dumpster.[4] The story of the he-said-she-said between Amy and her boyfriend is a horrifying tale about how a newborn baby's shattered skull and lifeless body are found in a plastic bag by an unsuspecting cleaning woman.[5] This wouldbe-rescuer cannot save the little baby boy's life, so she immediately calls the police and exposes Amy's horrible secret.

Melissa Wexler is a highschool girl who goes to the prom and gives birth to a little boy in the bathroom stall.[6] Melissa immediately cuts the umbilical cord herself, chokes, or smothers the little boy, puts him in a plastic bag, and throws him away in the trash.[7] The dead baby's body is found when Melissa's high school friends become suspicious of her actions, and search the bathroom for answers.[8]

When I hear these stories, I'm thrown into a tailspin. Older and repentant, I'm caught between hating the girls and sympathizing with them. My self-righteous mind asks how they could be so heinous? It quickly reminds me that this very question could have been asked of me. Years have not changed the fact that when I was eighteen I got rid of my child, too.

Media reports say that these upper-middle class girls could have had an abortion, put the babies up for adoption, or raised the babies instead of killing them. They say this as if an eighteen-year-old is mentally and emotionally developed enough to make these mature, well-reasoned decisions. Certainly, many girls do. But, I was not mature enough to make such a wise decision. Nonetheless, the consequences of my decision are extensive. I hid what I had done just like Amy and Melissa. Maybe I didn't hide my pregnancy or throw my baby in the trash, but I certainly hid my feelings, fears, and deepest desire to keep my baby and be his mother. Despite this, I could never hide the shame of my sin.

I am sure I should not judge Amy and Melissa, but as I'm older and finally reconciled to my undeniable desire to be a mother, an uncomfortable mix of jealousy and guilt reignites my bitterness towards them. It seems like they've gotten away with something. They've had an opportunity I did not. In reality, none of us have gotten away with anything. I'm no different than them. Our babies are gone. We are the blame.

Is there any relief to the bitterness?

Each time Amy and Melissa's stories, or the countless other stories of young women who needlessly harm their children appear in the news, my past and my self-righteous inclinations are pushed into focus. I refuse to see them. Instead, my late twenty-something self desperately desires motherhood. But my no-longer-eighteen body is not conceiving no matter what I try. That's why I turn my judgment on these girls. "How could they not value the life of their children? How could they be so cruel as to kill their own children? Do they know what I would give to have the chance they have?"

It occurs to me that this attitude of mine is no different than that of all the pro-life people who could not understand when I was eighteen. Back then, I conveniently wanted Jesus to come in and protect me from those uninformed activists. To my dismay, He didn't. So here I am, a decade later with my own ignorant opinions about what really happened with Amy and Melissa. It is funny how their actions look so much worse than my own. They're not. Whether our actions occurred from mental incompetence, domestic instability, or fear, they all resulted in the loss of a child and the loss of our motherhood. Youth and bad decisions are the common denominator. We each chose to believe the doomsday report that told us we had no other choice. We did what our immature and selfish minds said was best. Three babies died. Not because of the baby or the mother's illness. No. These babies died because of the mothers' ignorance, pride, and sin.

The result for me is a confusion of resentment. I'm mad at Amy and Melissa, every woman who has a healthy baby, and God for allowing all of this to happen to me. I am bitter.

The Unpleasant Mom

A bitter mother whose child has died is a hard woman to console. Her worldview is tainted by the distressing days to which she can imagine no relief. She doesn't realize that relief is available. She cannot see it because she doesn't look forward to anything. She only sees life through the tainted lens of her pain. A pain that she blames on God.

The book of Ruth tells a beautiful love story about how a foreign woman, Ruth, is rescued by a rich, elder of Israel named Boaz. Today, women are seeking their *Boaz* because of how this man cared for Ruth. But there's another story in this book that's not so sweet. It's the story of Ruth's mother-in-law, Naomi. A woman who responds to the tragic loss of her children by rearing bitterness in her soul.

> *"Now it came to pass in the days when the judges ruled, that there was a famine in the land. And a certain man of Bethlehemjudah went to sojourn in the country of Moab, he, and his wife, and his two sons. And the name of the man was Elimelech, and the name of his wife Naomi, and the name of his two sons Mahlon and Chilion, Ephrathites of Bethlehemjudah. And they came into the country of Moab, and continued there." (Ruth 1:1-2)*

Before we get to know Naomi, we need to understand the circumstances that surround her life. She lives "in the days when the judges ruled" in Israel. Let's do a little digging into this information to understand what this means. Who are the judges? What did they do? How did they rule?

We are first introduced to judges during the time of Moses, when his father-in-law advised the prophet to appoint capable, God-fearing, trustworthy men to serve as judges who handled disputes among the people (Exodus 18: 17-26). In obedience, Moses appointed these judges who became leaders among the people. Under Moses and the judges, Israel became a mighty nation. Over time, however, these judges died. The following generation of Israelites turned from God into the hands of neighboring nations. Despite their disobedience, "... the Lord raised up judges to rescue the Israelites from their attackers. Yet Israel did not listen to the judges but prostituted themselves by worshiping other gods. How quickly they turned away from the path of their ancestors, who had walked in obedience to the Lord's commands" (Judges 2:16-17 NLT).

This is where we find Naomi. In fact, in her day, "... every man did that which was right in his own eyes" (Judges 21:25). Judges rule, but the people ignore them. In response to their disobedience, God judges the nation with a famine that even hits the area known as Bethlehemjudah. This is bad, because Bethlehem means "the house of bread or food,"[9] while Judah means "praise."[10] This famine not only removes the food from this place, but the praise, too. Living in this ironic famine causes Naomi's husband, Elimelech, to do some considering. In keeping with the way of the times, instead of the way of the Lord, Elimelech weighs his options and does what he thinks is right. He decides to move, taking his praise away from the house of bread. On the surface, most of us can understand his decision. If you're hungry, it makes sense to go where there is food. It makes better sense, however, to go with the blessing of God. The problem with Elimelech's decision is that it's contrary to who he is. His name means "God is my king,"[11] yet he never petitions God before taking his family to reside in Moab, a foreign land where foreign Gods are worshipped.

It is under these conditions that Naomi stands by her man. She does not resist Elimelech's decision, but in keeping with the pleasantness her name implies,[12] conserves her family by agreeably uprooting to Moab.

"And Elimelech Naomi's husband died; and she was left, and her two sons." (Ruth 1:3)

Sometime after they arrive in Moab, Elimelech dies. It's not clear how long the family has lived here. If it is soon after their arrival, then this is quite a shocking turn of events. They've left their homeland, friends, family, and familiarity, and now, their patriarch is dead. The Bible describes the effect of his death by telling us that Naomi is left, as in left behind, abandoned and forsaken. Of the Elimelech-Naomi two-some, she is all that remains, with nothing except her two sons.

This might not seem like a big deal. Today, when a woman's husband dies, if she's fortunate, her husband leaves her a life insurance policy to provide for her after his death. He may also leave a will that distributes his wealth, property, and possessions to her. If he does not have a will, intestate succession laws or inheritance customs require that his wealth and property pass to his surviving heirs, namely his surviving spouse. In Naomi's day this is not the case.

The Bible instead says "If a man dies and leaves no son, give his inheritance to his daughter. If he has no daughter, give his inheritance to his brothers. If he has no brothers, give his inheritance to his father's brothers. If his father had no brothers, give his inheritance to the nearest relative in his clan, that he may possess it. This is to have the force of law for the Israelites, as the LORD commanded Moses" (Numbers 27:8-11 NIV).

Did you notice who's missing from this list of relatives? His wife! Accordingly, Naomi is left with nothing.

But Elimelech left two sons with Naomi. Shouldn't his property pass to them? And shouldn't they use their inheritance to take care of their mother who is now a widow? Yes. And, yes. The fact that scripture does not here mention Elimelech's property or its succession to his sons is curious. Maybe he failed to value his property, leaving it behind to obtain the foreign food. Once in Moab, Naomi's life now depends on her sons. They are her sustenance.

> *"And they took them wives of the women of Moab; the name of the one was Orpah, and the name of the other Ruth: and they dwelled there about ten years. And Mahlon and Chilion died also both of them; and the woman was left of her two sons and her husband." (Ruth 1:4-5)*

Are you kidding me? Bad just turned worse for Naomi. She's lived away from her homeland for more than ten years. Though widowed, she at least has her sons to protect and care for her. The three remain in Moab and become comfortable there. So comfortable, that Naomi's sons marry local, heathen women. Curiously, her sons do not have children. Like their father, they die in Moab.

Do you notice something about Naomi's sons' deaths? We don't know how they died. Think back. We know how Abel died. Cain stoned him. We know how David and Bathsheba's baby boy died. He was ill. We even know how Amnon died. Absalom directed his servant to strike and killed him for humiliating Tamar. But we don't know how either of Naomi's sons died. That could be an oversight by the writer. It's odd though, because the Bible is full of graphic details of deaths. What is this writer doing with Naomi's story? Who wrote this story anyway? Some believe the prophet Samuel wrote the book of Ruth. Since Samuel was a prophet, we know God spoke to him. Why wouldn't God tell him to add that information? Inquiring minds want to know.

It's my habit to ask God to fill me in on what's missing from scripture. It's a little arrogant, but I need to know what's going on here.

Most of the time, a commentary gives me an idea. For this passage of scripture, the commentaries suggest that these sons met their demise due to their disobedience to God's directive not to marry heathen women.

The Bible tell us that God said to Israel:

"Be very careful never to make a treaty with the people who live in the land where you are going. If you do, you will follow their evil ways and be trapped. Instead, you must break down their pagan altars, smash their sacred pillars, and cut down their Asherah poles... You must not make a treaty of any kind with the people living in the land. They lust after their gods, offering sacrifices to them. They will invite you to join them in their sacrificial meals, and you will go with them. Then you will accept their daughters, who sacrifice to other gods, as wives for your sons. And they will seduce your sons to commit adultery against me by worshiping other gods " (Exodus 34:12-13, 15-16 NLT).

Naomi's sons married forbidden women and they died.

That makes sense. We accept that death (not just physical death) is punishment for sin. How they died remains the open question. My studies give no inkling of the answer. My conclusion is God leaves this fact unexplained for you to dive into the passage. You have the privilege to imagine how they died by inserting your own facts. Let your story live with Naomi here. Will the disease, illness, murder, suicide, or accident that took your child unite your heart with Naomi's? Now consider how the manner of your child's death left you feeling alone.

For our girl Naomi, she's truly left with nothing. No husband. No sons. No grandchildren. She's a matriarch without a tribe. A woman without hope. That is until she hears that there's bread in Bethlehem. With no reason to linger in Moab, Naomi decides to go back home.

There is, however, the matter of the two daughters-in-law her sons left behind. They cling to her refusing to leave. Obviously, Naomi's been quite a role model to them. I'd bet she treats these young women better than their own mothers. She does not appreciate her impact on these young women. She tries to convince them to return to their

Moabite homes. When they refuse, Naomi's only recourse is to reveal what's been marinating in her heart.

> *"And Naomi said, Turn again, my daughters: why will ye go with me? are there yet any more sons in my womb, that they may be your husbands? Turn again, my daughters, go your way; for I am too old to have a husband. If I should say, I have hope, if I should have an husband also to night, and should also bear sons; Would ye tarry for them till they were grown? would ye stay for them from having husbands? nay, my daughters; for it grieveth me much for your sakes that the hand of the Lord is gone out against me." (Ruth 1:11-13)*

Naomi's greatest value is the product of her womb. To her, the only thing she has to offer the world is her offspring. Since she's too old to marry, she's too old to have children. She believes she has nothing to offer anyone, especially these two young women under her care because her condition grieves her to bitterness. She views her condition not in acknowledgement of the disobedient decisions her husband and sons made, but irrationally only on the result which she interprets as God's wrath-filled hand upon her.

Poor Naomi. She's so confused. She's so like me. My displaced grief clouded my view. I deemed every woman who gave birth as my enemy. I hated that they could have a child and I could not. My child's death, though at my behest, ignited a nastiness in me that I aimed at everyone.

Has that happened to you? What? You say you aren't bitter? You've never been bitter? What about jealous? Resentful? Judgmental? Have you looked unsympathetically upon another mother's choices? Have you been angry that you don't have the chance to be a mother again?

My sister, here's the truth God wants us to experience along with Naomi: we grow bitter. Our bitterness develops no matter the cause or manner of our child's death. It may arise immediately. Or it may take years to appear. It may not dawdle. Or it may last for years. No matter its manifestation, our grappling to reconcile this uneasy phenomenon of motherhood through unoccupied arms leaves us sour and disagreeable. It's not odd for you to be this way. It's normal, seeing that this is your child we're talking about!

The growth key in this is to acknowledge that the unpleasantness, or bitterness existed or exists. Then like an infectious disease that lays dormant until it metastasizes with little warning, we must take care to make sure it's effectively eradicated once and for all before it has a chance to contaminate everyone around us.

Pulling Up Roots

Naomi has to deal with her bitterness openly because her daughter-in-law, Ruth, refuses to leave her side. Having famously declared her devotion to Naomi and the God Naomi introduced to her, Ruth vows to leave her own home, mother, pagan gods and the only way of living she has ever known, to travel side-by-side to an uncertain future with Naomi. Despite Naomi's attempt to wallow in self-pity alone, she cannot walk off into the Middle Eastern sunset to disappear forever. She must give voice to her thoughts and conclusions.

> *"So they two went until they came to Bethlehem. And it came to pass, when they were come to Bethlehem, that all the city was moved about them, and they said, Is this Naomi? And she said unto them, Call me not Naomi, call me Mara: for the Almighty hath dealt very bitterly with me." (Ruth 1: 19-20)*

That Naomi is some kind of woman. Pagan women are drawn to her. Israeli women fondly remember her. Accompanied by Ruth, Naomi enters Bethlehem at the interest of everyone in the town. She becomes the talk of the town. Though she hasn't been there for more than ten years, everyone is anxious at her return. Can you imagine being a woman like that? Time nor distance erases you from the minds of your neighbors. The whole town welcomes you with open arms. Wouldn't you love to go home and receive the town's welcome like a soldier who's returned from war? Well, not Naomi. She doesn't see how special she is. Or how she is favored among men and women. Or how people like to be around her. She does not recognize her value as a God-fearing woman in their lives.

As great the anticipation of Naomi's return, the town's people are perplexed when they see her. Something is not as they remember. The years in Moab have affected her appearance. They ask, "Is this Naomi?" Her spiritual brightness is visibly gone. She responds by telling them she is no longer pleasant, as the name Naomi implies. To the contrary, she immediately tells them to call her Mara, a name and word that is not used anywhere else in the Old Testament. A name that implies a unique brand of bitterness that by her own renaming she embraces. She wants others to embrace it, too. It's her new identity. She is officially and permanently a bitter woman.

A Sure Relief

"I went out full and the Lord hath brought me home again empty: why then call ye me Naomi, seeing the Lord hath testified against me, and the Almighty hath afflicted me?"
(Ruth 1:21)

Here's where Naomi blows my mind. Not because I find her offensive, but because she is speaking my thoughts. Honestly, it's as if she's living my life. Though there's so much about her I do not know, like her age, how long she's been in Moab, what she did there, the age of her sons at their deaths, and how long she remained in Moab after their deaths, I know that she interprets her situation the way I interpreted my own. If Naomi were here today, I believe this is how her words would sound:

"I'm not who I used to be. When I left here, I strutted away with my head held high. I was pregnant with possibilities. Then, I had a full family, and full potential. Today, God has forced me to stagger back home abandoned and worthless. You'd be right to call me broke, busted, and disgusted. Why are you acting like you can't see it? You know

I'm not the same Naomi you used to know, yet you want to pretend nothing has happened. Since you last saw me, God has made my life hell. He has done this to me. Can't you see how God has ruined me?"

This is Naomi's "woe is me" song. It's her justification for her bitterness. By these words, she thinks she's cleared the way to be a mean, withdrawn, sarcastic, sad, and aloof woman. Isn't that how a woman should act when God takes her children from her? Shouldn't she wallow in her feelings without regard to the effect of her disposition on her neighbors and friends? That's not to mention her daughter-in-law, Ruth. Doesn't she matter?

I certainly didn't think about anyone but myself when I spoke like Naomi. Until I heard myself one day. As a confessed Christian, I realized that the scourge in my words threatened to discourage other people from wanting to know and serve God. It's the risk of unharnessed bitterness. Sinful accusations against God can scare people away from Him and me, too. Then life is certain to be bitter. The worst thing of all about my having become bitter and jealous is that I could no longer be effective.

Why? Because God can't use you when you are bitter.

Don't Fall Short of God's Grace

Thankfully, the story doesn't end here. No, Naomi doesn't have an Eve experience, she doesn't become a mother again. Rather, she renounces bitterness to give full attention to helping her daughter-in-law.

"One day Naomi said to Ruth, 'My dear, isn't it time that I try to find a husband for you and get you happily married again?'" (Ruth 3:1 TLB).

By her concerted efforts and Ruth's trusting conformity, Naomi gets Ruth a husband, and becomes a grandmother. Not just any grandmother, but an involved one. "Naomi took the baby and cuddled him to her breast. And she cared for him as if he were her own" (Ruth 4:16 NLT).

This grandchild rewarded to Naomi through the young woman she mentored returns her to normal. And everyone knows it. So much so that, "the neighbor women said, 'Now at last Naomi has a son again!' And they named him Obed. He became the father of Jesse and the grandfather of David" (Ruth 4:17 NLT).

Did you see that? After renouncing bitterness, Naomi becomes the great grandmother of King David. And you know what that means? She is also a distant great grandmother of Jesus Christ.

Yup. Ladies, it's time to ditch bitterness.

Reflection

Are you bitter?

Tell God about your bitterness. If you are artistic paint it or write about it.

Who do you blame for your child's death?

Prayer

Dear Father,

Forgive me for accusing You of being anything but a righteous and loving God. Even when I am wrong, You remain right. Lord, I have so often misunderstood my situation. In my rush to explain my loss in terms that make sense to me, I have become nasty, harsh, spiteful and ugly. Nothing like the kind, patient and gentle woman you created me to be. Lord, I have judged others with the judgment I am grateful You have not levied against me. Please God help me to deal with the bitterness in my heart. I've not always been as brave as Naomi. I have not stood up in the middle of town and shouted that I am bitter. I have tried to hide it for years, but I suspect I am not doing a good job at it. I've hurt people. I may have even turned others away from knowing You. I am sorry that I have not represented You fittingly. Lord, help me to come to terms with my actions and the death of my child. Let me feel the forgiveness that comes through Jesus Christ.

In the name of Jesus, Amen.

5
...

Seeking Grace in Grief

"But after you have suffered for a little while, the God of all grace, who calls you to share his eternal glory in union with Christ, will himself perfect you and give you firmness, strength, and a sure foundation."
(1 Peter 5:10 GNT)

This part of my story is vitally important to my recovery. No one has heard the entire dreaded story. By now, there are parts of it I'm sure I don't remember. As I write this, more of it is coming to mind, because I'm allowing myself to think about it. Referring to old diaries from that period to share this story with you helps to flush things out. The words from those journals are written on these pages, but in my heart and mind they are treasured commemorations time cannot fade.

It Starts With Disaster

Sitting at my desk on a summer-like Tuesday in September, a quiet panic falls over the office. I overhear a coworker talking on his cell phone.

"An attack in New York City? The World Trade Center? Really? A plane? A plane hit it? That can't be true!"

I don't take the words seriously, because I can only hear part of the conversation by eavesdropping. Besides, I have work to finish. All of a sudden, my coworker stands up and runs to the kitchenette where the televisions are located. Partners come out of their offices to go to the kitchenette, too. I don't move. My phone rings. It's my boyfriend, Timothy.

"Kim, are you okay?" he asked.

"What do you mean?"

"Did you hear that a plane hit the World Trade Center?"

My heartbeat quickens. "What?!"

"I'm leaving work now. I'm coming to pick you up."

I'm confused. I don't know if I should call my my mother and sister here in Philly, or my brother down in the D.C. area first. I only know I have to make sure they know about the planes. Without saying it, we all know to go to my mother's house. Even Timothy knows to go there.

Through intermittent cell phone coverage, crowded downtown streets, unmanageable traffic, and visible panic, we make the hour-long drive to my mother's house. When we arrive, the television is tuned to the *Special News Report*. My mother, sister, boyfriend, and I watch in horror as people in New York City scramble and run for their lives.

The date is Tuesday, September 11, 2001 or *9/11* as we've come to know it. The *9/11 attacks* shock us all. It disrupts our belief in our safety. It makes us rethink everything, including our lives, our loved ones, and our futures.

On this day, I'm more certain than ever that I want Timothy to be my husband and the father of my children. I pray for it and I pray that he feels the same way. Today is the day that it starts to become a reality. For the first time, he insinuates that he wants to marry me thereby changing our relationship. He's more caring. It's why I decide it prudent to stop taking the birth control pill. I don't want anything to hinder my ability to get pregnant.

As the terror of the *9/11 attacks* continues for weeks, likewise our changed relationship continues. Admittedly, I initiate most of the discussions, but he joins in. As the country regains normalcy, so do we, including my decision to get back in shape. After all, a bride has to be beautiful on her wedding day. I start a new treadmill and weightlifting routine at the local fitness center. A week or two into my workout, I start experiencing terrible stomach cramps that cut my fitness goals short. I can't imagine what's wrong with me until I realize my good old "Aunt Flow" hasn't come during the entire month October.

Maybe it's because I stopped taking the pill and my body is all mixed up. I figure I'll just power through it. That is, until mid-November when the cramps turn into nausea and my period still does not make a return. I tell Timothy what's been going on. He's a bit concerned, but not at all worried.

As is a requirement for any woman whose period takes a vacation, I go to the drug store and buy a home pregnancy test. There's fear and excitement in my heart. To think, after all these years, I might be pregnant again. This time with Timothy. But what will he do? What will he say? Will he say it's not his? Will he treat me the way Gary did? Will he leave me? Will he stay?

I take the test.

Positive.

I'm pregnant. I'm pregnant! Excited and scared. I feel for my stomach. It's another female requirement. This time for a woman who's just learned she is pregnant. Touching, feeling, and rubbing her stomach is automatic. It's involuntary at first. Then, it's reactionary, until it turns nurturing and all out loving. There, in my bathroom, my touch is everything. I have another chance at motherhood.

Brimming with Expectation and Excitement

Anxiously, I call and tell him. At first, he is silent, then he says, "Are you sure?"

"Well, the test is positive."

"Okay," he concedes.

I promise him I will call my doctor to confirm. He agrees to accompany me to the doctor's office. It makes me feel wanted that he's accepting of the potential *us*. Fortunately, the doctor sees me quickly and confirms my pregnancy. I'm six-to-eight-weeks pregnant.

The next few weeks are a whirlwind. Since I believe we're going to get married, I figure I may as well go ahead and buy my wedding gown. Surely, we're not waiting too long. Good thing I did because nausea and back pain over take my body. My doctor places me on disability from work, because being almost thirty-five years old with large, intra-uterine fibroids puts my pregnancy at high-risk of health problems for me or the baby. The fibroids continue growing faster than my baby, giving me tremendous pain. My doctor prescribes pain medications and orders weekly visits and ultrasounds to check my fluid levels. Sometimes the vaginal ultrasounds are uncomfortable. They always concern me. Results often send me to the hospital, but each time, Timothy picks me up and takes me. I'm grateful.

Obviously, this is going to be a very hard pregnancy. At only twelve weeks I look like I'm six months pregnant. The fibroids are taking up too much of the space where my baby needs to grow. By January, I'm desperately ill and hurting, but I want my baby to live. At night, I often sleep on the bathroom floor. My head hurts, my sinuses hurt, my stomach is upset, I have diarrhea, I'm nauseous constantly, and my back aches from the pressure of the growing baby and the growing fibroids. Crying feels good emotionally, but it just makes my head hurt more. So, I stop crying.

It's only mid-January and I need to go to the hospital again. In the emergency room, they check my baby's heart rate. Thankfully, it's strong. I'm relieved. The emergency room doctor decides to admit me due to my low blood pressure, heart rate, and fluid levels. The nurses are instructed to watch me closely. Early one morning, the nurse notices something. She calls the head nurse to tell her that my baby is trying to come out. But I'm barely eighteen weeks pregnant! They say I have to get to twenty-four weeks for the baby to be viable.

Wait!

Slow down.

Viable?

Please explain this to me. The viability issue has only come up in my constitutional law classes when we discussed the case of Griswold v. Connecticut.[1] I know about the word *viable*.

My state law defines it as:

> "That stage of fetal development when, in the judgment of the physician based on the particular facts of the case before him and in light of the most advanced medical technology and information available to him, there is a reasonable likelihood of sustained survival of the unborn child outside the body of his or her mother, with or without artificial support."[2]

The U.S. Supreme Court determined back in 1965 that a baby is deemed viable between the twenty-four to twenty-eight weeks of gestation.[3] I technically understood this issue in law school. I cannot comprehend it now. Am I now hearing this nurse use the word *viable* to refer to my baby? Is she saying that my baby might be born premature? My high-risk pregnancy never meant this to me before this moment.

"We have to push the baby back in, Kim," the head nurse announces.

"Okay."

"Are you willing to help us do that? Can we do that?" the other nurse chimes in.

"Yes!"

"Now, this is going to hurt. You must be strong. Don't let us push you down. Hold yourself up. We are going to push the baby back in, because he's trying to come out."

"Okay."

"Be strong, Kim. Okay?"

"Yes!"

The nurses tell me to get on all fours. I comply. They put on their gloves. The head nurse holds my shoulders. The other nurse inserts her hand inside me. She forms a fist and pushes. And pushes. And pushes. The head nurse continues to hold me, helping me to resist the pressure.

After several seconds, it stops. We're all exhausted. It did not work. We have to do it again. Three more times, again. It's excruciatingly painful. But it works, a little.

Afterwards, I'm so sore that I need the medicine in the intravenous drip to sleep. My previous refusals to take the medication were to protect my baby from being drug addicted. This child deserves me to be stronger, but the pain is so intense. I need the medication.

When I'm finally released from the hospital, I don't tell anyone about that ordeal. It's not something you want to tell people. I pray and ask the Lord to please let me get to twenty-eight weeks. "Permit me to avoid another failed pregnancy, dear Lord."

My doctor extends my work disability. He orders me to rest and limit my activities. My ultrasounds are rescheduled to biweekly on Monday and Thursday. And Timothy? He decides that even though he isn't quite ready to marry me, he's committed to his child. Especially concerned about my going up and down the stairs in my house, Timothy thinks it's best if he stays with me more often during the week. Furthermore, there are household chores a pregnant woman shouldn't perform while carrying his child.

As I continue to grow in size and concern, I hesitate to buy items to decorate my baby's room. Maternity clothes are another matter. Fortunately, there are fashionable options available since regular attire no longer fits. Everyone says I look happy and cute in my outfits. They also remark how big I am. They can't understand why I look like I'm about to deliver.

Tired of explaining the effect of the fibroids on my pregnancy, my full focus turns to helping this little one grow inside me. We've learned that I'm carrying a little boy. Timothy wants to discuss his son's name. Will he be a junior? No, we agree. We also agree that since my son's mother is not his father's wife, this little boy will have his mother's last name until her last name becomes his father's last name. Maybe now his father will reconsider our marriage. In any event, his first name will be biblical.

"Ananias!" Timothy exclaims.

"What?"

"Let's name him Ananias?"

"You mean the one who died because of his financial sin? No."

"Hezekiah."

"He'll get beat up every day in school with a name like that," I say. "I'll name him."

Fortunately, Timothy let the naming experiment go. There's no way he's going to screw up my son's name. A boy's name has to be well thought out. It has to mean something. I embark on studying and researching the meaning of boy names. Checking the popular names for the year, Jacob and Andrew jump out at me. I'm not getting warm fuzzy feelings when I say Jacob, so I cross it off the list. I remember that a woman I know just recently named her son Andrew, so I cross it off the short list, too.

Looking at the popular names again, I see it. The perfect name—Daniel. Reflecting on the character of the famous biblical prophet, how he stood up to the king, remained steadfast in his devotion to God, braved the lion's den, and positively influenced many including the three Hebrew boys, the name Daniel is selected. The name that means, "God is my judge."[4] Yes, Daniel. God will judge my baby Daniel's life and he'll be raised to fear and serve the Lord.

"I want to name him, Daniel," I tell Timothy.

"Daniel?" he asks.

"Yes."

"Hmm. Okay."

Only for a Little While

Settled.

Now, to get back to ensuring I remain pregnant for at least twenty-eight weeks. The nurses said twenty-four weeks, but I'm asking God for more time. Daniel must be more than just viable, he has to thrive and survive! Twenty-eight weeks is only eight weeks away. I'm determined to do everything right this time, so I touch and talk to my little Daniel constantly.

"Just rest baby, Daniel. Mommy loves you."

Monday, February 4, 2002. The next ultrasound test day. The radiologist comes into the exam room and asks me if they can perform a vaginal exam.

Bracing for pain, I say, "Sure."

As expected, the test is uncomfortable. She says my fluids are not at a good level. She'll check it out again on Thursday. Since the exam increases my pain, I'm advised not to do anything strenuous for the next few days. "Take it easy," she tells me. I listen and comply.

The next day is an unusually pleasing one, because Timothy is with me. I go to bed to rest in the early evening while he cooks dinner. Unhappily, the excruciating pain returns. My routine whenever I have that level of pain is to go to the bathroom. It's more comfortable to sit on the toilet than to lay in bed or on the floor. After shuffling my way to the bathroom, I feel an unusual amount of pressure as I lower myself. Suddenly, a gush of something comes out of me. It feels like I've lost control of my bodily functions. It's incredibly quick. When I look in the toilet, there's blood. A lot of blood. I scream for Timothy. I scream again, louder and more urgently. He comes rushing up the stairs.

"What's wrong?" he says.

"I need to go to the hospital. Something is not right. Something is wrong!"

I know what's happening. I can't tell him. I want to be wrong. I want someone to tell me I'm terribly wrong. Maybe the doctors will save him. Maybe he will not come just yet.

Maybe ...

At the hospital, they check his heart. I can see the monitor. It's moving slowly. Very slowly.

The doctor finally tells me, "Kim, you are losing the baby. We are going to have to take you up to labor and delivery."

"Why?"

"You'll have to deliver the baby."

Deliver the baby? I don't understand. I'm speechless and numb and sad. Actually, I'm furiously paralyzed with disbelief. The unfairness of this moment has crippled me.

"Will someone get my boyfriend? Will he be able to come up?"

"Yes. We'll get him now."

When Timothy comes into the emergency room, I tell him what's happening. He says nothing. He refuses to believe me. For the first time in our three years together, I witness him showing utter anger and sadness. He's been blindsided by this news. I ask him to call my mom and sister to have them to come to the hospital. He says he's also calling his cousin, the gynecologist. She will have something to say about all of this. I hope he's right.

When they wheel me to labor and delivery, I'm dismayed. Here I am, a pregnant woman with a dying baby inside of me that I'm about to deliver, yet I hear the joyful cries of newborn babies down the hall. It's an awkwardly cruel state of affairs. My only recourse is to try not to fall apart and concentrate on my loved ones. By now, Timothy is in full anger mode. When the doctor comes in to my room, he confirms that he will no longer try to save the pregnancy or our son. He asks me if I want drugs as we wait for my body to continue the premature labor. Daniel will be delivered when my body is ready.

Helpless to save my baby, there's nothing I can do. Not to help Timothy. Not to stop the tears that my sister's trying to hide from me. Not to comfort Daniel's grandmother whose hurt is indescribable. Not to save my precious little Daniel. My precious little baby boy.

God, why?

It's a sad, quiet and mournful process. I hold Timothy's hand through the delivery. He stays close by my side. We do not cry much during the delivery. At least, not with each other. I'm too drugged. He's too angry.

I deliver Daniel on Tuesday, February 5, 2002. Daniel does not cry, and no one smacks his bottom to check his lungs. He's taken away. The doctor comes back in to the room to tell us we will be able to hold him for a little while. He says they're cleaning him up and will bring him back to us soon. We are advised to not be alarmed when we see his chest moving. It's just his heart's still beating. It would eventually stop.

Though I'm drugged and reacting slowly, the doctor's words are the strangest, most inconsistent I've ever heard. If Daniel's heart is beating, why can't they save him? Timothy must be thinking the same thing because he is livid at this news. He asks his cousin for advice. She reluctantly confirms the doctor's report. Daniel cannot be saved. The events of the past few hours are foggy to me. This must be a really bad dream. A nightmare. A true nightmare.

The nurses bring my Daniel to me. He stunningly beautiful. A cocoa-colored dream who looks like me! He does not quite weigh a pound, yet he's long, with lengthy legs and arms. His little nose is as cute as a button. His lips are perfect. His eyes are closed. He appears to be sleeping. I hold him tight and kiss him. I stare to take in every bit of him. My baby boy. My Daniel. As I soak him in, I desperately want him to open his eyes and cry out a loud, screeching, newborn cry. Of course, he does not.

After what seems like twenty seconds, they take him and disappear. Then, we cry. Together, we cry. My drugged-out cry is slow and full of the agony of a woman who will never see her little baby boy again. Timothy's cry is full of despair of a man who can't solve this problem and save his child. The nurse or doctor, I'm not sure which one, comes in at that moment to tell me that I will need to decide if we want to donate Daniel's body for research. That's when I finally lose all control.

Donate his body for research? Why did she ask me? The mother? The childless mother. The words, the timing, the concept, the complete and total lack of decency overwhelms me. Timothy steps in to scream at them in his usual, precise way. He reminds them that we just lost our baby and the last thing they need to ask me is that question. We are both unaware that this health care provider is simply following the law that requires maternal consent for the procurement or use of fetal tissue or organs.[5]

Eventually, the drugs take over and I go to sleep. When I awake, I'm no longer in labor and delivery, but a regular hospital room. I'm no longer a new mom. Just a sick person in the hospital who's expected to leave without her baby. I went there pregnant. I'm leaving an empty woman. Empty womb. Empty arms. Empty heart.

Despite everything I know and all of my years with the Lord, no scriptures comfort me. None even come to mind. The tumult of the last few months, losing Daniel and Timothy's reaction leave me debilitated. The ultimate hope and utter despair of it all is too much to bear. It was enough to hold on to my sanity let alone my faith and integrity. I wonder what wrong I did that would lead to losing my son. What exactly is God punishing me for? Or is it Timothy's transgressions that procured this suffering? It must be him. He's getting over this too fast anyway. His life is back to normal while I'm still crying and missing my baby. I need comforting and an explanation from him. When I don't get it, I verbally lash out at him. My most vicious attack is reserved for him. Because he is supposed to understand me, and he doesn't.

There are a few people that are allowed to visit. When they come in they are devastated for me and say the things they believe they should say. Not much more. After all, what do you say to a mother who has no child?

The Lady Who Gets It

Once I'm able to grab my Bible again, I find a mother who surprisingly speaks to what I'm feeling. Tragedy, child loss, anger, relationship stress, and eventual healing are the name of the game for her. She gets a bad rap for her honest words of misunderstanding during grief, when she should be applauded for her authentic expressions of agony. In one moment, this woman lost ten children in a violent, desert windstorm. Her response to such horrific events, her words, fury and lingering distain for her husband make perfect sense to me. Woefully, not so among historic Christian theologians. They unfairly apply epitaphs without empathy, calling her "The Devil's Accomplice" and "An Instrument of Satan."[6]

My soul commiserates with this woman, finding that she is not the epitome of evil, but my sacred partner in genuine female hurt and humanity. Though only seven of the 1,070 verses in the entire book of Job mention or refer to her, how God and her husband graciously handle her brashness strikingly differs from what we have been taught about her. In truth, she gives women like me hope for a brighter future.

"Then said his wife unto him, Dost thou still retain thine integrity? curse God, and die." (Job 2:9)

These are the words that define my sister. We don't know her name. Only that she's "Job's wife." In lieu of continuing to call her that, and to help you get to know her as I do, we'll call her "Lady Job" or "Lady" for short.

Lady is a woman who just learned of the death of her ten children along with the loss of her home, business, and great wealth. If that's not enough, her husband is stricken with a sudden disgusting illness that includes "terrible boils from head to foot" (Job 2:7 NLT). Ostensibly, in the midst of her grieving, Lady must care for him.

Lady's question to her husband is troublesome, but not the worst thing a child of God can say. I'm glad Lady asked this question centuries ago. Her confusion about what happened and why is informed by one common lie inside her mind and many of ours.

Lies Fill My Head

Initially, I thought Lady's statements indicated that she wants to run from God. That her words represent her anger at Job's strength and faith during all this calamity while she's crumbling under the weight of her heartbreak. It appears that she's displaying a lack of faith in God. The more I study and reflect on this passage, I realize she's communicating something more theologically significant.

In his book, *The Lies We Believe*, Dr. Chris Thurman names the "religious lie" at work in Lady's mind and words. This lie says the only reason for my pain and suffering is sin.[7] In some cases, this is correct thinking. The principle that you reap what you sow is true. We cannot escape the consequences of our choices, including our choice to sin. On the other hand, it is not true that all pain, loss, and suffering are the result of sin. Not all cancer patients get the disease because they sinned. Not all mothers lose their children because they sinned. You know this. But this lie captured your thinking at one time or another. Usually, we believe our own sin caused our pain. Lady is different. She doesn't assume it's her sin, but her husband Job's sin that's resulted in the adversities befallen them. Logically, it makes sense because he's the one who's also physically stricken. In Lady's mind, if Job would just stop pretending he's upright, curse God and join her precious children in death, then these unimaginable mishaps will end. Furthermore, she won't be forced to care for the one who did this to her.

On second thought, it's puzzling that Lady accuses Job. As his wife, she has intimate knowledge of his devotion to God. She must know what God knows about Job, right? Two times, God says Job "is the finest man in all the earth. He is blameless—a man of complete integrity. He fears God and stays away from evil" (Job 1:8, 2:3 NLT).

Why is Lady blaming him for her loss? Because like us, her grief has taken control of her reasoning. Right now, she wants the pain to stop. She wants an explanation for what's happening. Deep down, she believes bad things should not happen to good people like her. She knows she's done nothing wrong, so someone else must be to blame.

That's certainly how I felt. Sure, I became pregnant before marriage and fornication is sin. But also, I forgot that since the fall of Adam and Eve, disasters, debt, disease, and death are realities of life. Such lapse in memory is particularly prevalent during my trials. My spiritual radar does not always bend towards believing that God allows trials to strengthen my faith in Him. That He would want to prove my uprightness is out of the question, because it doesn't make sense.

But the Bible says otherwise. It teaches us that God allows Job's suffering because of Job's righteous. By default, as Job's wife, Lady's faith and integrity are being tested, too. Their sort of suffering is not logical. That's because it's divinely ordained. At the time of her speaking, Lady can no more see this than any other hurting person can. In her ignorance, she says these unfortunate words.

> *"But he said unto her, Thou speakest as one of the foolish women speaketh. What? shall we receive good at the hand of God, and shall we not receive evil? In all this did not Job sin with his lips." (Job 2:10)*

Lady doesn't not want to hear this from Job. She wants him to admit his sin and end it all. In the alternative, it would be nice if he would empathize. Tell her, *this sucks*, Job! Tell her you didn't do anything but offer daily prayers for those children. Admit that you don't know why your prayers haven't worked. You don't know what God is doing. Let her know you're hurting, too.

He would do that if it was the right thing for him to do. The problem for Lady is that blameless Job does not lie to her by doing what she wants him to do or by telling her what she wants to hear. Intuitively, he lovingly corrects her misguided statements with the truth, practicing the principles articulated by the apostle Paul when he says, "Then we will no longer be infants, tossed back and forth by the waves, and blown here and there by every wind of teaching and by the cunning and craftiness of people in their deceitful scheming. Instead, speaking the truth in love, we will grow to become in every respect the mature body of him who is the head, that is, Christ" (Ephesians 4:14-15 NIV). Job is concerned for Lady's maturity. He's not enjoying their condition either. But he's also not willing to allow their condition to force them into believing a lie about God. God loves them, and they must continue to love God.

You know how spiritually blind your loss has left you. You too end up saying strange things. At these times, the forever-ness of love ought to supersede. But when the object of your hope and life is gone, the last thing you can do is 1 Corinthians 13 love. You need someone to show patience, kindness, and the rest to you while you are contrary. Initially, the more they love you the more you want them to disappear, even if they are among those who love you most and best.

Lady feels this way, too. As her spirit crumbles, her husband is steady. He faithfully blesses God and prays. He seems oblivious to how the fullness of all the years she raised, cooked, cleaned, and served their large family, spawned the hollowing drain of losing their children. Her most precious identity, her motherhood, has been torn away from her without warning and she doesn't know what to do, how to act, or what to say. Her faith is weakening, but Job knows it's not completely lost.

Notice closely what he says to her. His response tells us more about her than her own words do. When Lady speaks to Job, she speaks out of fresh torment. When Job speak to Lady, he speaks out of time-proven knowledge of her character. He knows the type of woman, business partner, wife, and mother she's been. Lady is Job's suitable woman of integrity. She is not one of the fools described in Psalm 14:1 who "say in their hearts, 'There is no God'" (NLT).

Even now, she still acknowledges God's existence and His involvement in their lives. Notwithstanding her present ill-advised language, Job knows this foolish speaking is not her style. He looks beyond her faulty words and reminds her of herself. He ministers that they must accept what God gives—both the good and the evil.

Evil? Did Job say that evil comes from the hand of God? Yes, he did. And more surprisingly, the Bible says he did not sin by saying that. You see, though Job knows nothing about the heavenly conversation in chapters 1 and 2 between God and Satan where God let Satan perpetrate these bad and miserable occurrences against Job, he trusts God. When he refers to evil coming from God, he's not attributing the immorality of Satan to God. Job rightly recognizes that the pleasant and unpleasant events of life are subject to God's sovereignty. At first glance, his words seem incredibly harsh, but they're actually his way of addressing Lady's incorrect doctrine. He's protecting his wife's heart. Unbeknown to her, Job sets her healing in motion.

If Lady is anything like me, Job's comforting words further infuriate her. He sounds like the calls I received from compassionate family, friends, and fellow church members who intended to help relieve the hurt. They didn't say much to me, but when they did, they told me things like: "hold on," "joy comes in the morning," "all things work together for good," "pray without ceasing," "in all things give God thanks."

You know the type. They mean well, but you want them to shut up. You want them to walk just five minutes in your shoes and stop with the cutesy, righteous words. The more they said these things the more my belly fluttered and cried for my baby. I wanted to holler and scream, not gracefully wait on God, or pray or thank Him that my dreams were ripped away from me. Their words felt extraordinarily uncaring and outlandish. Until Lady Job helped me recognize that big lie stuck in my own heart about God and how He is supposed to keep all suffering away from me. When Lady's husband spoke to her, he informed me that when in grief, it's best to listen to someone—spouse, partner, family or friend, who's faith and integrity can redirect me to the truth about God.

"My breath is strange to my wife, though I intreated for the children's sake of mine own body." (Job 19:17)

I used to think that Lady was only mentioned in chapter 2 of the book of Job, but her husband mentions her after that. In this verse, we see that she is still mourning and lamenting. She continues to take out her frustrations on Job. Instead of treating her husband like she did before their tragedy, she's now offended by his presence. Completely understandable. Healing takes time. Transforming your mind takes time. None of us recover at the same rate. But I want to make sure we understand her process.

This verse may be taken literally. Perhaps the smell of his breath is so stinky that when he speaks to her she has to turn away. After all, this chapter reveals that his illness is now causing him to lose a lot of weight. Longstanding illnesses like this can sometimes lead to unavoidable bodily odors. The correct response of course would be to help our loved one by cleaning and freshening them. But Lady is not ready to offer that kind of help. On the other hand, Job's physical breath may not be what's offending Lady. The life in the words Job continues to speak may be repulsive her. Not because she doesn't believe God. But like Job's lingering disease, Lady's still blaming Job for their dire straits.

It's now that we see how her treatment is affecting Job. Before this, we really don't think about it. We pity and understand her so much we fail to see that as she refuses him, she's inflicting more wounds on him. She, and we, totally overlook that not for his own sake, but for the sake of their family, and the children they lost, Job cries out to her. Job misses the children, too. He's also missing Lady. They need not suffer individually. They can still honor their relationship with God together as husband and wife. He doesn't understand her aloofness. A classic male/female stalemate exists in his brain and her brain.[8]

No matter his own turmoil, Job will never understand Lady's brand of anguish. That's not his fault. As a man, he can only give her what he has to offer—a dogmatic and systematic solution. He's likely wondering why she hasn't applied it yet. For her part, Lady equally cannot understand why Job won't admit his wrong and empathize with her. She and he are fearfully and wonderfully created to suit one another. If only they could see it!

Similarly, I could not understand why Timothy didn't know how badly I hurt. Why couldn't he stay with me longer as I cried? His own processing of our loss never really mattered to me. All of our thoughts were supposed to focus on me. "I'm the mother," I thought. "My loss is more important than his. My belly is no longer big. My child is no longer kicking inside of me. My body is changing. My heart is broken. My baby is gone."

His child is gone, too.

"If mine heart have been deceived by a woman, or if I have laid wait at my neighbor's door; Then let my wife grind unto another, and let others bow down upon her." (Job 31:9-10)

There it is. Job's grief. Twenty-nine chapters after Lady uttered those infamous words, the father of her children finally proclaims his innocence. He tells his friends (and her?) that he did not do anything wrong. He didn't commit adultery, the ultimate sin of husbandly sins to a married woman. Emphatically, Job goes beyond a mere admission of innocence to offer Lady some recourse. He says that if anyone can find who Job committed this most unimaginable sin with, then Lady would be right to leave him for another man and receive the righteous praise of others for what she has endured.

Up until now, Lady believes she's honored her marriage vows by remaining with Job, but she's rejected him by ignoring what we know today as the "to have and to hold, from this day forward, for better, for worse, for richer, for poorer, in sickness and in health, to love and to cherish, till death do us part" stuff. Since he's not dead, her wifely duties are woefully lacking, and their relationship is not good. By the way, since Job himself has not abandoned Lady, he is perhaps sick and tired of being sick and tired with her. At his wits end, he's desperately reaching for his wife. We know this because you can't be rejected where you don't reach.

Reaching for Love

Who's desperately reaching for you? Is it the father of your child? What if he's not reaching or has not reached for you? Do you give up or skip over this section of the book because it doesn't apply to you? Please don't! Please accept the reach of those who love you. If not him, then your other children, family, friends, and church members. Those who offer those words you don't want to hear. Allow them to keep reaching for you. They understand you're grieving, but they miss you. Your laugh, hug, and smile lights up their lives. Will you let them bring you out, or will you continue to make them suffer without you? The choice is yours.

If you have no one, seek out a church you can attend. Keep seeking until you find a place where people notice you as a new visitor or member and they reach for you. Most churches are full of loving people who can discern a new, needy heart like yours. Like Lady, it may take time to fully accept the offer, but place yourself in an atmosphere of love. Be willing to let them love you out of this hurt.

> *"So the Lord blessed the latter end of Job more than his beginning: for he had fourteen thousand sheep, and six thousand camels, and a thousand yoke of oxen, and a thousand she asses. He had also seven sons and three daughters." (Job 42:12-13)*

We have arrived at the hallelujah part of Lady's story. I know she's not mentioned here, but she's here nonetheless. Before we get to the victory in these verses, we need to see something that happens just before the blessing.

In Job chapters 38-42, God ends Job's whining by directly speaking to him. The weight of all of his suffering and the judgment of those closest to him cause Job to begin to complain against God. Out of another nature-bending wind, God answers Job through a series of questions and stern statements about God's own authority and dominion. Job must stand up before God and account for his own reproofs concerning Him. In true Job fashion, he repents before the Lord. God accepts Job's contrite spirit, and turns to discipline Job's friends, whose unrighteous doctrine were of no comfort. God tells Job to pray for their folly and He again accepts Job's prayers.

It seems that everyone in the book of Job is addressed for their words. Except Lady.

Why doesn't God speak to Lady out of the whirlwind? Is He ignoring her? Doesn't she matter? Absolutely! I do not know why He doesn't speak to her directly. It may be that Job's response to her in chapter 2 is sufficient, given her loss. Our God is the Father of compassion, after all. He is not vindictive and knows better than you what you can endure. "For he knows how weak we are; he remembers we are only dust" (Psalm 103:14 NLT).

In the most comforting way, God deals with us individually. How He responds to Job, each of his three friends, and Lady is as individual as His dealings with you and me. When I lost my children, I did not have a husband who comforted me. God gave me family and friends to minister to me and guide me through my sadness. They spoke to me gently because that's what I needed. In the same way, God spoke to Lady through Job until she came out of her grief.

Unto the God of All Grace

And come out she did. We see in these verses that God blessed her by restoring her home, business, marriage, and motherhood. Sure, the verses only speak of Job, but how did Job have another ten children without Lady? Nowhere in the book of Job does it state that he married another woman or had a concubine. Job is consistently called a blameless man. Therefore, he wouldn't have done this. Though the Bible is full of great men who had multiple wives and concubines, God never condones this behavior. We have no reason to think that Job did either. Therefore, when Job receives his blessing, Lady does too! No more blaming, no more repulsiveness, and no more rejection. Lady and Job are restored, and God gets all the glory.

My story does not track exactly with Lady's story. God has not given me two natural children in place of the two I've lost. But, oh how He's restored my faith and hope in Him! Through the constant prayers and love of others, my grief eventually subsided. Like Lady, I have a testimony that no one can ever take from me.

Reflection

Whose sin do you believe caused your loss?

Do you believe that the love of God and others will help you to restore your joy again?

Prayer

Dear God,

Like Lady Job, I have been misunderstood. I cannot describe my grief sufficiently to anyone. They don't seem to understand how hurt I am. It's causing me to lose things that were once dear to me, like my family and friends. I now realize I have believed lies about my loss that I need to let go of. In a strange way, they have been my comfort during this time in my life. But I want to be in a righteous state of knowing. Please direct me to Your Word and Your people who will teach me the right way to go. Give me an open spirit to listen to the truth even when it seems harsh and accusatory. Make me willing to mature. I want to be loved, but I'm afraid to love like that again. Remind me that Your love is not hurtful. Remind me that You have people who will not hurt me. Give me the courage to be loved. I need it so bad.

In the name of Jesus, Amen.

6
...

Seeking Grace in Acceptance

"Will the Lord cast off forever? and will he be favourable
no more? Is his mercy clean gone forever? doth his promise
fail for evermore? Hath God forgotten to be gracious? hath
he in anger shut up his tender mercies? Selah."
(Psalm 77:7-9)

No Words

When a mother loses a child, she needs an overdose of empathy from her man. Didn't we learn that from Lady Job? When her man didn't (or couldn't) comply, she built an angry wall of sarcasm. I discover I'm just like her.

Apparently, if you're a man who lost a child, you don't say much to the mother who's just lost your baby boy. In fact, you ignore her. You stay away from her. You do everything you can to keep from letting her know that you feel so sorry for her. You really don't know what to say to her. You can't imagine her grief and you don't want to share in it. It might be contagious.

If you have to see her however, you're stuck. Of course, there's your own emotions and questions. You refuse to confront those. You really don't have to because her crying is relentless. It's consuming. You can't handle her pain. Since you think you can't really help her, but you should do something, you finally figure out what to say.

"Kim, it's time to move on."

At least, that's what you say if you're Timothy. Within a week of Daniel's death, he decides he can no longer tolerate my agonizing tears. It's time to get on with his life. He tells me he wants to go hang out with his friends. I guess he no longer wants to hang out with me. This is cruel and unusual treatment. My mind can't picture that maybe he's unable to endure any more of my crying. Or that maybe this loss is getting to him. I only think about me. He doesn't tell me anything to defy my selfish thinking. He just tells me to move on. Oh, and that he's leaving to go spend time with his friends. It's up to me to deal with all that's going on inside, alone.

Understandably, my crying doesn't stop that easily. His leaving only makes it worse. Instead of ending within a few days of being home from the hospital without a baby to care for, genuine grief takes up residence in my baby-empty arms. The truth that I lost the baby I desperately wanted assaults me. My arms wrap around my chest. I cradle myself to sleep all day and all night. My Daniel is gone. The events of his death, those last hours, the hospital room, the smell, the sound of other mothers' crying babies, and my son's quietness replay in my mind. Over and over again I see his little face and body. His body. His tiny body that is still in the hospital.

After giving Daniel back to hospital staff, Timothy and I know we have to discuss the question that had been posed to me. Will I donate his body for research? We agree that we will not donate Daniel or any parts of his body to science. The thought of it just doesn't make sense to me. Cutting him up to examine the growth of his organs tears my heart apart. We want to honor him by treating him as a human being, not a science project. We want his body to remain intact. He must be returned to us. We don't fully understand that this means we will be subject to emerging federal and state law regarding live birth and fetal death.

On September 11, 2000, the U.S. House of Representatives presented a report to the White House entitled the "Born-Alive Infants Protection Act of 2000."[1] This bill responded to the partial-birth abortions performed across the country, and several court cases that deem the partially-born fetus not a "person."

Under this House Bill, the U.S. Code definitions of "the words 'person', 'human being', 'child', and 'individual' shall include every infant member of the species homo sapiens who is born alive at any stage of development."[2]

The bill specified:

"the term 'born alive', with respect to a member of the species homo sapiens, means the complete expulsion or extraction from its mother of that member, at any stage of development, who after such expulsion or extraction breathes or has a beating heart, pulsation of the umbilical cord, or definite movement of voluntary muscles, regardless of whether the umbilical cord has been cut, and regardless of whether the expulsion or extraction occurs as a result of natural or induced labor, cesarean section, or induced abortion."[3]

In our state, this is called a "live birth," which "means the expulsion or extraction from its mother of a product of conception, irrespective of the period of gestation, which shows any evidence of life at any moment after such expulsion or extraction."[4]

Where does my Daniel fit in to all of this? Was he a live birth? Was he born alive? After my premature labor, Daniel's heart appeared to be beating until shortly after his birth. That seemed to meet these definitions. My baby was alive. He was a human being, or homo sapien. The nurse at the hospital disputed this. She said he was not alive. He only appeared so.

His birth was his death.

Thus, his was not a live birth, but a "fetal death," meaning "the expulsion or extraction from its mother of a product of conception after sixteen-weeks gestation, which shows no evidence of life after such expulsion or extraction."[5] I disagree with her assessment. I held him. I felt the slight vibrations of his chest moving. He should be noted as having been alive. But he wasn't.

Years later, my state, Pennsylvania, would recognize this heartbreaking conundrum with the passage of the Senate Bill 326. This Bill amended the State Vital Statistics Act and allowed the provision of birth certificates for stillborn babies.[6] But my Daniel's vital statistics are documented by way of a death certificate. I wonder, how can someone who was never alive be officially dead? The effect of all of this legal stuff means that Timothy and I couldn't take him from the hospital. A funeral home had to retrieve his body. He requires burial.

Waiting and Waiting

We decide to give our son a proper Christian interment. The thought of seeing his little body again is too much for me to handle. I ask Timothy to make the arrangements. He says he will. I trust him.

After receiving no news about Daniel's funeral for more than a week, I ask Timothy for an update. He tells me he's not yet scheduled it. I'm horrified that my dead baby is still at the hospital but try not to panic. It's only been a week. Certainly, he won't leave my baby, our son, in the hospital, abandoned as if he wasn't loved and cherished. Wanting not to nag Timothy yet wanting to hold on to our relationship so that we can get married and try to have another child again, I don't say anything.

Days pass and still no word of when we're going to funeralize my Daniel. After two more weeks, I ask again.

"I said, I'll handle it," he tells me.

"When? I don't want Daniel to be left in the hospital like that. He's been there too long. When are you going to arrange his funeral?"

"As soon I have the money."

"What? What! Is he serious? Did he just say that he did not have enough money to bury our baby?" I ask myself. "Why not? Why wasn't this important enough to get the money any way he can? Ask your family. Ask my family. But, God man, don't leave him there any longer!"

"I have the money," I say.

I'm furious. This could have been handled long before now. It's ridiculous that he let this go on this long. How could he? Not only hasn't he scheduled the funeral, but he hasn't even called a funeral home to pick Daniel up from the hospital. My baby's body is just sitting there, in a hospital morgue, I suppose, abandoned.

"I don't want you to pay for it. I said I will do it and I will. Just wait, Kim."

I do everything possible to hold my tongue from severely cursing him. I feel my hands forming into fist, and my feet itching to contact his back side. I make myself ignore the chairs, lamps, coffee tables, and anything else in the room that I'm strong enough to pick up and throw at him. He's telling me to stay calm and keep my mouth shut, while he ignores the fact that our child's remains are sitting in the hospital. Every hair on the back of my neck stands to attention as I try to calm down. But, I explode.

"Get my baby out of that hospital. Make the arrangements for my child. Do not leave him there one more day. Do you hear me!" I scream at the top of my vocal ability. I want Timothy and everyone in the city to hear me as I say this. I want everyone to know that my child matters and that he deserves a funeral. I must protect his body.

My threat is to no avail. It takes a few more outbursts before my family steps in. Timothy contacts the funeral home that handled my dad's and my brother's bodies just a few years prior. He's informed that they have a casket that's the perfect size for my little baby boy's body. They advise Timothy that most people in our situation don't have a funeral, but a graveside burial service in which the casket is not opened. After I agree, Timothy works with the funeral home to secure Daniel's body from the hospital.

Finally!

My family also contacts the cemetery, who agrees to open a small plot next to my dad and my brother, for my son. They agree to not charge us for a full plot. Though my baby's burial is finally planned, my fury is not quelled. I hate Timothy for doing this. I vow to hate him for the rest of my life. I cannot stand to talk to him. I don't want him anywhere near me. Not even at the burial. I threaten to not appear if he's there.

Saying Goodbye

Finally, on a cloudy Saturday morning in April, my Daniel is buried. In attendance are my mom, brother, sister, pastor, the mortician, Timothy, and me. I did not want to sit next to him, but there are only four chairs. Since I'm certainly not going to stand, I sit. Then, he sits next to me. My mom sits next to me, too. I'm glad she does. There is only so much acting up I'll do in front of her. I'm certainly not going to curse Timothy out in front of my mother and the preacher. Besides, I've already done that during the phone call en route to the cemetery.

This burial is one of the saddest ones I've ever attended. Of course, because it's my son's burial, but also because it marks the burial of more than my precious baby, Daniel. This graveside service marks the burial of my last child, my relationship with Timothy, and my dream of trying to have another baby with him, too.

"And I saw the dead, small and great, stand before God; and the books were opened: and another book was opened, which is the book of life: and the dead were judged out of those things which were written in the books, according to their works." (Revelation 20:12)

My pastor reads this verse over the tiny casket. He tells us that the death of this little one, my Daniel, has not gone unnoticed by God. He reassures us that at the end of life, no matter whether your life has been long, or as short as Daniel's, God stands to receive you. All human lives would be judged. So, what then would be the judgment of one like Daniel who has not really lived? He says that Daniel is safe in the loving arms of Jesus, who received Him as His own. He tells us that Daniel is not roaming or without care, guidance, and nurturing.

Tears stream down my face. I'm sad that I will never hold my boy. I'm happy he is being held by Jesus. Though his life has not even been lived here on earth, in heaven, he's able to live an abundant, joyful life. I imagine that as his body went into the ground next to my dad and my brother, my little baby boy is now with Jesus. He has his grandpop and uncle to show him the way around heaven. He's never going to be alone. He's with his earthly family and his heavenly family. That makes me happy.

As we leave the cemetery, I know my relationship is over. I cannot forget what Timothy's done. How he could be so selfish as to let Daniel sit in that hospital that long troubles me. Back at home, I sit on the couch and stare at the walls for hours. Just a few months before, this house was brimming with the hope that the life growing inside of me would soon run its halls, eat at its dinner table, and play on its cherrywood floors. Now, there's no baby in my womb and there would be no baby within these walls. I'm a childless mother. Worse still, I'm a mother who just buried her son. I feel no honor in that.

The Best Way to Honor Your Dead

Daniel's burial bothered me for years. My perceived failure to protect his body is the biggest failure of my life. I never even visited him at that hospital. I didn't keep watch over his body. I often wonder where they stored him. How they preserved him. If they preserved him. Since I could not prevent his death, I should have done something more about protecting his body until his burial.

Though time cannot be recaptured, victory can be garnered through the strength of others. Those mothers who know what to do when their children die. Mothers who accept their death with grace and dignity. Who refuse to believe that God's forsaken them or that what seems to be His injustice cannot be turned to honor. Those mothers who know that acceptance is the beginning of healing.

Rizpah of the Bible is such a woman.

Like me, she never reaches wife status of the man for whom she bore sons. However, Rizpah is the acknowledged mistress of Israel's first king, Saul. The two sons she has with the king are ultimately murdered by hanging. Yet, Rizpah doesn't let their bodies remain abandoned. She protects them as only a mother can.

The infamy of her story fueled the writings of 19th century poets, including Americans William Cullen Bryant[7] and Joseph Lemuel Chester,[8] and British Poet Laureate, Lord Alfred Tennyson.[9] None, however, captured the essence of Rizpah's story so intimately as female poet, Menella Bute Smedly.[10] It may be that Menella felt a mother's despair at the loss of her children in a way the men could only describe. Her words tell of Rizpah's loss with careful empathy.

> "This is the doom
> Of women; evermore beside the tomb,
> Where some pale passionate hope is laid asleep,
> To sit, as in a wilderness, and weep.
> And I accept it. …
> "One, speechless, weeps for joys that never were,
> But might have been; her heart's unanswer'd cry
> Is starved into the silence of despair."[11]

Nevertheless, what Menella's poetry left untouched, God's Word beautifully unearths. Rizpah's fidelity reveals an inner-strength not covertly found in women of the Old Testament. Until we meet this concubine turned heroine in 2 Samuel.

Under Scandalous Circumstances

"And Saul had a concubine, whose name was Rizpah, the daughter of Aiah: and Ishbosheth said to Abner, Wherefore hast thou gone in unto my father's concubine?"
(2 Samuel 3:7)

We are introduced to Rizpah in a strange set of circumstances. Saul, her man, is dead. As a result, the kingdom of Israel is severely divided. David is king of Judah, while Ishbosheth, Saul's son, has become king of Israel. As David continues to grow strong, his men defeat Ishbosheth's men in hand-to-hand battle. Consequently, Ishbosheth fears losing the throne. That's why it's irrational for him to accuse his own army commander, Abner of sleeping with Rizpah. You see, were it not for Abner, Ishbosheth would not be king of Israel. By accusing Abner of sleeping with his father's concubine, Ishbosheth essentially accuses Abner of severe betrayal. In doing that, he risks Abner's loyalty and the throne.[12] In the end, he loses both.

It curious why Ishbosheth brings Rizpah into this indictment of Abner. Abner seems to deny the crime. What then of Rizpah? Did she do something to suggest an affair with Abner? Or is this simply Ishbosheth's insecurity talking? Is he unsure of Rizpah's loyalty to the house of Saul? Why does that matter? Notice Ishbosheth refers to her as his "father's concubine." She holds a unique status as Saul's only concubine in the days when men, especially prominent men, had many wives and many more mistresses. Still, Rizpah is set apart. Even Abner honors her. As the mother of two of Saul's remaining sons, she thus poses a distinctive threat to Ishbosheth's reign. Her influence is substantial, especially if her sons are young men. It makes sense that Ishbosheth would want to taint her reputation before the people of Israel, making her and her sons appear unfit to succeed the throne. This makes Rizpah a noteworthy mother.

We find Rizpah again after Ishbosheth is killed and David becomes king of a unified Israel.

With David as king, you would expect that Israel has God's favor. The nation is not so fortunate. It finds itself in a three-year famine. Confounded, David seeks God about the reason for this plague. He learns that the famine is punishment for Saul's reckless slaughter of the Gibeonites, a people who entered into a treaty of protection from killing at the hand of Israel's armies. Wisely, David approaches the Gibeonites, offering to make atonement for Saul's misdeeds. He agrees to give the Gibeonites whatever they request. In response, the Gibeonites ask for seven of Saul's sons that they "will hang them up unto the Lord in Gibeah of Saul…" (2 Samuel 21:6).

Say what?

> *"But the king took the two sons of Rizpah the daughter of Aiah, whom she bare unto Saul, Armoni and Mephibosheth; and the five sons of Michal the daughter of Saul, whom she brought up for Adriel the son of Barzillai the Meholathite: And he delivered them into the hands of the Gibeonites, and they hanged them in the hill before the Lord: and they fell all seven together, and were put to death in the days of harvest, in the first days, in the beginning of barley harvest."*
> *(2 Samuel 21:8-9)*

David agrees to the Gibeonites' request. He chooses to take the sons of two women from Saul's family. Fittingly, David takes Rizpah's two sons as restitution. Since Ishbosheth is dead, to David's knowledge, these are the only direct sons of Saul that remain. As heart-wrenching as this must be, nevertheless, David hands these sons of Saul over to the Gibeonites to be killed. These verses don't tell us whether Rizpah knows what's about to happen to her sons. It doesn't tell us if she follows David, pulling at her son's arms, begging the king to let them go, but this heart-wrenching scene is clearly plausible.

William Cullen Bryant imagines it this way:

"Oh, what an hour for a mother's heart,
When the pitiless ruffians tore us apart!
When I clasped their knees and wept and prayed,
And struggled and shrieked to Heaven for aid,
And clung to my sons with desperate strength,
Till the murderers loosed my hold at length,
And bore me breathless and faint aside,
In their iron arms, while my children died.

> They died—and the mother that gave them birth
> Is forbid to cover their bones with earth."[13]

It is curious, however, that David hands Michal's five sons over to the Gibeonites, too. She is, after all, his own wife! But these are not her own children, or David's children. These are the sons of Adriel. A man from David's past. As the saga goes, for killing Goliath, Saul promised to give his oldest daughter, Merab, to David as a reward. However, "when the time came for Merab, Saul's daughter, to be given to David, she instead was given in marriage to Adriel, who was from Meholah" (1 Samuel 18:19 NET). These sons of Michal, then, are actually the sons of Merab, Michal's deceased older sister. To further complicate this part of the story, Michal and David have a strained marriage. Not because David has other wives, namely Bathsheba, but because of Michal's infamous behavior. You see, she "despised [David] in her heart" when she observed him praising God by dancing when he brought the ark of the Lord into Jerusalem (2 Samuel 6:16). In her words, "He exposed himself like a fool in the sight of the servant women of his officials!" (2 Samuel 6:20 GNT).

Ouch! For the record, it's generally not a good idea to call the king a fool. For this attitude, Michal was cursed and "had no children to the day of her death" (2 Samuel 6:23 NIV). These sons, therefore, who are actually grandsons of Saul, are handed over because David has no reason to protect them. Since Rizpah's two have already been taken, these five complete the Gibeonite demand.

The delivery of these sons must tug at David's heart. Michal's sons are his nephews. I'm sure he knew them. Even if he and Michal are estranged, delivering them to their death has to affect him, and Michal. Surely, this does not make him more endearing to her. And what of Rizpah's psyche? She's been loyal to the kingdom despite accusations to the contrary. What is her reward? A new king who does this? How can David deliver such a dramatic sacrifice to atone for Saul's sin, knowing that these sons, Rizpah's only sons, will be killed disgracefully by hanging?

We know too well that the death of a child by any means is devastating for a mother. But in these days, hanging is especially heinous. Per Israel's law, "If a man has committed a crime worthy of death, and is executed and then hanged on a tree, his body shall not remain on the tree overnight. You must bury him the same day, for anyone hanging on a tree is cursed of God. Don't defile the land the Lord your God has given you" (Deuteronomy 21:22-23 TLB).

In this case, the sons (and grandsons) truly suffer for the father's sin. Not just that, these sons, who were accustomed to grand living as the king's sons, are "cursed of God" in death. They die hungry at the beginning of the harvest. Whatever hope existed with the burgeoning harvest is replaced by this misery. What decency is there to salvage?

> *"And Rizpah the daughter of Aiah took sackcloth, and spread it for her upon the rock, from the beginning of harvest until water dropped upon them out of heaven, and suffered neither the birds of the air to rest on them by day, nor the beasts of the field by night." (2 Samuel 21:10)*

It's here where Michal and Rizpah are distinguished. We don't know what their feelings are about the sacrifice of their sons. We can suspect. Based on what we already know about Michal, she probably gives David a strong tongue lashing. If she hated him for dancing, you can only imagine what she feels for him at this. Rizpah is another story.

She accepts the deaths of her sons. She knows there is nothing she can do to bring her sons back. In her mourning, she determines that she can do something to ensure their honor. The sackcloth she takes out is at once the fabric of mourning and her bed of grace. She spreads the sackcloth on the rock where she can perch to stay with the bodies as she laments their deaths. All seven of them. Her sons and Michal's sons. Out on the stony hillside with them, Rizpah waits. Hungry. Protective. Motherly. All day and night. Not allowing these sons' bodies to be ravished by the ravenous birds or beasts. This living scarecrow fights back anything that would further disgrace the bodies of these men. Amid the smells, her growling stomach, the intense heat, the burning sun, she keeps watch.

For how long?

Until the rains come. Some commenters suggest she's there "days and weeks."[14] Others estimate her vigil last five to six months.[15] However long, she's there enough time to show that a mother's love can endure human vengeance, ravenous birds and animals, devastating weather, and death. While the curse remains, she's there. When the rains of deliverance arrive, she leaves. Now the remains of her sons can be removed from the tree and buried.

Laid to Rest

"And it was told David what Rizpah the daughter of Aiah, the concubine of Saul, had done." (2 Samuel 21:11)

It takes a strong woman to do what Rizpah does. To look on the decaying face of her sons, day after day. Knowing they will never again cry, see, or breathe. Remaining as loyal to them as she had been to their father. This is an uncommon act. An uncommon resolve. It is remarked throughout Israel and carried to the king as something that the highest officials of the land need to know. This woman, this mother is commendable. She is more valiant than Adriel, the father of the five killed, who Rizpah also protects. He's not here with her. No, it's the mother, Rizpah, who insists these human remains require dignified treatment. They cannot be left as if no one cared for them or knew them. Abandonment of a dead son's body is not an option.

Not for Rizpah.

Not for Kim.

And not for King David.

*"And David went and took the bones of Saul and the bones
of Jonathan his son from the men of Jabeshgilead, which had
stolen them from the street of Bethshan, where the Philistines
had hanged them, when the Philistines had slain Saul in
Gilboa: And he brought up from thence the bones of Saul and
the bones of Jonathan his son; and they gathered the bones of
them that were hanged. And the bones of Saul and Jonathan
his son buried they in the country of Benjamin in Zelah, in
the sepulchre of Kish his father: and they performed all that
the king commanded. And after that God was intreated for
the land." (2 Samuel 21:12-14)*

Rizpah's actions are not just remarkable, they are inspirational.
Not just for us today, but all those years ago for David, the king.
When he learns what she did, he realizes his own failure. Her valor
reminds him of what he's left undone. How the remains of his pre-
decessor and his best friend sit forsaken in foreign territory. It's time
for him to take extraordinary action to secure their remains. They all
deserve a proper burial. David then oversees the domestic burial of
Saul, Johnathan, Armoni, Mephibosheth, and Saul's five grandsons.
Then, thanks to Rizpah's wake, God shows Israel that he has not
forgotten them. His anger is lifted. He heals the land of the famine
curse. Rizpah's selfless act of love releases her sons' memory from
the ignominy of hanging. Without one spoken word, this mother's
acts unleash God's favor. Innocently, she frees herself to live with
the sweet memories of her sons, knowing that she has respectfully
honored them.

Don't we all need to do the same? So many of us remain pent up
with frustration, shame, and anger that our children have died. We
refuse to accept their deaths by doing what is necessary to honor their
lives. Moving on from death does not mean their deaths do not matter. Or that you are forgetting their lives. To the contrary. It means
that their lives matter so much that you use their deaths as a trigger

to release the best life in those you touch. You are willing to influence others to be strong in the areas of life that they secretly ignore.

My sister, allow for the proper burial of the unsettled remains of your child. Bury the negative thoughts, attitudes, and behaviors you continue to pursue. Discharge those who caused your child's death from your judgmental disgust. Allow the cleansing rains fall on your life to feed the mother's love that remains deep inside you. At the right time, the famine of love will end. Harvest time is coming.

God's Always Gracious

I eventually took my own advice. I laid to rest my anger-fueled, sarcastic attacks on Timothy. His seeming lack of thoughtfulness became a fact that no longer ignited negative emotions. My focus instead became remembering Daniel by honoring the gift of the brief moments of his life we shared together, not on Timothy's missteps or on making him pay for the pain. In return, God's loving grace has filled my heart and lifted my countenance. I believe that if He can do that for me, my best response is to accept what He's allowed and let Him handle the rest.

Reflection

What actions will you take to publicly accept your child's death? How will you release yourself to live and love again?

Prayer

Dear God,

Show me what to do. Nothing hurts like the death of my child. I am afraid to accept it. It seems like the wrong thing to do. If I accept it, I'm afraid I'm a bad mother. It's already too much for me to bear that my child is gone. Every time I think I'm okay, I remember another fact that reminds me of who wronged me, who caused this, or whose failure complicated my child's life. The controversy surrounding these events are convoluted and unfair. My child deserved better. Show me what to do to bury all the things I think and feel that do not bring You honor. Show me how to respectfully cherish my child's memory. Mostly, God, show me how to live now. Give me future hope. Remind me that the rains will produce fruit. And the harvest is coming.

In the name of Jesus, Amen.

7
...

Seeking Grace in Prayer

"The Lord has heard my supplication [my plea for grace];
The Lord receives my prayer."
(Psalm 6:9 AMP)

Three's Too Many

How many abortions are too many? One? Two?

For Raza, her two abortions mean that she graduated cum laude from college and was accepted into law school. What they don't mean is that she's changed her behavior. Sitting in her 3L, elective Family Law class, she can't believe she's pregnant again. This is her third pregnancy. What is she to do now? Have a third abortion? The other two were no big deal. She pretends she hasn't thought about those babies since the abortions. It's true enough, except each year on her due dates and the dates of their termination procedures, she counts the ages of her children. Then she prays that God can forgive her for what she did.

Today, finding out she's pregnant again, she thinks of her two children again. And prays. She can't talk to anyone but God about this. It's nothing to talk to anyone else about. This time around, Raza's concerned about the effects of a third abortion on her body. Can she have a third abortion? Should she? She thought she wouldn't face this decision again. She swore to herself that she would never again be faced with that woman outside the clinic. The one who gave her the little booklet with the pictures of abortions gone wrong. Raza promised herself she will never again be called what that woman called her. Nonetheless, here she is. Concerned for the first time about what she used to think was just a blob. This one this time is her baby.

"Why does it matter this time?" she asks herself.

She knows why it matters. What she doesn't know is what to do about it. Abortion has been her go-to proclivity. Pregnancy and child-rearing are scary propositions. Raza cannot fathom the idea of raising a child. She'll need her parents. She'll have to tell them about this one. She'll act as if it's the first. Their disappointment will be palpable. Once they're over the initial shock of her out-of-wedlock pregnancy, they'll choose the right decision for her, making sure she lives comfortably. Even if that means they raise the baby themselves. Relying on her mommy and daddy for this seems more selfishly immature than Raza is comfortable with. Yet, there are those plans her family has made for her life. The dream that Raza join her mother's law firm one day and follow in her mom's footsteps. No one, not even this child is going to interfere with her mother's plan.

Raza calls home to talk to her mother. For days, she's rehearsed her script. It did not prepare Raza for her mother's tremendous disappointment. As expected, her mother is livid.

"I am not having this discussion about how you are messing up your future with this little problem you've managed to get yourself into. Not now. Not on the phone," her mother, founding law firm partner, former District Attorney, wife of a judge, instructed her daughter.

"Mom, let me explain."

"I don't want to hear anything you have to say. When I agreed to let you go to down there to that second-rate law school, I knew you would be influenced by the wrong people. I never imagined this! I arranged for you to have a seat in the best school in this state. But because you convinced your father to do your bidding, you went to that god-forsaken place. And, for what? For this? I knew you would be wrongly influenced there. When you left for school, you said you would make me proud. Do you think I am proud of you, now?"

This is not following the script. Raza is paralyzed by her mother's words. Her heart races. Her mind races as well. "I have to open the windows. I'm burning up. I'm suffocating. I'm about to die. My skin is on fire. I wish somebody could help me. She's going to disown me. How am I supposed to live with the disappointment in the tone of your voice, Mommy? What am I supposed to say? I'm sorry? I don't know what to do. Will you help me, Mom, please? I'm sorry. I'm so sorry!"

The words are not spoken. Raza knows better than let her mother hear weakness. She can't cry. Her hands shake. Sweat beads on her forehead.

"You're going to have an abortion, Raza."

Without warning, Raza hears her own voice. "No. I'm not, Mom. I am not aborting my baby." Raza cannot believe the words escaped her lips. For the first time, she's not deferring to her mother and she's not going to call on her father for help. Though she's depended on their money and influence her entire life, it's time to change that. Her mother can't speak for her any longer.

"Excuse me? What did you say to me, young lady?"

"Mom, you always tell me, 'be a leader, not a follower.' You tell me to challenge everything. And to trust God. I've not done that. I always wait for you to tell me what to do. I always act in total dependence on you and Daddy, and in total independence from God. It's not right. I can't do that anymore.

"I know that what you're telling me to do is not the right thing for this baby. I don't know why, but it feels like God wants me to do something else. I know He's out there for me. All those years of you sending me to Sunday School as a child, and the stories I learned about Jesus tell me that He has to be able to help. I've made silly decisions. My choices got me into this mess. It's easy for me to run to you like a little kid for direction and answers. And you know what?

I planned to do just that. But Mom, you don't have the answer. God does. And I don't think He wants me to have an abortion. Not this time."

"Not this time? Is that right? Well, since you have all the answers, handle this by yourself. I'm done with your mistakes. Do not call us when you fall flat on your face. Goodbye, Raza." With that, her mother hangs up the phone.

Time to Grow Up

Not sure what that means, Raza exhales. She is on her own. No longer does she have to be what she's not for her mother. No more secrets. This cleansing feels like a new beginning. One that includes the new life growing inside her. She still doesn't know what to do about the baby. All her talk about Jesus and Sunday School makes her want to go back to her childhood church. Reverend Jordan will be surprised to see her. Maybe the Reverend can also offer some hope and advice. There has to be a better option. She knows her mother wouldn't approve of her going to the old neighborhood. Raza's grandmother's neighborhood. Where 'the good-ole church folk' live. She needs those folks today. She gathers her coat and drives to the church.

"Raza? Is that you, dear?"

Raza turns to Reverend Jordan who hugs her tight. She's exactly as Raza remembers her. "Yes. It's me. Hi, Reverend Jordan. I know it's been a long time since I was last here. I'm sorry I haven't been to church."

"Oh, dear, you don't have to apologize to me. I'm just awful glad to see you. What brings you here?" Reverend Jordan graciously guides Raza to a chair in her office. She's completely unlike Raza's prosecutor mother.

"Reverend Jordan, my life is ruined! I hope you can help me to ask Jesus for help," Raza tells the preacher.

"Dear, you know you can talk to Jesus yourself. You don't need me for that. Have you done that?"

"Yes. I have. At least, I've tried to pray, but I'm so bad that He hasn't answered me."

"Nonsense. You can't be too bad for God. The very fact that you care what God thinks tells me that. What did you do, dear? What's so bad?"

Raza tells Reverend Jordan everything. No matter what she said, Reverend Jordan did not judge her or turn her away. Three hours after Raza arrived at the church, Reverend Jordan asks a question.

"Do you want this baby?"

"It's crazy. More and more, I'm starting to love this baby. I feel like this child is special and deserves a chance to live. There's nothing I can offer him or her. This child needs to be in a family where they'll be loved. That's not my family. My mom has disowned me, again, and my dad just goes along with what she says. I don't want her involved anyway. It's my problem."

"Well, Raza, you have a choice. You can keep the baby or give the baby to someone else."

"Like who?" Raza doesn't understand how she can just give the baby away. Who would take her baby?

"Like someone who will love the baby and raise them as their own. You can give the baby up for adoption." Reverend Jordan holds Raza's hand.

"Adoption? You mean go through with the pregnancy and then hand the baby over like I don't care about him? I can't do that. I'm not one of those women. What do they call them? Birth mothers? I'm not one of them. I'm not a teenager or strung out on drugs.[1] I'm twenty-three. I'm in law school. I'm going to be a successful lawyer. It's just that right now I can't raise a baby. But, I want this baby to have a good life, a better life that I can give them. I want him or her to be loved. Really loved. Loved without strings and heavy, unbearable expectations. You know?"

Reverend Jordan doesn't speak. She lets Raza talk.

Finally, Raza ask, "Reverend Jordan, what should I do?"

"I can't tell you that, dear. What I can do is make a suggestion. Would you talk to the people of the Caring Hearts Ministry here at the church? It's our pregnancy center. They can give you better advice than I can. Except this, continue to pray. The Lord will show you the way."

Now What

Thanks to Reverend Jordan's advice, Raza begins working with the ministry. In four months of counseling and looking at parent profiles, she can't find anyone she wants to raise her child. She'd hope to hand her baby over to the adoptive parents in the delivery room, but perspective parents keep rejecting her fearing the future lawyer will change her mind.

On the day of her son's birth, Raza's in a quagmire. She can't believe he's here. Or that he's in her arms. He's so little. The thought of keeping him haunts her. She planned to give him to his adoptive mother, not to hold him or feed him and bond with him. It doesn't seem right that she should still have him. Holding the newborn son she can't afford to raise, Raza wonders why she's being forced to spend this time with him. In a way, she's happy, yet she imagines this is only going to make giving him up harder. Since he's with her, she decides to name him. She calls him Jack. Short for her grandmother's last name, Jackson. Then she prays, asking the Lord to please give him a home. Crying she also asks for direction.

"Is there a family here at the church that can raise my son?" Raza asks her ministry counselor the day after Jack's birth. "Maybe we'll be more successful with someone here in the ministry. I don't want my baby to be stuck in foster care. He needs an always family," Raza says.

"Why yes, Raza. Jill's been cleared for adoption. Would you like to talk to her?"

"Who's Jill? Her name is, Jill? Really? Ironic, isn't it?

"What do you mean?" the counselor probes.

"Nothing. Yes. Can I talk to her? Who's Jill?"

"Reverend Jordan, silly. Reverend Jill Jordan. Certainly. I'll arrange it right away."

Raza is dumbfounded. She never knew Reverend Jordan's first name. Could she possibly raise her son?

Weeks later, Raza's anticipating the meeting with Reverend Jordan. This time, the call is different. It's strange calling Reverend Jordan by her first name, but Jill's excitement is palpable. Jill's almost like the big sister Raza never had. She even gets the irony of Jack's name, but Raza's relieved that she promises not to change it. When the day comes for Raza to bring Jack to Caring Hearts for the last time, she smiles as she watches Jill and Jack begin to bond. Raza can't believe this is happening. Reverend Jordan is the answer to Raza's prayers for Jack's forever.

After a period of emotionlessness, Raza begins to process her loss. She feels guilty for missing Jack when she's the one who chose to place him with Jill. Though the adoption is open, she knows Jill and Jack need time to bond. Instead of calling Reverend Jordan for guidance, she picks up her Bible. Unsure reading it will help, Raza doesn't know where to turn. She recalls that story Reverend Jordan told her about in 1 Samuel 1 and a mother named, Hannah.

The Power of Prayer

> "Now there was a certain man of Ramathaimzophim, of
> mount Ephraim, and his name was Elkanah, ...: And he had
> two wives; the name of the one was Hannah, and the name of
> the other Peninnah: and Peninnah had children, but Hannah
> had no children." (1 Samuel 1:1-2)

Here we go again. We have here a man named Elkanah who is from Israel during the days of the judges. Like his kinsman, Elimelech of Naomi fame, this man Elkanah makes a bad decision. No, he doesn't leave Bethlehem for a pagan city called Moab. Elkanah, instead, decides to keep two wives in the same house. That can't possibly be good, because God never endorses it. Not convinced? Well, consider this practical problem of the bigamist.

"If a man has two wives, and he loves one but not the other, and both bear him sons but the firstborn is the son of the wife he does not love, when he wills his property to his sons, he must not give the rights of the firstborn to the son of the wife he loves in preference to his actual firstborn, the son of the wife he does not love. He must acknowledge the son of his unloved wife as the firstborn by giving him a double share of all he has. That son is the first sign of his father's strength. The right of the firstborn belongs to him." (Deuteronomy 21:15-17 NIV).

What a mess, right? Two wives mean disproportionate affections, multiple children, fights over birth rights, and hard feelings. This is the nature of dysfunction in the household of the two-timer.

Like Elkanah.

The two women in his home, Peninnah and Hannah, are importantly distinct. Peninniah has children. Hannah, on the other hand, does not. Though Peninniah is mentioned first, it is Hannah who is believed to be Elkanah's first wife.[2] She is certainly his preferred wife.[3] And that fact irked Peninnah. Wouldn't you be bothered, too? Think about it, if you were brought into a home to do what the first wife could not, that is, to bear children, and you do it, wouldn't you expect to also gain some favor or priority in that home? Yet, for Peninnah, Elkanah's favor eludes her. What is she to do? Bully her rival.

"And her adversary also provoked her sore, for to make her fret, because the Lord had shut up her womb." (1 Samuel 1:6)

We act as if bullying is a new phenomenon. It is not. It has biblical roots. And roots in woman-to-woman relations. Remember Sarah and Hagar?[4] Sarah was Abraham's wife. After years of trying, Sarah and Abraham did not have children, despite God's promise of an heir and decedents too numerous to count. Desperate to bring God's promise to fruition, Sarah offers her Egyptian servant girl, Hagar, to her husband, to be his wife and to give him a child. When Abraham obliged, and Hagar became pregnant, Hagar turned on her boss and the two women became rivals. Accordingly, Sarah turned their happy home upside down. Sure, she gave Abraham the business for listening to her, but when he told her to handle her servant herself, the bullying began. Sarah tormented Hagar so severely that pregnant Hagar ran away into a deserted place.

In that same way, Peninnah and Hannah become adversaries due to a man's bad choices and the unproductive womb of his wife. Impatient and disbelieving, Abraham and Elkanah allow the women in their lives to wreak havoc in their homes. Resulting in the child-bearing, second one disrespecting the preferred first one. And that first wife? Well, she reacts with rage. Now, I know you have never heard about Hannah's rage. Every sermon I've heard about Hannah has painted her as a poor, crying victim of the headstrong Peninnah. But that's not how the Bible presents the story. The words used to describe Hannah's response to Peninnah indicate strong reactions. Hannah, like Sarah, does not meekly run to her bedroom to bury her head in her pillow to sob like a spurned, teenager. No. Hannah publicly responds with an audible, weeping rage.

This reminds me of how Jesus wept in John 11:35. He does not do this because He's sad. His tears reflect exasperation due to the unbelief of those He loved. Similarly, Hannah's weeping is heavy with annoyance. It not uncommon.

Haven't you ever been so bothered by life's circumstances that all you can do is cry? Especially, when you are powerless to change the situation? Not that "I'm so sad and hurt" cry, but the "I'm going to tear some stuff up" cry. The Hannah cry that painfully asks, "What am I to do?" For Hannah, is she supposed to get herself pregnant and have a child? Sure, she would choose to do that, but God Himself is preventing her from getting pregnant. Talk about frustrating! "God, how could you make my womb dead? What did I do to deserve this?" They're the questions I asked, too.

"Then said Elkanah her husband to her, Hannah, why weepest thou? and why eatest thou not? and why is thy heart grieved? am not I better to thee than ten sons?"
(1 Samuel 1:8)

His love for Hannah is admirable. It's not enough to comfort and return her to normal, though. She's wailing and refusing to eat. Hannah is inconsolable. And Elkanah has nothing to do with it. Peninnah hit the nail on the head. This is a woman thing that a man just doesn't understand. No one, not even a husband, can substitute for what Hannah wants most. A child. Especially, in this house where children abound. Peninnah's children, that is. Ten of them, most likely. The number Elkanah broadcasts and at the sound of which Hannah trembles with anguish.

About Elkanah's "aren't I better than ten sons" comment. Doesn't that seem extremely self-centered? Easy for him to talk about ten sons. He's the one who married that second woman who flaunts his sons before Hannah to taunt her. Is Elkanah now in a position to talk? What is he thinking?

Well, before you determine that he isn't thinking, let me tell you something about Hebrew culture. It is the man, not the woman, who is obligated to procreate.[5] Relying on God's words to Jacob in Genesis 35:11 which says, "And God said unto him, I am God Almighty: be fruitful and multiply; a nation and a company of nations shall be of thee, and kings shall come out of thy loins." Jewish culture deems the man who fails to have children as forfeiting his legal and religious rights.[6]

For me, this male-centered responsibility is hard to reconcile, however, against the Lord's command to both Adam and Eve to "be fruitful and multiply" in Genesis 1:22.

Nevertheless, knowing the ancient Jewish perspective helps to humanize Elkanah. The way he sees it, Hannah is grieved because she concludes her position in his home is at risk, since she has provided nothing to solidify Elkanah's legacy and earn her keep. Maybe

Peninnah is right. But no. Despite that evil mind game, the truth is to the contrary. Elkanah is actually saying to her that not only won't he banish her, he will keep her because he loves her. Shouldn't that be enough? Okay, maybe that's not better.

To be fair, Elkanah's not Hannah's enemy. He's doing the best he can in a situation he has no idea how to handle or fix. Men are fixers. Especially of things that affect the ones they love. And without a doubt, Elkanah loves Hannah. Seeing her tears, her refusing to eat, her despondency and sorrow hurts him as much as it hurts her. After all, she's bone of his bone. She's the wife he married and kept despite the circumstances. He wants to fix this for her, but he cannot supersede God. His words are his best efforts to take her focus off what she can't change.

You can imagine what it's like living with Hannah. It's no fun for him either. On top of that, he has to somehow keep Peninah occupied so that she stays away from Hannah. You know, the more I think about it, I'm kind of feeling sorry for brother Elkanah. He's not as bad as I first thought.

By the way, aren't you bothered by the use of the word "grieved" to describe Hannah's condition? Why is she grieved? As a mother who's lost her children, I know grief. It comes from the loss of life. Hannah on the other hand, has not lost anything, yet she is grieved. This is one of the reasons I have such a hard time with Hannah's story. I just want to say to her, "Girl, stop it and go get something to eat!"

With a more empathetic eye, however, you can see what she's lost. Imagine that Hannah married at a young age. She's hopeful and bright-eyed. Her husband is a Levite and they will surely have a home full of children just like every other woman in her town. Year after year, her dream is renewed, until after a decade, she can no longer dream. Her hope is lost. Thus, she grieves.

Now, I get it.

Grief Leads to Bitterness

"And she was in bitterness of soul, and prayed unto the
Lord, and wept sore. And she vowed a vow, and said, O
Lord of hosts, if thou wilt indeed look on the affliction of
thine handmaid, and remember me, and not forget thine
handmaid, but wilt give unto thine handmaid a man child,
then I will give him unto the Lord all the days of his life, and
there shall no razor come upon his head."
(1 Samuel 1: 10-11)

Bitterness is not a momentary reaction to a singular event. It is a brewing stew of hurt, sadness, confusion, and despair that culminates into a lingering, subtle anger so gnawing that you don't care who sees or hears it. As it was with Naomi, it is with Hannah. Reaching to the depths of her identity, bitterness grips her very soul. Since God is the one who orchestrated the triggering events that result in her bitterness, He is the ultimate object of her acrimony. But how exactly does a Levite's wife mount a challenge against the Lord, who's name in the Hebrew, *Yehovah*, is so hallowed that it is not to be spoken?[7] As the perpetrator of this perceived wrong, and the keeper of the gate to her womb, only He can undo her condition. If asked.

The one thing that I did not want to do when my Sunshine and Daniel died, was talk to God. Most certainly, I did not want to ask Him for anything. Hadn't He done enough? What should I say? He already knows what happened. Do I ask for Him to bring them back? To undo what's done? Do I tell Him how angry I am with Him? Describe my wretchedness? Doesn't He know?

I chose to yell at Him. Through my tears, I screamed inaudibly and challenged His actions against His word. From my bowels I said, "Didn't You say, 'Lo, children are an heritage of the Lord: and the fruit of the womb is his reward'"? (Psalm 127:3) Is that for everyone except me? Why is my womb a tomb? Why does it have to remain empty? Where are You God? Why won't You answer me? I'm so angry with You! Why should I talk to You when all You do is hurt me? God? God? Do you even hear me?"

Little did I know that I was acting in the spiritual heritage of my biblical ancestors. Even this woman Hannah who "wept sore" just like me.

Without warning, though, Hannah turns on me. She does the thing that for years made her the most difficult biblical woman for me to understand. She makes a treaty with God that boggles my mind. How can a woman weep, moan, and cry about being childless, then offer to give the potential child away? She must be delusional. That's the only logical explanation. Who asks God for something, then pledges to give that something back to Him? Come to think of it, I've done that.

When I was in law school, just prior to graduating, I begged God for a job. Firm after firm had rejected me. My future was bleak. Only divine intervention would change things. So, I asked Him to please give me a job making a particular salary. Out of my desperation, I told God that if He did this, I would tithe 15 percent of that salary. To solidify the deal, I wrote it on a piece of paper and kept it in my wallet. Back then, this did not at all seem schizophrenic to me. This was strategic faith. Downright lawyerly, too. Guess what I did after that? When my first job did not get me to the salary I requested, that contract remained in my wallet. I continued to expect God to come through. After a while, when the first check came that sealed God's side of the deal, I proudly walked down the aisle at church to deposit my tithe check for 15 percent.

But, a salary is not a son. That tithing example didn't change my mind about Hannah. Surely, she won't do this ridiculous thing. No way God will expect her to follow through.

I keep reading.

"And they rose up in the morning early, and worshipped before the Lord, and returned, and came to their house to Ramah: and Elkanah knew Hannah his wife; and the Lord remembered her. Wherefore it came to pass, when the time was come about after Hannah had conceived, that she bare a son, and called his name Samuel, saying, Because I have asked him of the Lord." (1 Samuel 1:19-20)

Hannah and her family are devout followers of God. Every year, they go up to Shiloh to worship God.[8] Why Shiloh? The name of the city means a place of rest. It is the place where the Ark of the Covenant and the Tabernacle of God temporarily rest.[9] A place of tranquility where the Jews journey in holy submission to God. It's here where Hannah receives a word of comfort from God through the priest.

And she worships. While she's with her vengeful adversary, she worships. While she watches her stepchildren play and grow, she worships. As her situation lingers, she worships. In the midst of her despair, she takes the time to bow her head, implore and honor that same God who closed her womb, yet has the power to open it.

You know what else Hannah does? She honors God in her marriage by having sex with her husband. Sure, Elkanah's out of touch, but he's also key to her deliverance. Withholding sex from him would mean withholding a child from her womb. Don't get me wrong. I understand the uneasiness the married woman feels about being intimate with the husband who's said stupid things about her infertility or miscarriage. On the other hand, 1 Corinthians 7:5 warns about withholding sex from your spouse, except for during a time of prayer. Since Hannah and Elkanah have prayed at Shiloh, once they return home it's time to be husband and wife.

Good thing, too, because God "remembered" her. Stop for a minute. Does that mean that God had forgotten her? No. God does not forget His daughters. Nor does He forget the prayers of His daughters. The word here simply implies that God granted her request and opened the womb that He had temporarily closed. Hannah's honest prayer, faith in God and faithfulness to her role as a wife leads to her pregnancy. Hooray for her! It's a boy!

"And the man Elkanah, and all his house, went up to offer unto the Lord the yearly sacrifice, and his vow. But Hannah went not up; for she said unto her husband, I will not go up until the child be weaned, and then I will bring him, that he may appear before the Lord, and there abide forever." (1 Samuel 1:21-22)

What is Hannah talking about when she says, "I will not go up?" Does she have a choice? We are still in ancient Israel, right? She's supposed to go where her husband goes, right? Fortunately, her loving husband is understanding enough to respect her position. Elkanah agrees to her not going to Shiloh to worship this time. (That's another feather in brother Elkanah's cap!) Yet, there's more to the point of her remaining behind than just that. All that time Hannah has gone with the family to worship, prepared her for this moment. Her attendance in the previous visits was no more required than on this occasion. Only the men were required to go up each year.[10] In those previous visits, Hannah went for a blessing.

That's how she received her breakthrough. It's the key to you receiving yours, too.

If you want your situation to change. If you want your crying to end, then you've got to be willing to get into God's presence while you are in your low point. That's what Hannah did. She went to Shiloh year after year to worship God there in the midst of her hurt, humiliation, and bareness. She did not shy away from it. Hannah didn't wait until her battle with childlessness was over to pray. While she was in the worst of her storms, she took her request to the Lord.

Maybe you are not a member of a church. Or maybe it's been years since you last went. You're wondering where are you supposed to go? Well, like Hannah and Raza, go back to the place you last worshipped. Whether it was last year, or a decade ago, go back there. The faces may be different, but the Spirit of God remains. Both Raza and Hannah went seeking an answer to their motherhood dilemma when the normal solutions no longer worked. They sought a godly intercession. At the risk of being misunderstood, Hannah and Raza dared to better understand God's hand in their lives. With open honesty, they poured themselves out before God by way of the leader of the place of worship. In both cases, God used His appointed man and woman to offer His compassion and grace. If you have no place to return to, then I urge you to find a Christian counselor who can guide you as you navigate your circumstances.

It's Giving Time

Even with the great direction Hannah received and blessing she's experiencing, there's something she must do. Remember that promise Hannah made saying, "I will give him unto the Lord"? Umm, well, it's giving time. Otherwise known as integrity testing time. You know, thinking about it, it's not clear what she meant by that statement. How is she going to "give" the child to God? Is she going to do an Abraham? Will Hannah one day take Samuel up the Shiloh mountain to sacrifice him? God forbid!

My mind still tries to understand this woman's conviction. Maybe she's going to figuratively "give" the child to Lord by being really prayerful and obedient to God throughout the child's life. No decision regarding him will be made without consulting God first. He'll be God's child. Instead of asking Elkanah about the boy's haircut, clothing, discipline, and schooling, she will ask God. Yeah, clearly that's what she means because she's not even taking the boy to annual worship meeting this year. Certainly, she wants to train him in the ways of Israel knowing that one day, the man Samuel will take his family on the annual pilgrimage like his father does. Practically then, if she is going to literally give Samuel to God the best place to offer him would be at the place where God lives, which the Jews believe is in the Tabernacle, where the Presence of the Lord dwells.

Hannah resists taking him there. Why? Probably because taking Samuel there would mean leaving him there. But, at a year old or less, he's too young to travel while still breast feeding. She needs to wean him. Actually, that weaning bit sounds a little like a lame excuse, doesn't it? Well, it's not. Staying back with Samuel means giving the boy a chance to live. Ancient Israel is not an easy place for an infant to thrive. For little Samuel, born to a mother who's been infertile for at least a decade, the odds are not in his favor to live past his earliest days.[11] It is his mother's responsibility to make certain he survives. Preserving Samuel's life is Hannah's greatest gift.

"And when she had weaned him, she took him up with her, with three bullocks, and one ephah of flour, and a bottle of wine, and brought him unto the house of the Lord in Shiloh: and the child was young." (1 Samuel 1:24)

Many texts suggest that Samuel is about three years old when Hannah decides he is ready to go on the annual trip to Shiloh. Hannah is not emptyhanded. She brings a holy offering when she brings Samuel to the Lord.

It never occurred to me that a child can or should be an offering to the Lord. Offerings are monetary. They are based on income. At least, that's the way I'd always viewed it. Yes, I offered my talent and my time, but my tithe and finances have always been my main source of offering. Especially offerings that I give at church, in the house of God. Hannah enlarges my view of this most holy act. She makes me see the product of my womb as an offering. Here's why.

In Hebrew, the word offering is *teruwmah*.[12] It means to make a contribution, to give a gift to the temple of God, especially sacrificial-ly. A true offering means nothing if it doesn't cost the giver anything. Anything you can give to God without missing is an inconvenience. A hiccup. God wants an offering. The best of what you have. Not the rest of what you have. Think back to chapter 1 of this book and our discussion of the Genesis 4 story of Cain and Abel. That's where the concept of an offering is first mentioned in the Bible. We learn what's an acceptable offering and what's not. Cain gave God an unacceptable offering because he gave God some of what he had. God could not respect it. Abel, however, gave God his first and his best. This offering pleased God. Hannah gives an Abel offering.

My Plea for Grace

"For this child I prayed; and the Lord hath given me my petition which I asked of him: Therefore also I have lent him to the Lord; as long as he liveth he shall be lent to the Lord. And he worshipped the Lord there." (1 Samuel 1: 27-28)

Not only does Hannah remember her promise to the Lord, she keeps it. Out of her gratefulness, Hannah gives her offering to God. There is no reason to be sad about it. It's a time to celebrate.

Before we go on, there's a word in this verses that troubles me. Hannah told God she would "give" her son in verse eleven. Here in verses twenty-seven and twenty-eight, she refers to this transaction as a loan. What's that all about? When Raza gave Jack to Jill, she didn't get him back. Neither did you get your baby back, right? I certainly haven't received Sunshine or Daniel back into my arms. Our girl Hannah doesn't get Samuel back either. Nor did she expect him back. When she says "lent" she's not referring to a loan such that God is required to repay her in kind. It means that Hannah commits Samuel to a life of service to God for as long as Samuel lives. Read these verses in the NET version of the Bible: "'I prayed for this boy, and the Lord has given me the request that I asked of him. Now I dedicate him to the Lord. From this time on he is dedicated to the Lord.' Then they worshiped the Lord there" (1 Samuel 1:27-28 NET).

Hannah and Raza epitomize what those of us who've lost children have painfully learned. "The greatest joy in having a child is to give that child fully and freely back to God."[13] For those of you reading this now, who have offered your child a better life through blessing of adoption, realize the gift of your offering.

God does.

Reflection

Does Hannah's choices change anything about how you view the child you lost through adoption?

Like Raza, will you allow Hannah to be your mentor and soul sister by letting her willing sacrifice encourage you to think of your loss as an act of worship through sacrificial giving?

Prayer

Dear God,

It's hard to think of the loss of my child as an offering. My choice has never been to give them away. Frankly, not even to You. I wanted my child to be with me. To raise them, to see them mature. Not being able to do that hurts beyond what I can articulate. Yet, I know there is a reason Hannah is in the Bible. Her willingness to serve You in this way is hard to digest. Change my perspective. I did the best I could. Like Raza, I knew that I could not care for my child at the time of my pregnancy. Adoption was the best choice. It still is. Just as Hannah's sacrifice is etched in history, so is mine. My child is Yours. I pray that they are giving You pleasure. God, accept my offering. They are Yours.

In the name of Jesus, Amen.

8

...

Seeking Grace in Christ

"For sin shall not have dominion over you, for you are not under law but under grace." (Romans 6:14 NKJV)

Looks Sometimes Matter

Karla is beautiful. As a seventh grader, she's often mistaken for a high schooler, but she doesn't believe she's ever mistaken for beautiful. When she looks in the mirror, she sees every pimple.

"I'm not beautiful. I'm ugly," she says to herself.

When Karla's small-town youth choir is introduced to the new community center's youth director, Mr. Foster, a man in his early twenties from New York City, the other girls giggle and say he's cute. Karla doesn't join their comments because her grandmother doesn't allow her to talk like that. So, she sits alone.

Mr. Foster notices and bets she needs a friend. "Hi Karla, I'm Mr. Forster."

"I know who you are, sir," Karla answers.

"You don't have to call me sir. You can call me, Mr. Tony. Or even Tony, if you want. I don't care much for titles."

"No, sir. I'll just call you, sir. Or I can call you, Mr. Foster," Karla replied, respectfully.

"Very well, young lady."

Karla thinks Mr. Foster is strange. And she doesn't like the way Mr. Foster looks at her. Especially when he asked her to lead a song. Scared and shaking she tries to sing, but no sound comes out. The other kids snicker. She is so mortified she just wants to die. Instead, she runs out of the rehearsal hall into the handicapped stall in the girl's bathroom to cry. Mr. Foster follows her.

"Mr. Foster? Boys, uh, men aren't allowed in here!"

"Well, I'm not leaving until you come out."

Unsure what to do next, Karla comes out of the stall looking at Mr. Foster. He rubs her shoulder and tries to hug her, but Karla pulls away.

"You've been hurt. I can tell. I won't hurt you, Karla. I just want to help you. I am only here to help you."

Karla doesn't say a word. She hurriedly walks out of the bathroom and runs home. She doesn't tell her grandmother or anyone about Mr. Foster or about the funny way she feels when he touches her. But she doesn't know how to resist his hugs and shoulder rubs. As the months progress, she becomes less uncomfortable around him. In time, she looks forward to seeing Mr. Tony. And his closeness. She believes him when he says she's beautiful, and she dreams about him.

"Oh, Karla. You don't have to be ashamed to talk about your dreams," Mr. Foster tells her. "You are a woman. It's natural. That's why I am here to help you. I can help you to explore what it means to be a woman."

One day, Karla hears footsteps. The familiar heavy, deliberate steps of the center's president. As the sound of his shoes against the wood floor gets louder and closer, she turns to see him standing in the doorway of the music room.

"What are you doing?" Karla feels his intense anger.

"Sir, she enticed me." Mr. Foster quickly turns away, fumbling for his pants. "She's been after me for months. I'm ashamed, President Burke. Please forgive me, sir. Please don't fire me. Please." Mr. Foster chokes back tears.

"Come to my office immediately, young lady," President Burke demands Karla.

Mr. Foster zips his pants and scurries out of the music room without looking at Karla. Confused, she pulls down her dress. The president's office assistant seems to know what happened as she retrieves Karla to escort her to the office.

"Do you know why you're here, young lady?" President Burke ask Karla.

"Sir?" Karla asked.

"Don't be coy with me. You have disgraced your family. You are no longer welcome here. I will have your grandmother come to get you."

Karla's grandmother can't hold her head up or speak. All of the town's women gossip and gather around as she walks into the center.

"We knew that girl was fast. She's like her momma. Poor Mamie. She just doesn't know how to raise no girl child. A woman should know how to raise a girl child. It's a sin and a shame."

Grandma Mamie sends Karla up North to her Aunt June and Uncle Theodore. They're nice enough to take her in after she embarrassed the family like she did. At least, that's what Grandma Mamie said.

That next spring, Karla returns home to Grandma Mamie's house. She's not the same. Everyone knows there is something different about her. Sure, she's taller, but there's something else. Soon they'll learn about the little baby girl Karla left behind. The baby daughter who will one day call Aunt June, Mommy.

All Too Familiar

Does Karla's story sound eerily familiar? I've spoken to many women with similar tales of innocence and indignity. Sisters who learn to live with the family secret and the situation they got themselves in. Too many of us try to forget the hurt that unwarranted accusations of reckless promiscuity lodges in our hearts. Secretly, we wonder if the accusations are justified. Was I being fast? Did I lure him? I've been there and I know I am not alone.

We cannot overlook how we feel. To be free to live and love again, we must confront sin and accusation. For some, like Karla, this story of lost innocence includes the loss of a child. No matter what the cause of our loss, the accusations hurt us so much that we may overlook our own sin. Even if the accusation is one sided and unfair, the underlying sin must be addressed. Especially if the sin has been hidden so many years that we no longer view it as sin. We blame others for our condition.

It's time for us to break free from sin and accusation and find liberty in Jesus Christ.

The Only One Caught

We should turn to another of our biblical sisters for some help here. There's one in the book of John who is mistreated, abused, and ridiculed, too. Her story is a familiar one, so I'm not going to preface it. Let's just dive into it and find our hope in Jesus.

> *"And early in the morning he came again into the temple, and all the people came unto him; and he sat down, and taught them. And the scribes and Pharisees brought unto him a woman taken in adultery; and when they had set her in the midst," (John 8:2-3)*

On this occasion, many people from the city come to the Temple, the Jewish holy place, to hear Jesus teach. The audience includes Jewish religious leaders—the scribes and the Pharisees who are men who study, write down, and profess to know the religious law. The Pharisees are often seen in the Bible as outspoken and outraged at the nerve of Jesus to call Himself the Christ, the Lord, the Savior, and the Messiah. It's no wonder that the scribes and the Pharisees are not noted here as people who came to hear Jesus teach. To the contrary, they show up bringing in a woman they caught in the act of adultery.

The Bible does not identify this woman. It also does not mention her accomplice, the man with whom she commits adultery. It seems to me these religious men set this woman up. How else do they happen to "take" her this way? Was she doing it on the street, in the public square? Of course not. I will speculate here that the scribes and Pharisees went looking for her to do something wrong all so they could be evil to her. I say evil, because Satan is the only one who always tries to make a fool of you. He always uses the most uncomfortable times, to make the most uncomfortable appearances, in front of the most uncomfortable people in your life.

To understand why the scribes and Pharisees are concerned with this woman's affairs, we need to learn a little bit about ancient Jewish law. In ancient Judaism, adultery is a serious crime. The law of Moses is clear about God's standards regarding adultery.

The seventh commandment says, "Thou shalt not commit adultery" (Exodus 20:14).

In the book of Leviticus, the law further describes what's to happen to the man who commits adultery: "If a man commits adultery with another man's wife—with the wife of his neighbor—both the adulterer and the adulteress are to be put to death" (Leviticus 20:10 NIV).

The law treats the man, the adulterer, and the woman, the adulteress individually, but equally. Why only the woman is here in the Temple is a thought-provoking, timeless question. Even today, when a woman gets pregnant by a man who is not her husband, the father of the baby is seldom shamed. The woman, or girl in Karla's case, is humiliated, shunned, and called names. If she aborts the pregnancy, she is called a selfish, baby murderer. If she carries the baby to term, then gives the baby up for adoption, she is called a child abandoner, or the one who didn't quite do enough to give the child a good life. She's rarely called brave for recognizing that she could not care for the child herself. But I digress.

Though this woman is not noted to have become pregnant, I feel and share her shame, humiliation, and shunning. It is a universal indignity that is uniquely female. It leads to the same aloneness that many women share, even though she can never commit this act alone. Here, this woman, my sister, is left to stand in front of an entire Temple congregation to suffer the exposure of her sin, alone.

> *"They say unto him, Master, this woman was taken in*
> *adultery, in the very act." (John 8:4)*

The scribes and Pharisees address these statements to Jesus, the Master. However, they are not honoring Jesus as their Master or seeking to be taught by Jesus, but they will learn a lesson. Before the congregation, they announce her sin. Not to inform Jesus of her actions, because as the all-knowing, omniscient God, Jesus already knows everything about her. No, they announce this in order to selfishly prove that Jesus is not who He had claims to be, but a fraud. The woman is their pawn. Shining a light on the fault of another is a mere game to them.

Being the light that saves from all darkness is Jesus' mission.

The Writing on the Ground

I wonder if that was how you got into the situation that led to your loss. For me, I became pregnant because I didn't know my own worth. Like Karla, I didn't think I was beautiful. I exaggerated every flaw instead of embracing my uniqueness. Being young, athletic, and smart became my albatrosses instead of my butterflies. Not unlike this woman now standing before Jesus, and the woman reading this book. We are left to deal with the accusations and condemnation, feeling too unqualified to handle any of it. Consequently, as a young, pregnant woman facing the prospect of aborting my child, I was confused. The idea became attractive because society convincingly said it's the way to a better future and asked—do you really want to raise a child alone?

It told me abortion will be quick, easy, and complete. But, sin never is quick, easy or complete.

I too was set up. Not merely by my sinful nature or my choice, but by a broader system. I am not espousing the pro-life agenda, nor am I espousing the pro-choice agenda. Instead, I am wondering where is the love agenda? Where is the love for this exposed woman? Where is the grace and truth to inform her that she's loved and accepted despite her misdirection? It turns out, He's standing right there with her.

"Now Moses in the law commanded us, that such should be stoned: but what sayest thou?" (John 8:5)

These scribes and Pharisees just won't let up! As self-proclaimed keepers of the law they tell the giver of the law what the law says and requires for punishment for this woman. Their remedy is to stone her, loosely referencing the law in Deuteronomy, which gives specific procedures for handling adulterers:

"If a man is found sleeping with another man's wife, both the man who slept with her and the woman must die. You must purge the evil from Israel. If a man happens to meet in a town a virgin pledged to be married and he sleeps with her, you shall take both of them to the gate of that town and stone them to death—the young woman because she was in a town and did not scream for help, and the man because he violated another man's wife. You must purge the evil from among you. But if out in the country a man happens to meet a young woman pledged to be married and rapes her, only the man who has done this shall die. Do nothing to the woman; she has committed no sin deserving death" (Deuteronomy 22:22-26 NIV).

Let's dig into this a bit. The first thing that we see in these verses is that the law clarifies that if a man commits adultery with a married woman, both of them are to die by stoning. But the law focuses on the man being found, not the woman. Why then do the scribes and Pharisees find this woman and not the man? After all, it takes two to tango, right? Was it maybe because this man is there in the crowd of the scribes and the Pharisees who are now handling this woman?

Maybe.

There's a legitimate reason the law requires death. Though it may seem outdated to punish people for sexual crimes today, the punishment is not to ridicule or expose the adulterers only, but to remove the influence of the evil of adultery from Israel, God's people. Yet, in all their speaking, finding and accusing, the scribes and Pharisees never pledge to rid the community of evil.

Next, the law says if a man meets an engaged woman in a town or city and he sleeps with her, both the man and the woman are to be brought to the edge of the city and stoned. Here's where stoning comes in to play. It seems that they are to be stoned together, but for different reasons. Him for the adultery. Her for failing to cry out for help since the act occurred in town where there is a denser population and her cry for help will be heard.[1] Thus, if she fails to cry for help, the law infers that she's a willing participant and worthy of stoning.[2]

On the other hand, if the adultery occurred in the country, or a rural area, and the man forces himself on the woman and rapes her, then only the man is guilty and stoned. Why? Contrary to the city situation, a woman in the country which is not as well populated might not be heard when she cries for help.[3] The man does not sleep with her, he rapes her. Notice that in no scenario is the woman to be stoned alone.

Interesting.

The scribes and Pharisees know this law. By their actions, it seems they forgot. However, Jesus, knowing the law and being put on earth to fulfill the law, continues to teach and illustrate proper application of the law.

> *"This they said, tempting him, that they might have to accuse him. But Jesus stooped down, and with his finger wrote on the ground, as though he heard them not." (John 8:6)*

The scribes and the Pharisees' true intentions are revealed. They want to tempt Jesus to deny God's standards, just as Satan before them tried to tempt Him. Though his response to their accusation is unanticipated and odd, it's in keeping with His character. He stoops down and starts writing on the ground with His finger. Many theologians and biblical experts imagine what Jesus wrote. I, on the other hand, marvel that Jesus writes on the ground with His own hand. You see, Jesus' hand is the hand of God, and now it's writing on the dirt. I could go on here about the powerful hand of God, or about God's power over the humanity that He created out of the dirt of the ground. I won't do that, except I will mention that whatever Jesus, the all-knowing God writes must express His dominion over human beings and over humanity's sinful nature.

I believe in response to the question the scribes and Pharisees ask, Jesus writes what is written in the law. I believe He simply writes out each of the sins the law determines worthy of stoning. Remember when Satan tried to tempt Jesus, He stated four times, "It is written" (Matthew 4:1-11). Therefore, in this case, Jesus again refers to what is written. Only this time, Jesus doesn't speak about what is written, this time, He writes it, bringing their focus down to earth, giving them a chance to humble themselves before God.

The Bible says Jesus does more than write on the ground. As if God writing on the ground isn't enough, He doesn't verbally respond to them or buy into their evil plan. Jesus gives each accuser a chance to see the sins written on the ground, their sins, and themselves in their accusations. Just like accusers today, these ancient accusers are so blinded by their own self-righteousness, and so set on proving their malicious point, they fail to see their own sin. Jesus uses the ground as a mirror for the people in that Temple. Unfortunately, they refuse to look, but continue wanting the stoning and trying to tempt Jesus to follow their plan.

I Dare You

*"So when they continued asking him, he lifted up himself,
and said unto them, He that is without sin among you, let
him first cast a stone at her." (John 8:7)*

Just then, Jesus addresses the accusers directly. With that one statement, He makes them collectively and separately confront their own
sin. Maybe even their own adultery, or murder, or blasphemy. All of
which are punishable by stoning. Jesus doesn't deny the law. The Light
of the World illuminates the law by imprinting it on the ground, making it clear that the law applies to all—men and women, adulterers
and adulteresses, equally.

With those few words, Jesus also protects the woman. I can see
the Lord standing there, just like a loving Father, between the accusers and the woman, saying, "Go on. I dare you. Throw a stone at her
in front of Me. Since you are so righteous and full of the law, which
one of you accusers can stand here and throw even one stone at her
while I am in the way." I imagine the scribes and the Pharisees are
not standing close to her. They likely threw her into the center of the
Temple to make a spectacle of her and are prepared to throw stones at
her with enough force to kill her. As you know, you cannot effectively
throw stones at someone who is standing next to you.

How can I see all of this when it's not described in these Bible
verses? I see this, because for my continued healing, I have to see this
vividly. I have to see them, because I have to see me. This woman
caught in sin, standing alone, accused, and scared is me. Then, I see
Jesus standing in the middle of the accusations with me. Protecting
me from my accusers; even that accuser inside of me. I am behind
Him, protected.

Before I move on, I must note that it's interesting that Jesus said,
"Let him cast a stone at her." If we take another look at the law in

Deuteronomy for a second, we will see what the law says about how many stones are to be thrown at the adulterers. The law requires: "and ye shall stone them with stones that they die" (Deuteronomy 22:24). Stones are thrown at the adulterers, not just a single stone, until they died. This is as much to anonymize the killer as it is to ensure the killing. Of course, there are supposed to be two subjects, but we will not go back to that right now.

Logically, I must ask, why does Jesus say, "cast a stone?" He certainly knows the law. Did He only refer to one stone because before you can claim the righteousness of the scripture, even one piece, stone, or one pebble of it, you must first be righteous, clean, and without sin? The lesson here for the scribes, Pharisees, crowd, you and me is this: we cannot stand on even one letter of the rightness of the scripture if we are not standing in the right, or proper relation to the Lord, the One who takes away our sin and makes us righteous. The scribes and the Pharisees are physically and spiritually standing on the wrong side of Jesus. They're not standing in a right relationship with Him. Behind Jesus is where I place my wounded, lonely heart alongside this woman.

"And again he stooped down, and wrote on the ground." (John 8:8)

Why do you suppose He writes on the ground a second time? And why doesn't He say something this time? Is it perhaps to leave a lasting impression? Get it? Seriously, though, I believe Jesus does this for three reasons.

First, the scribes and Pharisees misunderstood the first time. He has to teach them. This time, I believe He adds to what He wrote the first time. Next to the laws, He adds something that clearly associates the people with the sins. Maybe He writes the exact locations or dates when these sins were committed, making their recognition personal and individually felt.

Second, Jesus writes on the ground to level the playing field. He brings the scribes and the Pharisees down from their self-appointed, exalted positions of accusation to remind them that they, like this woman, are standing on equal ground before Him. All of their sins are as vile and punishable as this woman's sin. Now, they're all caught.

Third, Jesus writes on the ground to inform this woman, and you and me, that though evil lies want to convince us that we are the only sinners, the truth tells us we are not. Why do you suppose He writes on the ground instead of speaking? There's power in His words. After all, Jesus is the Living Word and by His word all things, including the heavens and the earth were created (John 1). Is it perhaps to make the scribes, the Pharisees, and the crowd contemplate His words? After all, the scribes are the ones who write out the law, thus the written law matters to them. Though His words are not detailed in this Bible passage, these verses should cause us to think about how His writings might be different if you or I were in that room on that day.

"And they which heard it, being convicted by their own conscience, went out one by one, beginning at the eldest, even unto the last: and Jesus was left alone, and the woman standing in the midst." (John 8:9)

Thus, with the knowledge that the Master knows the intimate details of their lives, these accusers leave the Temple. No one in that room could throw a stone at this woman, without ducking to avoid that same stone boomeranging back at them. Now that their sins are exposed too, they cannot bear the embarrassment. Can you see them with their heads down, eyes to the ground, reading what Jesus wrote, seeing their own sins written there, turning and leaving the Temple, one by one?

Not Condemned

"Then Jesus stood up again and said to the woman, "Where are your accusers? Didn't even one of them condemn you?"
(John 8:10 NLT)

Once the accusers leave, Jesus stands up and speaks to the woman. Prior to this, she's never asked any questions. The scribes and Pharisees didn't care to hear any explanations about her sin or how she'd been found. Even now, as she stands with Jesus, she doesn't speak. Because of His knowledge of everything, He doesn't need to ask anything about her sin, either.

So why does He ask her this question? And why does He call the scribes and Pharisees her accusers? The Bible says in verse six that the scribes and Pharisees intended to accuse Jesus, not her. Yet, Jesus lovingly teaches her a lesson. Although the accusers are gone, the thoughts of this woman's mind and her sinful condition are not gone. Both have to be addressed.

Certainly, she knows that according to the law she deserves to be stoned. Perhaps she has condemned herself. Jesus however, takes time to talk to her to explain that just as none of the scribes or Pharisees could condemn her, neither should she condemn herself. Sure, she sinned, but the Bible states, "For all have sinned, and come short of the glory of God" (Romans 3:23).

"No, Lord," she said. And Jesus said, "Neither do I. Go and sin no more." (John 8:11 NLT)

This is the bottom line. Jesus forgives her. He doesn't accuse her nor does he condemn her. And He blesses her. God's forgiveness is always a blessing. Only Holy God can condemn us for our sins. However, for those who follow Him, He does not condemn us.

For you and me today, the punishment for sin may not be stoning, but sin is still punishable by death. That is because sin is a failure to observe and meet God's holy standard. Jesus is the Holy God who cannot dismiss sin. So, why doesn't He allow sinners to be stoned? Why does He ignore the law? Oh, friend, the answer to this question is where I found my liberty!

Jesus never ignores the law. He always fulfills it.[4] Through His life, and His presence in the Temple that day, He carries out the law.

Someone was stoned. It was not the woman who caught in adultery, nor the scribes, Pharisees or crowd. The one stoned would be Jesus Christ, Himself.

The final stones for these sins were thrown at Jesus on Calvary where Jesus died for the sins of the whole world, including this woman and everyone in that Temple. I know you are thinking how that could be, because when this story occurs, Jesus has not yet gone to Calvary. That is true. But, He's already being prepared to endure the punishment for the sins of all the world by coming to earth to live as a human being. Jesus, therefore, did not execute the stoning required by the law in the Temple that day, because through His life, death, burial, and resurrection, He received the stones of every punishable sin that every human being has ever committed or would commit, so that those people, that woman, you and me do not have to. He substituted Himself for you and me. He took our stones!

Because of Jesus, we must not allow other sinners to condemn us by their words and attitudes. Even when our sins have been publicly exposed, there's redemption and comfort available to us through Jesus Christ who sweetly tells us, "Go and sin no more." We need to heed His words by accepting His salvation and repenting from the sin that put us in these situations to begin with. We can blame no one else for our sin. Even when we were overtaken and forced into activities that we would not have chosen for ourselves, or where we willingly joined in, did not scream in the city, or were confronted in the country, all of us now have access to a Master who doesn't condemn us, but protects us and directs us to sin no more. All we need to do is accept His love and protection by standing behind Him and following Him.

As I reflect on this passage and think back on the stories of Amy and Melissa, I'm struck by how quickly I picked up a stone with the intention of throwing it at them. I wonder if I had been in that Temple crowd, would I stand with the scribes and the Pharisees, or behind Jesus?

There are many unanswered questions about the woman in this passage. Was she young like Karla? Was she married? Engaged? Found in the city? Found in the country? Was she a willing participant? Or forced and raped? All we know is that Jesus told her to "sin no more," implying that she sinned. Then Jesus chose to love her. Therefore, I choose to love her, Amy, Melissa, Karla, and Kim, too.

Now Under Grace

Some of us have had multiple losses of our children through several abortions or adoptions. There are some who are reading this right now who are considering having another abortion or giving another child up for adoption. There are some of us who became pregnant out of wedlock or because of an affair with a married man and are now facing a pregnancy decision. I don't know your specific circumstances, but like the woman in John 8:1-11, the facts about how you got here does not matter right now. What matters is that when you stand with the Master, Jesus, no one can accuse you nor condemn you. He stands in the way of those people. But He stands in front of you and faces you. He asks you, "Where are your accusers?" Who can stand before Him to accuse you? Who else matters? There is only you and Him.

He's saying to you, "I do not condemn you. I love you. I have standards for you. I have abundant and full life for you. I have a life of righteousness and good for you. Do not subject yourself to this sin any longer. Go away from that sin. Go and do not do it anymore."

Reflection

Despite the foolishness of your accomplice, have you accepted the forgiveness that Christ offers?

Are you heeding His command to "Go and sin no more"?

Prayer

Dear God,

I know I have sinned. I know my own sin brought me to this difficult situation. I accept my part in the creation of my child. But,

I am not in control of my life, You are. Where I have sinned, Lord, please forgive me. For those actions that were contrary to Your Word and Your will for my life, please forgive me. I name it specifically right now. God, please forgive (insert the name or title of the person who you need to forgive) who was involved in the sin by (name what the other person did). Lord, please, forgive my doubt and lack of faith. Help me to turn that situation and the feelings that linger over to You. And Lord, I will not come before You without acknowledging that You know my sin. Lord, I give it up now. I want to break free from this hurt and pain. I want to accept Your forgiveness. Teach me Your ways. Direct my thoughts this week when those things, those convenient emotions and reactions, come back on me. Instead, give me the strength to lean on You and Your Word. Make me remember that I am fearfully and wonderfully made (Psalm 139:14). Let me remember that I am not rejected by You (Romans 8:1). Let me remember that I have been chosen by You and I am Your treasured possession (Deuteronomy 7:4; 14:2). Even when others try to throw stones at me by reminding me of what I have done, by Your love, remind me that I am protected and safe.

In the name of Jesus, Amen.

9
...

Seeking Grace in Mercy

"Let us therefore come boldly to the throne of grace, that
we may obtain mercy and find grace to help in time of
need." (Hebrews 4:16 NKJV)

"Let your speech be always with grace, seasoned with salt,
that ye may know how ye ought to answer every man."
(Colossians 4:6)

The Questionnaire

"**D**o you have any children?"

This is the question every woman is asked at some point in her
life. After a certain age, I suspect you are required to have children.
My belief that motherhood is a woman's responsibility put a lot of
pressure on me.

I planned to have children. Three to five boys. No girls. Of course,
if I'd had a girl I would have loved her immensely. She would have
been my pride and joy. But, I wanted and prayed for a house full of
boys. I thought I deserved them. Thus, this question reminds me of
my spoiled plans.

"Number of pregnancies?"

Some of you read that question and had no idea why it's there or what it means. Others read this statement and thought about a specific place and a specific process. Still others cringed and cried.

That dreaded question is usually accompanied by a blank box or space on a questionnaire. It must be answered. If you do not answer it with a pen or pencil, you are asked verbally by a not-so-caring medical staff member who mercilessly waits for an answer. The full question is sometimes asked in two parts:

"Have you ever been pregnant?"

A yes or no answer is expected. Your reply is then followed up with, "How many times have you been pregnant?" Hence the, "number of pregnancies" statement-question rears its head again. This should be an easy question to answer.

For many women, it's just a question on a form. But for women like me, it is a reminder of life events that are most conveniently not recounted. Especially, not with strangers. And for God's sake, not with uncaring, unsympathetic medical personnel.

"Number of children?"

There it is. The real question. The one that all the other questions lead up to. Even the, "Do you have any children?" question winds up leading to this question. It's easy to just give a number. Right? Either you have children, or you do not. Why not answer boldly? Say one, two, three, five, or none. It's simple. Except, when it's not and the answer requires an explanation that's too much information for the person asking, and too much painfully, complicated information for the woman answering. The thing is, a complete answer is not only necessary, it's therapeutic. The answer is not just an answer, it is a healing, a revelation, an admission, a confession, a testimony, and a statement from you and about you.

The answer is loaded with emotion, guilt, confusion, fear, anger, despair, remorse, condolences, hurt, hate, and pain. There is always pain. Invisible pain. Pain more awful than labor pain. It is the worst kind of pain, because it is the silent aching that the bearer avoids giving voice to until provoked. Such as when confronted with these statements and questions on a physician's intake questionnaire.

"How do I answer this?"

This is as much a reflexive response as a self-asked question. The woman confronted with these questions asks herself this one automatically. What are her choices? She can ignore the question. But then she risks being rude. She can lie, but lying only leads to more questions like: What are their names? How old are they? What schools do they attend? This constant stream of questions creates a level of anxiety that only this woman, this certain kind of woman, can understand. When she is sure she's no longer affected by these questions, a new question from an unexpected source slaps her in the face and takes her back into this tailspin of emotion.

These questions anger me. I avoid them like the plague. With each passing year, the effect of these questions never lessens in severity. I long for the boldness to answer them. Then, I recall a woman I met in Mark 7. She teaches me what to say.

The Sincere Request

This woman's story seems ripe for mercy. When she hears Jesus is in town, she goes to Him for healing. Once before Him, she falls at His feet and pleads, not for her own healing, but for the curing of her sick, demon-possessed daughter. In response, Jesus implies that she's a lowly dog. That does not sound like appropriate words from the Savior. With a remarkably blunt response, she insists He restore her child. Her honesty results in Jesus mercifully filling her request. Though this mother's child does not die, her perseverance in the face of ostensibly humiliating statements and questions can encourage us to press forward and not give up no matter the words we're sometimes forced to address.

"For a certain woman, whose young daughter had an unclean spirit, heard of him, and came and fell at his feet." (Mark 7:25)

This mother is just like you and me.

The Bible does not tell us her name, age, or marital status. Instead, she is called a "certain" woman meaning she is of uncertain specificity. This is perfect because the Greek word for certain, *tis*, means anyone.[1] So when we read this story, you are free to make this mother anyone you need her to be. Whether she is short, tall, young, old, rich, poor, single, married, or widowed, we already know this one thing about her—she will stop at nothing to help her sick child.

What is her child's sickness? The young child has an unclean or evil spirit. Though the Bible does not say that the little girl died, I suggest that the little girl is not living. Her spirit is not her own. She's under the influence of filthy wickedness that's not in keeping with the purity and innocence we associate with a young girl. The little girl needs to be returned to abundant life in Christ. I suspect the mother does, too. That's why as soon as the mother hears help is near, she drops everything and goes where help can be found. When she finds Jesus, she falls at His feet in humble submission.

"The woman was a Greek, a Syrophenician by nation; and she besought him that he would cast forth the devil out of her daughter." (Mark 7:26)

We're beginning to learn something about this woman. Not her physicality, but her nationality. Jesus, of course, is Jewish. This woman is Greek, a gentile. As a Syrophenician, her people are historical enemies of the Jews.[2] Not only should she, a woman not speak to Jesus, as a gentile enemy, she shouldn't request or expect a spiritual blessing from Him. Despite this, she seeks His assistance.

"But Jesus said unto her, Let the children first be filled: for it is not meet to take the children's bread, and to cast it unto the dogs." (Mark 7:27)

Jesus!

Every time I read His response it's shocking. Since everything Jesus does is right, we must understand His message to this mother. First, Jesus does not ignore her. He responds to her request. There's such consolation in knowing that Jesus does not ignore anyone who pursues Him.

Second, Jesus upholds the Jewish tradition. Through analogy, He refers to a household, perhaps God's household, calling the Jews "the children"[3] of the home and the gentiles the pets, or "the dogs." Jews regularly referred to gentiles as dogs.[4] But Jesus here uses the word for "little" dog, lessening the viciousness of the term.[5] Jesus tells this mother that the children should be fed to satisfaction before the puppies are allowed to eat from the table.

This is a hard response. How would you respond? If you need healing from your pain and sorrow would you miss your blessing if called a dog? Perhaps we need to better understand this statement before we answer.

Today, in the United States, we treat our pets like family members. We sometimes dress and feed them better than our children. But dogs, even little ones, are not the same as children. They are subordinate to children. In that way, Jesus communicates that the gentiles are in the homeland of the Jews, but not of God's household.[6] The gentiles can access God's blessings, but the Jews, God's chosen children, have priority.

You can imagine the scene He provides. Children often play with their food and fail to appreciate the price their mother pays to obtain it and prepare it. Kids scoff at what is put on their plate, and sometimes give their food to the little family dog. What does the dog do? Devour the food. What the child fails to appreciate, the dog joyfully consumes.[7] By using the analogy of the children at the table and the puppy under it, Jesus shrewdly acknowledges this mother's determination to receive mercy from Him. Whatever bit of it He happily drops before her.

Why doesn't Jesus just give her what she asks? Sometimes, God tests and stretches our faith.[8] He does so with this woman.

"And she answered and said unto him, Yes, Lord: yet the dogs under the table eat of the children's crumbs." (Mark 7:28)

Right on, sister!

Without hesitation or thought, she finds the words to answer Jesus. She says to Him, "Yes sir. You are correct. I am not worthy of Your abundant blessings. The Jews deserve the best. I just want the rest." What a show of humility! Succinctly, this mother expresses her understanding of her position in society and Christ's power to change her life forever. She accepts that she has no right to ask for a blessing of the magnitude of the feeding of five thousand men,[9] but just a morsel or crumb that drops from the table is sufficient. She's only seeking a healing for her daughter.

Just a Little Bit of Faith

I have to stop and say that this woman has faith. Do you know what sized faith she has? Mustard seed faith. Consider this scripture: "Jesus told them another parable: 'The Kingdom of heaven is like this. A man takes a mustard seed and sows it in his field. It is the smallest of all seeds, but when it grows up, it is the biggest of all plants. It becomes a tree, so that birds come and make their nests in its branches'" (Matthew 13:31-32 GNT). Add to that scripture this proclamation of Jesus: "Then the disciples came to Jesus in private and asked him, 'Why couldn't we drive the demon out?' 'It was because you do not have enough faith,' answered Jesus. 'I assure you that if you have faith as big as a mustard seed, you can say to this hill, 'Go from here to there!' and it will go. You could do anything!'" (Matthew 17:19-20 GNT).

Let's see what this mother's bit of faith does for her.

"And he said unto her, For this saying go thy way; the devil is gone out of thy daughter. And when she was come to her house, she found the devil gone out, and her daughter laid upon the bed." (Mark 7:29-30)

The ironic thing about mercy is that it is effective when it is accepted and acted upon. This mother does both. When Jesus announces the daughter's deliverance, neither the mother nor Jesus are with the little girl. The mother cannot view the healing. She has to believe Jesus and make the trek home to see for herself. She does not linger or repeatedly ask Him for help. Her faith propels her. I believe His mercy sustains her.

This mother came to Jesus seeking only a morsel of help. That's the faith she had stored up. In the end, she received His mercy. That's more than she bargained for.

I don't want you to get upset about this. I did not forget the purpose of this book. Yes, the little daughter is healed and does not die, but I ask you to see beyond that to consider the mother's blessing. You need to see this. It is the mother, not the child, who encounters Jesus. The mother exhibits faith and perseverance. Ultimately, Jesus responds to the mother's "saying." Not merely her response, but her interaction with Him. Her attitude, posture, and words all communicate reverence for Him and faith in Him to deliver. This mother's life expresses a need for Him and is changed after their meeting. Though she fully understands she deserves nothing from Him, she believes she might be able to convince Him to give her a little something. He grants her favor on par with what He offers the Jews. She directly experiences God's mercy. Jewish tradition instructed Him to send her to the back of the line, rather Jesus immediately has mercy upon her and grants her full request.

Seasoned with Salt

This woman's boldness inspires me. She doesn't avoid statements or questions. She knows she needs a healing and she lets nothing stand in her way. She automatically answers Jesus despite any discomfort the questions present. Because of her, today I am not consumed with crippling anxiety at the mention of these questions, though admittedly, upon signing up with new doctors and reunions with old friends, they rear their ugly heads. I'm again confronted with how to answer.

I think about this woman whose child was lost to a demonic spirit. We do not know how long the little girl suffered before her mother met Jesus. We can assume the mother lived with the shame of being the mother of a demon-filled child. Yet, she answers Christ honestly and tastefully. When reminded of her lowly position, this mother doesn't suffer disgrace, but receives grace. Her answers preserve her child's life and the life of her own motherhood. I think of her and am grateful she persisted. How she answers Jesus is a profile in courage. None of His statements sway her. Would they sway you?

As a woman who aborted or terminated your pregnancy, do you still believe you do not deserve Jesus' compassion? I used to believe that. What about you, the mother who lost your child prematurely to accident or murder? Do you believe you can't go to Him for help? I understand. The inability to openly mourn my prematurely born child weighed heavily on my psyche, making me feel subhuman and unworthy to raise my voice to cry out for mercy. For years, I didn't seek God's help. I didn't honor my children or my motherhood before God or others. I avoided entering into discussions about children with other women just so that they would not ask me about mine. When asked, I eluded the questions and hid my debilitating anxiety. Try as I might, I unsuccessfully avoided all inquiries until I couldn't any longer.

The breakthrough for me is in being bold like my Syrophenician sister and refusing to be uncomfortable. Today, I answer these questions directly because the merciful healing is in my response, my "saying." When asked if I have children, my answer is, "Yes, but they both passed away." This is a direct answer that is truthful and sincere. It's not provided to solicit sympathy, or to shock the questioner. It's a direct response to a direct question. It sometimes stops the inquisition. More than that, it's my victorious proclamation of the peace that God has given me through His kindness, care, and understanding. This answer describes my hope in a future reunion with my little ones, one day, on the other side.

Upon occasion, someone will ask me what happened to my children. This is rare, but I do not avoid it. "My first was aborted. My second was born prematurely and died." With confidence, I answer. It is alarming for someone to admit abortion without also communicating condemnation. It's equally stunning for a woman to discuss the premature birth and death of her child. And yet, while both of my babies died, and both deaths hurt for years, any follow-up sympathies offered to me are only extended for the premature delivery and death of my Daniel. Remember, premature labor is a tragedy. Abortion is murder. Right?

"Why should anyone sympathize with a woman who aborted her child?"

"How can she feel comfortable about her grief over the loss of that child?"

"What right does she have to expect understanding when her child died at her hands?"

More questions. Except these are never verbalized. The woman never has the chance to speak up. She's to remain silent and be forever remorseful about her decision. She should never be comfortable with it. She should never receive mercy.

That's what I believed for many years. My acceptance of this way of thinking was so deep-seated that I never gave my aborted child a name. I did name my prematurely born son; the son I held and felt. My Daniel. Not so for my first child. For so long I tried to ignore the child that resulted from an intense conception and was aborted at eight weeks in utero. I tried not to view this child as a child, a male or female, or a human being. Partly to lessen the pain, but mostly to make myself forget what I can never forget. The witness of the audaciousness of the Syrophenician mother does not let me forget. If her demon-possessed daughter did not embarrass her, how can I continue to let my aborted child embarrass me? I can imagine the unasked questions that might swirl around that mother today:

"Why should a Syrophenician woman receive help from Jesus?"

"Who told her she could talk to Him?"

"What right does she have to expect healing for her little demon daughter?"

When in the presence of our gracious Lord, she found the right words, and received mercy.

So. Can. I.

With Grace

Even though television commercials, news articles, legislation, and general discussions routinely remind me of the child of my youth, naivety, and ignorance, the feeling of motherhood at the first notion of being pregnant told me like nothing else that this child, my child, was a significant part of me and integral to my motherhood. That little ray of light I could not talk about never, ever left me. Long after the abortion, the light did not completely dim. So, I took on the boldness of my sister and accepted God's mercy by taking a confident step. That's when I named my aborted child. Using the words of the song that my best friend sang to her infant children, my baby is my "Sunshine."

Through the questions, the many, many questions, and the strength of my ancient sister, I love my children equally and embrace the fact that I am their mother. I preserve my motherhood. With all my flaws, mistakes, and ill-informed decisions, I embrace my babies and honor their memory. The new questions for me are not those posed on questionnaires, but, "How do I honor my babies? How do I encourage the mothers of babies like them to live to love unapologetically?"

The answer is, I do it by sharing my "sayings" regarding them. I inhale the mercy God gives me that I do not deserve and exhale His grace.

Sunshine would be thirty-three years old today. Daniel would be sixteen years old. Though the years continue to mount, they are forever my babies and I am forever their proud mother. I live today to love them through the testimony of our lives.

Reflection

What questions or statements regarding your child(ren) do you avoid and refuse to answer?

How are you receiving God's mercy and honoring the memory of your child(ren)?

Prayer

Dear Lord,

I haven't been very bold at all. In fact, the only thing that I've been persistent about is being in despair. Though I know this is not what You want for me, I cannot seem to stay of out of my own way. I don't want to confront what people have been thinking about me and my child, why they died, how they died and my part in it. Even where I had no part in it. I don't trust that I will be able to answer in a good way like this woman. Lord, but now I realize that I need Your mercy. I can no longer avoid the difficult questions. I can no longer act as if this didn't happen. It has. It has shaped who I am. Please help me to not allow it to limit my future. God, guide me and show me how You want me to use this and the answers that lie in me to make me into the mother my child would be proud to have. Help me to honor my child though my own perseverance. I can't do it without You Lord. Guide my feet as I make this first step, in You.

In the name of Jesus, Amen.

10
·····

Seeking Grace in Faith

*"God the Father knew you and chose you long ago, and his
Spirit has made you holy. As a result, you have obeyed him
and have been cleansed by the blood of Jesus Christ. May
God give you more and more grace and peace."*
(1 Peter 1:2 NLT)

The Choice

Few women sanely live through the choice I have to make.

That's because some women get pregnant and don't even know
it until they go into labor. Then, there's me. For years, my life was
consumed with dreams about being pregnant and planning to be
pregnant, until losing my two chances to realize the dream. Since
Daniel died, my full desperation is to replace my failed pregnancies
with another successful one, quickly. But, until those pesky fibroids
are removed, the same thing is sure to happen again. My mission to
get pregnant is in full effect. I know it should matter, but it doesn't
matter to me that God has forgiven me and commanded me to sin no
more. I want what I want. I want to be a mother. Though I feel God's
grace tugging at my spirit reminding me to heed His word, I plunge
ahead with my plan, overshadowing the real supernatural power at
work within me.

Two months after we bury Daniel, I undergo a myomectomy to remove the large fibroids that suffocated and crowded out my baby boy in my womb. Recovery takes months and months. Many more months pass before I can start trying to be a mother again. Because I don't want to be a woman who's been pregnant by multiple men, I'm determined to have Timothy's child, even if I can't have Timothy's heart. Sadly, he doesn't want to have a child with me. Not anymore.

When we break up, severing all communication between us, I convince myself that my every chance of being a mother is over, for good. Fortunately, I'm brave enough to start dating again, and for a desperate woman like me, any date introduces the hope to begin planning the next pregnancy. As a woman in her late thirties with the biological clock tick-tocking louder and louder every month, my anxiety convinces me to do outlandishly dangerous things with men who are ill qualified to be my child's father. None of that matters, though. There's a singular goal: for me to be a mother. The identity of the father serves a small technicality. No matter what I try, however, nothing works. I never get pregnant again. Two tries appear to be the allotment for my lifetime.

One day, my most trusted doctor says to me, "It's sad you are not going to be able to be a mother, because you are such a good person."

Hold it.

Full stop.

What did he say?

"It's sad you are not going to be able to be a mother, because you are such a good person."

I think I heard him clearly, but the words make no conceivable sense. The combination of "sad", "not going to be able to be a mother", and "good person" can't possibly apply to me. What is he talking about? Why would he even form his lips to say such a thing?

I'm graceful and stoic. I affirm, "Yeah."

And, I sit there. Trying to reconcile those words. He's caring and gentle as always. He gives me time to process this. I assure him I'm okay.

I check out of the doctor's office, get in the elevator, walk to the car and pay the parking lot attendant. I'm completely numb until I notice that I've pulled up to my own garage. As I walk in the door, this house that was to be a home for my family, has suddenly become so very big and very lonely. Finally, I hear the words in the ears of my gut.

"It's sad you are not going to be able to be a mother, because you are such a good person."

The crying starts and continues without ceasing for hours. I sink into my bed and further into the tear-stained sheets and pillow until there's not a dry spot on the queen-sized bed. It's there that the real conversation begins.

Can You Hear Me?

I ask, "God, is this really it? My children have died. Are You saying that my dream to be a mother has to die, too? What are You saying to me? Where is my child? I've heard from my doctor. Now, I need to hear from You. Why aren't You talking to me? Where are You God? Where are You?"

The Lord does not answer. Not that day, and not for many months. Though I don't sense the Lord's presence during this very dark time, I keep crying out to Him. I keep demanding that He step in and correct this disarray. He's officially on notice that I expect Him to correct this mix-up that has been my life. It's not supposed to be those teenaged girls who have the successful pregnancies, it's supposed to be me! Me! The one who's wanted this for decades, who's an adult, has a career, a home, and an income that can comfortably provide a secure future for a child. The one who has endured. Who's forgiven. I'm the one who's supposed to be a mother. I deserve it. I've earned it. I deserve it.

"Do you want to be a wife or a mother?"

For a minute, I'm not sure who's speaking to me. Since my ears are not engaged, the lack of natural sound vibrates loudly within me. It's a bit strange. That's when it hits me what's happening. God is speaking to me. He's responding to my earnest cries!

When I feel Him speak to me, it's not quite like in the Bible. There's no cloud, mountain, burning bush, or talking animal. There's not even a preacher or prophet in the room. Just me and my senses. In what is nothing less than a miracle, the presence of the Holy Spirit fills my room and my life. He doesn't declare anything. He doesn't push me to stand and acknowledge Him. Or bow and worship. Instead, He simply, quietly whispers the question that permeates the air and my own spirit.

"Do you want to be a wife or a mother?"

I cannot sufficiently tell you how I know this is His question for me. Only that I can feel it seep from the atmosphere through my skin down inside of me. It comes like an out of place calmness in my gut. It reminds me that I am not forgotten. At the same time, the question pierces my psyche. The words are wrenching and alarming, yet I know this is really God's peculiar question to me. There it is. Here He is. The Lord has spoken. He's answered my prayer when I asked to be heard. Not at all like I wanted.

Now, He's listening.

How do I answer that? This inquiry is worse than those pesky doctor's office questionnaires. God's appeal to me is of biblical proportions. Of all the questions Jesus asked the Pharisees in the Bible, this one, posed to me, takes the parabolic cake! But this isn't an opening question to a story. This is a real-life-to-be-answered-today teaching. It's an eye-opener and a relief at the same time. It makes me take notice of the state of my Christian walk during my pursuit of motherhood. I used to sometimes wonder if Anyone was walking with me. This question settles that concern. It also makes me grateful that God has not cast me off for my immoral and promiscuous ways. I feel that He is with me like I have never before. For this reason, in an inexplicable way, I feel compelled to choose. There, in that question, the issues of my heart are exposed. My life's deep desire to be a mother is equal only to my deeper desire to be some man's wife. And, here's God's Holy Spirit, putting it out there in plain spiritual sight.

A Watershed Moment

In this question, my desire to please myself is rigidly juxtaposed with my desire to please God. (Seems I have quite a few desires). It's my defining moment. I must choose: wife or mother; God or me. I know what I have to choose. I know what the answer has to be. That's why I don't want to hear the question. But that's not the biggest problem with God's query. The tension it poses is in the fact that it is not an audible bid. It's spiritual. It's with me. Which means I cannot escape it or move from within ear-shot of it because it resonates in the ears of my heart. That question echoes in my mind, joints, and breath. This is the question that's ushering me into a new relationship with God.

A fellowship of faith.

If I chose to be a mother, then I'm essentially choosing to continue to disobey God. The prospect of motherhood for me has only meant sex out of wedlock. I know that adoption is acceptable, but that's not a worthwhile option for me. As a single woman, I believe the adoption agencies don't prefer me. Everything I've been told implies that married couples are more attractive to birth mothers. The one time I tried adoption, the agency's information session confirmed that baby purchase is not for me. Thus, old-fashioned baby-making is my preference. Given that I'm single, fornication can no longer be my choice. I can try to take the fertilization route. After all, my doctor is one of the top doctors in the country for this sort of thing. That just doesn't seem right either. Besides, needles filled with eggs and sperm are not what I want. Moreover, it's not what I believe God's Holy Spirit is guiding me to do.

I have to choose.

It seems that the choice to be a wife would please God as long as I'm willing to marry whomever He chooses. Being a wife is as honorable as being a mother. Just in the proper order. Eve taught me that marriage should come first. You know, "First comes love, then comes marriage, then comes Kim with the baby carriage." Making the choice to be a wife means choosing God. God. God. He has to be the choice. The only choice. Nothing else in my life can matter more than Him. Not even my desire to be a mother.

Through the abortion of my Sunshine, God kept me safe. Through the accusations of other people, He protected me from abuse. Through my many attempts to get pregnant again, He blocked me from contracting a deadly disease. Through the premature birth of my Daniel, He steadied my mind. Through learning that my body can't carry a child to term, He comforted me. He has become everything to me. He loves me like no one else has or can. It's now my time to take the step towards loving Him more than anything and anyone else. Even the anyones who are not yet born. It's my time to be a sinful woman who dares to worship Him with my everything.

God has to be the choice. I want to obey Him, to worship Him, to please Him. I choose to be a wife. Little do I know that He will please me.

I hesitate to share this spiritual crossroad, because it sounds so unfair. You might ask, "How can a good God require someone to make that choice? Holy God would never make someone do that. If He does, then I don't want to know a God who would do that."

God is always merciful and gracious. The God who asked me this question is the same God who sent Sarah's husband, Abraham, to the mountain to sacrifice her only son. The son she had to wait until she was ninety years old to give birth to. (Genesis 22). This is the same God who compelled Hannah to wean her son and "lend" him to God for the rest of his life, after she cried for the chance to have this child for more than fourteen years. (1 Samuel). This is that God. The God of Sarah, Hannah, and Kim. His request of me is the best thing to happen to me, because my resulting faith re-evaluation put my plans and goals in their rightful place. That is, because of God's inquiry, I've placed Him in His righteous place. He is the Most High God. Up to this point in my life, He had been merely the God I called on when in need. The God I acknowledged at church. The God who protected me from my accusers. The God who forgave me. The God I read about every day on the pages of the Bible, who I did not trust into every detail of my life.

His attention-commanding question showed me that He wants to be more to me and for me. All the events of my life led to this question; this encounter with God. Though I'd accepted Christ as Savior of my life three years after my Sunshine died, I had not yet accepted Christ as Lord over my life. He was not directing my life. I wasn't letting Him. Sure, I talk to Him and receive benefits from knowing Him, but I was not listening for Him or giving myself to Him.

This question changes all that.

After this question, and the answer I give, His love becomes what I look for, expect, desire, and adore.

I choose to be a wife. I choose God.

In making that choice, I learned one thing that might help you, too. You are able to push through what you previously thought unbearable. Losing what makes us most uniquely female is the unfathomable. For me, losing my children and the ability to have them prematurely could have led me to lose all hope. By God's grace, I didn't. That doesn't make me an anomaly or a phenome. Rather, it points to the transformative power of God to the woman who by faith, reaches for Him.

The Female Issue

Wouldn't you know, we have a phenomenal older sister who humbly teaches us to let no loss take away our yearning to reach for God. Who is this woman, you ask? Since we are not told her name, we'll have to gather some background information about her from what proceeds her story in the Bible. The thing that strikes me most about her is that her encounter with Jesus is repeated three times in Matthew, Mark, and Luke. Even in a patriarchal society, it's incredible that this woman retrospectively commands such attention. In fact, in the town of Capernaum[1] where Jesus has healed a man with an evil spirit, Peter's mother-in-law, a leprous man, a paralyzed man, a man with a deformed hand, a Roman officer's servant, and many others, she disrupts His healing plans. As He's on His way to heal the only daughter of a synagogue leader, we meet her. You'd think Jesus, who loves the little children, would let nothing distract Him on route to this child. This woman does. Proving one thing each of us knows— when a special woman enters the scene, she changes the issue.

"And a certain woman, which had an issue of blood twelve years," (Mark 5:25)

We should never treat a comma like a period. I know that, but this pause in our sister's story is there for a reason. We need to explore it.

The Bible tells us that this woman, like the Syrophenician mother, is a "certain" woman. She's you. She's certainly me. Though no name is given, there is nevertheless something eccentric about this woman that accentuates her existence in this crowd. You might expect that it's enviable. To the contrary. In obscure KJV phraseology, we are told she has "an issue of blood." Besides the times this term refers to her in the New Testament, it's only used elsewhere in the book of Leviticus in the Old Testament. We'll go back there to try to understand exactly what this term means.

As primarily a worship how-to manual for the Levites and priest, Leviticus guides the Israelites in proper conduct and holiness.[2] Common human situations are addressed in its verses, including topics that most contemporary churches keep hush. You wouldn't expect God to mention these no-nos, but since He's sovereign, He does. Items like male and female bodily discharges are detailed. That's where this "issue of blood" comes in.

As a most femininely embarrassing circumstance, the "issue of blood" is first mentioned in Leviticus 12:7 referencing the discharge of blood new mothers experience after childbirth. It's next mentioned in Leviticus 15:19 in reference to a woman's monthly menstruation, followed by a final reference in verse twenty-five explaining, "And if a woman have an issue of her blood many days out of the time of her separation, or if it run beyond the time of her separation; all the days of the issue of her uncleanness shall be as the days of her separation: she shall be unclean." Like other human discharges, the woman with the issue of blood must be separated from others while bleeding and during a specified number of days of purification, after which she is to bring a sin offering to the priest.

Before you get too offended, let me address the uncleanness and sin-offering questions swirling around your head. It's important to note that calling a person unclean is not reserved for women. The Bible is full of chapters addressing unclean men, women, animals, fish, insects, foods, and things. In each case, during the period of impurity, the ceremonially unclean is not permitted to participate or be used in religious ceremonies, offerings or places of worship where Jews believed the presence of the Lord's dwells. No ceremonially unclean person or thing may enter His presence. Because the Lord desires to be with His people, impurity must be purged. Not simply by water cleansing, but by the sacrificial shedding of animal blood followed by "an offering made by fire, of a sweet savour unto the Lord" (Leviticus 1:9). There's an obvious segue here, but we'll come back to that later.

Conditionally Ill

Can you imagine bleeding for twelve years? Even through what I considered the excessive bleeding my fibroids visited on me, at its worst it didn't last for twelve consecutive years. My compassion for this woman is great. I can only hope that the common companions of pain, cramping, backache, and nausea aren't added to her symptoms. Undoubtedly, her prolonged hemorrhaging has developed into what doctors today call anemia with its flanking symptoms of fatigue, weakness, pale skin, irregular heartbeat, dizziness, chest pain, cold hands and feet, and headache.[3] Any manifestation of these symptoms or a combination of them in an Israelite would further sequester her because she's ill.

> *"And had suffered many things of many physicians, and had spent all that she had, and was nothing bettered, but rather grew worse," (Mark 5:26)*

For the love of God!

Is this verse telling us that for twelve years this woman has tried to be a responsible healthcare consumer, yet no one has provided any relief? They've only made her worse? How can that happen? Professors Mark Hall and Carl Schneider explain the crippled bargaining position of the ill.[4] According to them, illness "erodes control … enforces dependence … disorients … baffles … terrifies … [and] isolates… Illness is 'always a place where there's no company, where nobody can follow.'"[5]

If this is true of the modern patient, what do you think this ancient, unclean female faced as she sought relief from many ancient physicians? If they claimed to have the cure, she readily bought what they proposed. Drinking, eating, burning, inhaling, injecting, inserting, laying in, on and under whatever the physician promised would work, including things like frightening the illness out of her.[6] Surely some of these physicians were sincere in their bids, while plenty of other quacks and frauds took advantage of her. Year after year, she continues to try and try. Spending good money after bad. Having nothing to show for her efforts. Where's the fairness in that? She's only gotten worse.

Don't you wonder where her money came from? We don't know. Nor do we know her age. She may be divorced, widowed, or the child of a wealthy man whose financial provision has given her enough money to last each rescue attempt until the money has finally run out. At the end of her resources and wits, she epitomizes the sentiment of the psalmist: "I get nothing but trouble all day long; every morning brings me pain" (Psalm 73:14 NLT).

Many people are like her. Trying everything we can think to fix our problems. I did. When my doctor compassionately concluded that I could not have children it was after I'd undergone several surgical procedures, taken x-rays, MRIs, pills, potions, and herbs, used water bottles and heating pads, visited holistic practitioners and Googled anything that remotely claimed to shrink my fibroids and stop the excessive bleeding. All in an effort to save my fertility. Specialists said my pain and bleeding was all in my head. They referred me for psychiatric care. Friends who'd had similar experiences shared how some "experts" advised them to buy adjustable beds and wear looser fitting clothes. No matter how wacky the advice, we tried it all.

None of it ever works. It only makes us worse.

Just A Simple Touch

"When she had heard of Jesus, came in the press behind, and touched his garment. For she said, If I may touch but his clothes, I shall be whole." (Mark 5:27-28)

After many years and many ancient dollars spent, stares and jeers don't scare her. She's finally ready to try Jesus. It's not so exceptional that she sought Jesus for a cure. We're told elsewhere in the Bible, "Everyone tried to touch him, because healing power went out from him, and he healed everyone" (Luke 6:19 NLT).

In that regard, our sister is doing what others have proven effective. Except her act of touching Jesus is not exactly what others have done. Her "issue" requires a touching quarantine. Leviticus 15 explicitly directs that anyone who touches the woman with the issue of blood, or lies or sits where she has been, will also become unclean. That person must not only submit to purification but must also wash their clothes. It stands to reason that the same duties apply to the person whom she touches.

Diseased, desperate, and determined, she defies customs, norms, expectations, and taboos. This brave woman doesn't summon Jesus to her house like the synagogue leader. She goes to Him. On a swarming public street, she pushes her way through the crowd, allowing herself to be pushed and jostled. She lets her contaminated clothes touch others. There's so many of them they conceal her issue. They don't recognize she's the bleeding woman, because for the last twelve years, she's been sequestered. She persists until she gets close enough to reach Jesus. Matthew describes her as almost lunging as she reaches from behind, just managing to touch only the hem, edge or tassel of His clothes. (Matthew 9:20)

What a strategic move, my sister. An insignificant fact to us, but first century Jews know the significance.

The Holy Scriptures record:

"The Lord commanded Moses to say to the people of Israel: "Make tassels on the corners of your garments and put a blue cord on each tassel. You are to do this for all time to come. The tassels will serve as reminders, and each time you see them you will remember all my commands and obey them; then you will not turn away from me and follow your own wishes and desires. The tassels will remind you to keep all my commands, and you will belong completely to me. I am the Lord your God; I brought you out of Egypt to be your God. I am the Lord" (Numbers 15:37-41 GNT).

Though our sister is not the only person to touch Jesus in this way,[7] she does this knowing the issue, the law, and the risk of her doing so. She reaches for and touches the symbol of the very thing that declares her unclean in order to make her whole.

"And straightway the fountain of her blood was dried up; and she felt in her body that she was healed of that plague."
(Mark 5:29)

Did you notice that our sister's condition has advanced from an "issue" to a "fountain of her blood"? She's not just bleeding but gushing. This is again not uncommon when you put it in context. Many of our conditions get worse just before relief arrives. It's how life works. It's also how God works. He sometimes allows our issues to decline to what is humanly impossible to fix so that His glorious power may be noticeably exhibited. When my doctor pronounced the death of my motherhood dream, my condition seemed hopeless. Maybe the years you've mourned your child have convinced you that no one can revive the death of all those dreams you had for your child's future. Don't give up! "For with God nothing shall be impossible" (Luke 1:37). Not even your situation. Through blood, sweat, tears and death, reach for Jesus. He is the only One who can change you.

> *"And Jesus, immediately knowing in himself that virtue had gone out of him, turned him about in the press, and said, Who touched my clothes? And his disciples said unto him, Thou seest the multitude thronging thee, and sayest thou, Who touched me? And he looked round about to see her that had done this thing." (Mark 5:30-32)*

Without being too graphic, when she touches Jesus' clothes, her bleeding ceases. She knows immediately her condition is healed. Her body feels different. There's no need for a parting of the clouds and a grand announcement from on high. But it happens when Jesus feels something, too. Not inside His body, but through the extreme edges of his clothing. He knows that His power has been accessed.

Look at how Luke describes this portion of the story: "Coming up behind Jesus, she touched the fringe of his robe. Immediately, the bleeding stopped. 'Who touched me?' Jesus asked. Everyone denied it, and Peter said, 'Master, this whole crowd is pressing up against you.' But Jesus said, 'Someone deliberately touched me, for I felt healing power go out from me'" (Luke 8:44-46 NLT).

Jesus appears to ask a ridiculous question. Of course, nothing Jesus says is without purpose. He brings attention to the activity of this woman's faith. While the disciples fail to distinguish her from the crowd, Jesus does not. Purposely stopping in His tracks, He focuses the disciples and the crowd to her. Despite the law declaring her an unworthy candidate for a blessing, she is the only one to manage to access His curative power. It doesn't make sense that such a simple touch should lead to her transformation.

Grace doesn't make sense.

Jesus gives grace where He will. No one deserves it. Everyone can have it. Few receive it, because many won't dare to reach for Him.

"But the woman fearing and trembling, knowing what was done in her, came and fell down before him, and told him all the truth." (Mark 5:33)

When the Lord asked me that simple question, I felt compelled to respond. I didn't know exactly how to answer Him at first, but I knew He deserved the truth. (Lying to Jesus is never a good idea). I had to confess my past. Admitting our faults is a scary thing. You tend to pour it all out withholding nothing. Especially when Jesus asks you directly.

It never occurred to me to consider this woman a sinner like me. To see her mind racing to find the words, trying to figure out how to answer Jesus. Should she first admit that she violated the law by appearing in public? In complete submission, should she divulge her secret in front of everyone? Or beg Him to not take her healing from her? Just when she thought the risks were over, she reverently prostrates herself before the Lord, doing what the apostle Paul famously directs when he says, "So then, my friends, because of God's great mercy to us I appeal to you: Offer yourselves as a living sacrifice to God, dedicated to his service and pleasing to him. This is the true worship that you should offer. Do not conform yourselves to the standards of this world, but let God transform you inwardly by a complete change of your mind. Then you will be able to know the will of God—what is good and is pleasing to him and is perfect" (Romans 12:1-2 GNT).

Her faith leads to worship. And worship results in rescue.

More and More Grace and Peace

"And he said unto her, Daughter, thy faith hath made thee whole; go in peace, and be whole of thy plague." (Mark 5:34)

Jesus' track record gives our sister hope. She believed that healing from Jesus would make her a restored woman who could be accepted back into the community. He did not disappoint. In fact, He gives her more than she bargained for.

First, He calls her "daughter." This is the only time in Jesus' earthly ministry that He refers to anyone by this term.[8] Instead of chastising her for touching Him, He welcomes her into relationship with Him. She belongs to His family. Second, He lets her know that it's not His clothes that healed her, but her faith in Him that accessed the healing. Faith is not a magical hocus pocus act, but "confidence in what we hope for and assurance about what we do not see" (Hebrews 11:1 NIV). Third, He lets her know that she received the rescue she'd hoped for wrapped in the assurance of eternal wellness. She will never be spiritually plagued again.

Oh, to be comforted by Jesus. He's still calling women "daughter" today. Women who are willing to faithfully touch Him. Those of us who for years haven't belonged anywhere because of the plague of mourning, but who find comfort in the family of God. Won't you, with one not-so-simple touch, dare to be healed and whole?

This is where you probably think I'm going to tell you that my fibroids disappeared, and I became pregnant again. No. That's not how my story goes. Yet, like this sister, Jesus healed me and made me whole. The reason this woman ministers to me is because like her, He rescued me from the isolating reality of what my doctor confirmed about my condition and made me whole. That is, when I chose Him.

By reaching for Him, He fixed my mind, the hope within me, my faith and my love for Him. Like her, I was no longer afflicted by my past condition. I was made new. I experienced peace. And so, my sister, I say to you, if he did it for this ancient woman in Capernaum and for this modern woman in Philly, He'll do it for you wherever you are, too. By faith, touch Him.

Reflection

What's preventing you from touching Jesus?

Will you reach for Him now, wherever you are, and choose to tell Him "all the truth" about you?

Prayer

Dear Lord,

My suffering has made me miserable. Years of trying to "get over it" have not worked. I've tried everything from self-help books, positive thinking, counselors, and church. I'm tired of trying this and that. I need You. I know I do, but I'm afraid to reach for You. What if You don't heal me? What if You do? What will I do without this pain that has been my companion in isolation all this time? Like the woman in this scripture lesson, I'm emotionally and spiritually quarantined. I'm taking the chance to worship You, Jesus. Allow Your grace to give me the strength to live whole. Lord, at this moment, I hear You speaking to me the words of Moses: "Today I have given you the choice between life and death, between blessings and curses. Now I call on heaven and earth to witness the choice you make. Oh, that you would choose life, so that you and your descendants might live! You can make this choice by loving the Lord your God, obeying him, and committing yourself firmly to him. This is the key to your life. And if you love and obey the Lord, you will live long in the land the Lord swore to give your ancestors Abraham, Isaac, and Jacob" (Deuteronomy 30:19-20 NLT).

In response, Dear God, I speak by faith, the words of David, "But I keep praying to you, Lord, hoping this time you will show me favor. In your unfailing love, O God, answer my prayer with your sure salvation" (Psalm 69:13 NLT). God, there is no other help I know but You. Today, I choose You! Make me whole Jesus! I need Your peace and comfort. Please hear Your daughter's prayer.

In the name of Jesus, Amen.

11

Seeking Grace in Giving

"But since you excel in everything—in faith, in speech, in knowledge, in complete earnestness and in the love we have kindled in you—see that you also excel in this grace of giving." (2 Corinthians 8:7 NIV)

Dreams Come True

Liana promised herself that if she didn't have a child by thirty-five, she'd adopt. At three months past her thirty-fifth birthday, she researches adoption agencies. Since she can financially afford a child and has a three-bedroom house in a good neighborhood, she knows it's time. She schedules to attend an information session with a recommended Christian adoption agency.

On the day of the session, Liana is welcomed and told to make herself comfortable. The information session will start soon. To her surprise, there are others in attendance. They all seem to be couples. Not deterred, Liana is feeling good about moving forward on her dream. She's certain this agency will understand her desire to become a mother to a motherless child. After all, she's a childless mother. It's a perfect, if not blessed, fit. The agency representative hands out information describing the adoption process. She discusses how they facilitate open adoptions where the birth mother is free to choose who she wants to meet as possible parents. The birth mother will get to know the chosen adoptive parents for the remainder of her pregnancy. At the birth, if selected, and all paperwork is completed, the adoptive parents are called to the hospital. With the birth mother, they will decide if the adoptive parents will be present in the delivery room for the birth. Immediately after delivery, however, the baby will be handed over to the adoptive parents. While the birth mother will not be in the child's life every day, she'll have the ability to follow up from time to time through the agency. The adoptive parents are therefore required to keep in touch with the agency during the life of the child.

Of course, the potential parents have many questions. Liana observes how the agency representative is attentive to each couple. They laugh and share many wonderful stories about couples who've successfully gone through this process. They even share how the birth mothers are happy to hand off their children to loving families with fathers, mothers, and big brothers and sisters who cherish them. The representative gives examples of how she presents the couples to birth mothers every day. She even shares that her agency has a higher adoption success rate for eager couples than any other agency in the region.

Liana observes how each couple and the representative talk as if she is not there. They look at her as if they are waiting for her husband to arrive. As if they're waiting for him to properly introduce her. Though Liana is incensed by this ill-treatment, she remains silent.

Noticing Liana's discomfort, the agency representative remarks, "Oh, Liana. I hope I haven't given you the impression that you're not important to us. Every kind of loving home is represented in our agency. We have been very successful with single women. In fact, if you'll agree, I'll have someone call you to share her adoption experience. I'm sure you will be pleased to hear it."

Liana smiles. "Thank you," she responds. Relieved that she's been noticed.

The next day, a woman named Stella calls to share her adoption story. Her appeal to continue the adoption process is compelling. Liana's grateful. With perseverance, the week before her thirty-sixth birthday, Liana becomes the mother of Liam, a vibrant eight-week-old boy who's not just handsome, but smart and attentive. Life is exactly as she dreamed. Her family rallies around her, helping her with everything she needs. Especially her mother who comes to live with her and Liam, making Liana's adjustment to motherhood and the return to work easier.

Liana is devoted to Liam's care. Every morning before she leaves for work, she prays over her little boy as he sleeps. In the evenings, she sings, counts, reads, talks, hugs, and kisses him. On weekends, they participate in a mommy and son exercise group. With the other mothers, Liana shares dreams, experiences, and all the things he can do. Here, she's included in the group, being acknowledged as "Liam's mom." That makes her proud. "Liam's mom" is the best thing she's ever been called.

Mommy's Big Boy

When Liam turns three years old, Liana's mother decides she wants to return to her southwestern home. Living with Liana and Liam is wonderful, but the harsh winters are too cold. She asks Liana to relocate, but Liana can't afford to uproot her life. Besides, she and Liam have a routine. He has playmates and he's thriving. Now that the "terrible twos" are over, Liam is starting to tell fantastic stories about his new best friend, Brutus, who Liana quickly realizes is not really real. Since Liana won't move, her mother tries to convince her that Liam may do well to start the local preschool instead of daycare. The neighborhood preschool can teach him to speak more clearly. He can even learn another language. He's clearly smart enough to pick it up quickly.

"In this day and age, Liana, he'll need to be bilingual," her mother says.

"You know mom, that's a great idea," Liana replies. "He'll do well if he doesn't just play, but can learn and explore, too."

Liana's mom stays with them until the weekend before Liam's first day of preschool. That Saturday, as they return from driving Liana's mother to the airport, Liam asks if Brutus can come to school with him. He's assured that Brutus can go to school, too. When Monday morning arrives, Liana and Liam are excited. They walk to the pre-school two blocks away. Liana cries as she leaves him. But, Liam is ready to go. He pats her hand and tells her not to cry.

"It's okay Mommy. I'll be home for lunch."

"You're right, baby. I'll pick you up for lunch. I love you."

"I'm not a baby, Mommy. I'm a big boy!" Liam corrects her.

He gets in line with the other children. Carrying his little back-pack, he runs to catch up with Roger, his friend from the mommy and son exercise group. As he enters the school building, Liam turns and waves to his mommy. Liana waves back and leaves her son to his new beginning.

Three hours feels like a lifetime. Liana is a nervous wreck while Liam's in school. She calls her mother, resisting the temptation to call the school. While parents are always welcome to call and visit, the school advises them to use restraint. They must let the children adapt during the first week. Against her better judgment, Liana complies.

Finally, it's time to pick up Liam. She can't wait to hear about school. She goes in the building and finds no one there. It's an eerie feeling. She knows something is wrong. Frantic, she searches for her son. His backpack is on the table. His jacket is on the floor. There's a faint cry in the next room. Liana runs to follow the sound. She finds a school worker crying into her palms. When Liana runs up to her, the woman directs "Liam's mom" to the playground at the back of the building. Liana looks out to see a small crowd.

Barging through the doors, Liana pushes everyone aside. There he is. Liam. He's at the bottom of the swings. He's lying there, on the ground, unconscious.[1] No one's doing anything. No one's trying to save him.

Liana screams, "Liam! Liam! Get up!" He doesn't respond.

Liam is transported to the hospital via ambulance. It's there that Liana learns how he fell off the swing and hit his head on the concrete.

"I should have been here earlier," she thinks to herself. "He wouldn't have fallen. This is all my fault. I should have called. I should have ..."

Liam's on life support for two days. The doctors tell her they won't be able to save him, because he's lost too much oxygen to his brain between the fall and the time he arrived at the hospital. Liana doesn't cry. Shock and guilt won't allow it. On Monday, she walked her son to school. By Wednesday, he's brain dead. Liana decides to take him off life support. Within minutes, he's gone. Liana kisses her son's forehead and leaves his hospital room. She goes to the chapel. There she asks God to receive her Liam.

"Lord, he's the best I have to give. He's Yours now. Please, care for him as Your own," she prays. The tears escape her eyes without her permission. Weeping, she stretches on the chapel floor.

It's Better to Give

As hospitals do when little ones die, Liam's nurse meets Liana as she leaves the chapel. There, she asks Liam's mother the question that enraged me when my Daniel died.

"Would you be willing to donate his organs, Liana?"

Unlike me, Liana wipes her eyes and consents. It's as if she instantaneously knows that Liam lived for this moment. To be an organ donor. He will live on in another mother's child.[2] Liana is relieved by the request. Liam's corneas, heart and kidneys are harvested and transplanted into three waiting children. Weeks later, Liana learns that children in Iowa, Florida, and Maine can see, run, and thrive due to Liam's gift of life. For Liana, by humbly agreeing to donate his organs, she receives a more generous present in return. The unspoken love of three grateful mothers.

The Real Sinner

There are many women in the Bible who inspire me to "Run on and See What the Ends Gonna Be."[3] We've already met a few of them. There's another who like Liana, teaches that no matter what happens in my life, charity is the greatest expression of gratefulness. Some say her name is Mary. The story about her in Luke chapter seven, however, does not provide her name. I like that, because after studying her story, I think she's more likely named Kim. But you determine. After you meet her, I think you'll find a familiar name to give her, too.

"And one of the Pharisees desired him that he would eat with him. And he went into the Pharisee's house, and sat down to meat." (Luke 7:36)

Do you remember who the Pharisees are? They're the Jewish leaders who want to prove that Jesus Christ is not the Messiah and the Son of God. We saw them in chapter 8 of this book when they publicly embarrassed the woman caught in adultery. Here one of them invites Jesus home for dinner. This seems like the last thing Jesus should agree to, but He goes. I love that about Jesus. He's never afraid to show up where He theoretically should not. He dines with people the Pharisees would not. It makes this visit to the Pharisee's house all the more interesting. By going there, Jesus puts Himself in the company of those who do not think they need a Savior. Of course, they do. And this Pharisee is no exception.

"And, behold, a woman in the city, which was a sinner, when she knew that Jesus sat at meat in the Pharisee's house, brought an alabaster box of ointment," (Luke 7:37)

Take notice. Though we should find the Pharisee's dinner invitation remarkable, it pales in comparison to this scene-stealing sinner woman. I know it's not a nice thing to say, but the whole town knows it. Kind of makes you wonder what in the world did this woman do? Some Bible commentaries over zealously call her a prostitute. The Bible doesn't specify her sin. I guess they assume this about her because prostitution is the only sin that a woman can commit, right?

Of course, not! Women commit all kinds of sins. Even in the Bible. Specifically, the Greek word for sin used here, *hamartōlos*, describes those who don't believe in God, those who don't follow the Jewish laws and customs, and Jewish people who work for the Roman government to extort taxes from other Jews.[4] I suppose this woman might be a heathen prostitute who extorts money from Jewish men. That would win her city-wide notoriety. But, like her name, not knowing her sin just makes it easier for me to insert my own and identify with her more.

Another thing about this woman is that she knows about Jesus' dinner plans. How does she know this unless she follows Him or pays close attention to the news around the city about Him and His whereabouts? Whether she follows Him directly or the citywide news about Him, she's a disciple of Christ. I know some of you are upset at the notion of a woman being called a disciple because the Bible says the 12 that walked with Jesus were men. Not a sinful woman, right? Well, we must understand that a "disciple" is a follower of Christ.[5]

Though our sister dares to follow Jesus to a place she's not been invited, she has manners. What? A sinner with manners? Yes. As a guest, she doesn't arrive to this home emptyhanded. Since she's an unusual guest, she brings an unusual gift to this unusual dinner. Not a dessert, a bottle of expensive wine, an exquisite delicacy, a unique jar of preserves, or some other dinner appropriate present. No. Our sister brings a box or jar of ointment. My research does not indicate a food related, ingestible use of ointment in biblical food preparations. Only that ointments are topically applied to the body for healing or cosmetic purposes.[6] Odd gift, isn't it?

At the Dinner Table

"And stood at his feet behind him weeping, and began to wash his feet with tears, and did wipe them with the hairs of her head, and kissed his feet, and anointed them with the ointment." (Luke 7:38)

I'm not sure where to start with this verse. Trying to visualize the scene set by the story, I imagine Jesus sitting in a chair at the dinner table when this woman approaches Him. This woman stands behind Him, crying such that tears stream down her face, off her chin, and towards the floor. Then, my vision gets cloudy. How can her tears reach His feet? The previous verse says Jesus, "sat at meat at the Pharisee's house." We assume this means He's sitting in a chair at the dinner table as we would. But this term means that He is reclining with His feet extended behind Him.[7] Those tears wetting His feet make sense after all.

Except she's washing His feet with her tears. She must be crying pretty hard. Can you imagine? I can because I've cried that hard, shedding so many tears I could've washed something. Haven't you cried like that before? I know the circumstances that led to my tears. Do you remember what precipitated your tears? What do you suppose is making her cry like this? Maybe something she's done. She is a sinner, you know.

Then there's the hair situation. Though the Bible says a woman's long hair is her glory (1 Corinthians 11:15), it's notable that our sister has greater regard for Jesus than her probably long, lush hair, using it to wipe the tears from His feet. I offer no offense when I say this, but when you consider that Jesus' feet were probably quite dusty, having recently walked the unpaved Judean roads, her foot-drying process is a unique offering. Why does she do this? Doesn't she have access to a towel? Why not use her clothes?

You see, she uses her tresses because she wants to be close to Jesus. Having made it to Him, her overwhelming delight at the sight of Him brings about foot-wetting tears. Bowing in esteem to Him to wipe His tear-soaked feet, she uses what is most readily available, the strands that fall in front of her, sticking to her face, as she kisses where she wipes.

Wait. She kisses His feet, too? Wow! What a party-crashing scene this is. Can you see her in your mind's eye, down on the dirt floor with her face bowed to His feet and her mouth close to the floor to kiss them? That's a woman with some level of affection for Jesus! But why?

In territories governed by a king, townspeople lower their heads in complete deference to kiss the monarch's hand or ring in respect for him. It's an ultimate display of reverence to his position, authority, and power. This is not an appropriate way to greet everyone. It's only reserved for the king. Our sister, you see, understands that if this level of respect is proper greeting for an earthly king, then there must be a more extreme way to show reverence for the King of kings, Jesus Christ, whose name alone warrants every knee to bow before Him (Philippians 2:10).

About His feet. There's a lot that can be said. Generally, I don't touch anyone's feet, except my own. And sometimes, I don't want to touch my own feet. When I get a pedicure, it's astonishing how the nail technician touches, cuddles, and massages my feet without any reservation. Feet are not attractive, no matter how cute the polish chosen for the toes. But in this Bible scene, these aren't just any tootsies. These are the divine feet that would soon be "wounded for our transgressions, … [and] bruised for our iniquities" (Isaiah 53:5). Of course, this woman doesn't know what's about to happen to them. That makes what she does all the more remarkable.

You may still ask why so much care for His feet? Well, recall she's a disciple and they are known to sit at the feet of their master or teacher.[8] This woman simply chooses to fall at His feet, not in order to receive from Him, but to give to Him.

This woman knows that her healing, recovery, liberty, salvation, living, and loving depend on Jesus. The gift she brings to the dinner party is not for the host, but for Jesus, the honored guest whom she greets and anoints. Her only desire is to worship at His feet by giving her most precious possession to Him. She pours it out upon the only part of Him to which she's worthy to lift her eyes. His feet. In front of everyone in that room, and in front of you and me, she lives David's words when he said, "Bless the Lord, O my soul: and all that is within me, bless his holy name. Bless the Lord, O my soul, and forget not all his benefits: Who forgiveth all thine iniquities; who healeth all thy diseases; Who redeemeth thy life from destruction; who crowneth thee with lovingkindness and tender mercies;" (Psalms 103:1-4).

Who could possibly have a problem with this act of worship?

"Now when the Pharisee which had bidden him saw it, he spake within himself, saying, This man, if he were a prophet, would have known who and what manner of woman this is that toucheth him: for she is a sinner." (Luke 7:39)

Oh, I think I forgot. A Pharisee would disapprove of a woman showing up to the dinner party to display this level of commitment and love. In the condemnatory mind of a Pharisee, a true prophet would not accept such behavior. Though people like this usually express public disregard for such women, it's curious that this conversation occurs secretly, where personal opinions are confirmed by internal judgments. Errant thoughts are safe there in his mind where interpretations and conclusions are not questioned and challenged.

"And Jesus answering said unto him, Simon, I have somewhat to say unto thee. And he saith, Master, say on." (Luke 7:40)

Oops! I guess those secret thoughts can be challenged and questioned. Though Jesus could ignore the Pharisee's mean-spirited thoughts, He does not. He responds to this Pharisee as He responds to us today. Hearing this self-talk Jesus confronts it, compassionately teaching the Pharisee, named Simon, a spiritual lesson. As He's known to do with people who do not believe, Jesus teaches Simon through an illustrative story.

Debt of Love

"There was a certain creditor which had two debtors: the one owed five hundred pence, and the other fifty. And when they had nothing to pay, he frankly forgave them both. Tell me therefore, which of them will love him most?" (Luke 7:41-42)

Talking about a creditor and his debtors appears to completely miss the point of Simon's self-righteous attitude, doesn't it? Of course, there's an impeccable reason Jesus uses this parable to teach him. Knowing that people hear the truth He teaches and observe the truth He lives yet cannot accept the truth about who He is,[9] Jesus directs Simon's attention to the easy-to-understand tale about debtors and creditors. Even if Simon doesn't have outstanding debt, like you and me, he understands the setting. In this story, one debtor owes a large sum of money to a creditor, while another debtor owes a fraction of the other's debt to the same creditor. The gracious creditor cancels both debts.

Before we move on, we have to notice that Jesus is often accused of friending publicans or tax collectors. As I suggested earlier, perhaps this woman's sin has financial motivation. If everyone in the room knows this about her, maybe Jesus wisely chose a parable that directly addresses the questions in everyone's mind. Here she is, a financially-influenced sinner, in the house of a judgmental, unbelieving Pharisee who's secretly offended that she touched Jesus. And that same Jesus tells a story involving financial responsibility.

Such irony!

"Simon answered and said, I suppose that he, to whom he forgave most. And he said unto him, Thou hast rightly judged. And he turned to the woman, and said unto Simon, Seest thou this woman? I entered into thine house, thou gavest me no water for my feet: but she hath washed my feet with tears and wiped them with the hairs of her head. Thou gavest

*me no kiss: but this woman since the time I came in hath not
ceased to kiss my feet. My head with oil thou didst not anoint:
but this woman hath anointed my feet with ointment."*
(Luke 7:43-46)

Simon is caught! He cannot pretend he doesn't understand Jesus or His lesson. Of course, the answer to Jesus' question is the person with a greater debt is more grateful and deferential to the compassionate creditor. Notice however how Simon's hard heart won't allow him to wholly agree with Jesus. Have you been like Simon? Though you know it's time to change your thinking about the circumstances that led to the loss of your child, or about the mistreatment you suffered at your choice to abort or offer your child for adoption, have you become hardened like Simon? Is it time for you to stop blaming yourself or someone else? Will you also continue to avoid hearing or seeing the love of Jesus while He's near you? In the same way he offers charity to Simon, He's offering it to you. Please accept His love.

Unfortunately, Simon not only refuses to accept who Jesus is, he fails to honor Him. By doing that, He also declines the opportunity to experience the beauty of this woman. This is where my fondness of this story is solidified. While so many people in our society are like Simon and those folks in the adoption agency information session, willfully dismissing this woman, Liana and at times me, Jesus does not overlook us. Instead, He speaks directly to the Simons, asking them to observe us, her. Don't dismiss her. Don't avoid her. Look at her. See what she's doing. Understand her story and her actions. Regard her in light of her sin, the lesson of the parable, and your own shortcomings.

Jesus contrasts the woman's acts of commission with Simon's omissions. Simon didn't supply water for Jesus to wash the dust from his feet before entering his home. A simple custom. Simon didn't greet Jesus with a kiss as He entered his home. A common welcome for a house guest. Simon didn't anoint Jesus' head with oil. The mark of blessing that Simon, the outward religious leader, should know to apply. Simon not only steers clear of this woman, he keeps his distance from Jesus, too. In stark contrast to Simon's lack of common etiquette,[10] the unwelcomed, sinner-woman goes above and beyond each norm to embrace the Lord. She doesn't use everyday water to wash His feet, but her personal, unending supply of tears to shower Him. She doesn't greet the Lord with a routinely polite kiss on the cheek, but in ultimate humility, silently bears the shame of her past sins to lower herself to caress and kiss His feet. Finally, she doesn't mindlessly anoint His head with usual oil, but brings to Him her most prized possession.

You see, this woman brings an alabaster box filled with oil to the dinner party. If she follows her own previous example, then we can assume this is no ordinary ointment. It must be precious oil, above and beyond the norm. And, if her crimes are financial, then this oil is likely very expensive, too. Yet, she empties out her cherished possession on Him. Again, not limited to the usual custom of annointing the head of the guest, she offers a greater honor. Fully aware of who she is in relation to who Jesus is, this woman drains the costly contents of the stone vessel at His feet, not daring to stand face to face with Jesus. Isn't that a waste? Yes, usually it would be. But these are the feet of which Isaiah said, "How beautiful upon the mountains are the feet of those who bring the happy news of peace and salvation, the news that the God of Israel reigns" (Isaiah 52:7 TLB).

This woman knows Jesus is her salvation and peace. She loves Him. To show it, she gives. Her offering to Him is not a waste. Neither is Liana's offering of Liam's organs. That beautiful package of a son, wrapped in the box of human flesh, contained life-giving panaceas. Unselfishly, Liana freely poured out his corneas, heart, and kidneys to save the lives of other children. In this, Liana's love for the One who filled her promise to herself is expressed. Both Liana and this woman live out before us the spirit of the scripture, saying, "Give unto the Lord the glory due to His name; worship the Lord in the beauty of holiness" (Psalm 29:2).

Giving is plain and simply beautiful, holy worship.

In the end, the comparison Simon crafts in his mind between this woman and himself is dismissed. Jesus teaches that the proper comparison is not based on the identity of the two debtors, but on their response to the creditor's forgiveness of their debts. Simon therefore should concern himself with his own relation to Jesus, and not to this sinful woman. She, on the other hand, gets it right. She does not let Simon's opinion of her stop her from honoring, anointing, and worshiping Jesus.

I cannot move forward without making this point. For years, I didn't share my story because I was afraid of what people would say when they heard it. Sure, I'd shared it with a few people, but not publicly. Fear of jeering, sneering, and shunning kept me from speaking up and speaking out. Despite knowing that I'd overcome much and that my story might encourage others, my concern centered on what judgmental people would say, rather than giving the Lord the obedience, worship, and praise He deserves. That is, until this woman and Liana's generosity convicted me. These two teach me it doesn't matter what the Simons in my life think about me, because each of them have prideful conditions that also need forgiveness. Understanding this, I am able to push towards gratefully giving unabashed adoration to Jesus.

This Grace Of Giving

"Wherefore I say unto thee, Her sins, which are many, are forgiven; for she loved much: but to whom little is forgiven, the same loveth little. And he said unto her, Thy sins are forgiven. And they that sat at meat with him began to say within themselves, Who is this that forgiveth sins also? And he said to the woman, Thy faith hath saved thee; go in peace."
(Luke 7:47-50)

You know what? On second thought, Simon is correct to see her as a great sinner. What he misses however, is that he is also a great sinner. The secret of Jesus' story is that there's no one who's been forgiven little. We have all been forgiven much, my sisters. Those of us who terminated our pregnancies and those whose child died accidentally. We should thus be like this woman. With an uncontrollable overflow of gratefulness, we too must lovingly give our everything to the great creditor, Christ. None of us should be like Simon, tricked into thinking we owe no debt, therefore giving nothing, forfeiting forgiveness and peace, while Christ stands nearby.

My sister, "You are forgiven."

The three words the news, your friends, your family, and you fail to say to yourself—You are forgiven.

No matter how many abortions or terminations. No matter the reasons. No matter what you tried to do to get pregnant. No matter that you weren't there to protect your child from that murderer or accident. You are forgiven.

The three words that matter. Words that bring life. Words that have the power to change you, your outlook, your actions, and your future. You are forgiven.

Not just for one sin, one action, or one wrong. But, for all. You are forgiven.

Reflection

Are you ready to give yourself, which is your most precious gift, to the One who has authority to forgive your sin debt?

Will you believe Him and accept that you are forgiven?

Prayer

Dear God,

Let me never be ashamed of what I've been through. Where I need to repent and seek Your forgiveness, I'm ready to do so with boldness and reverence to You as Forgiver God. I'm coming to You knowing that, "If we confess our sins, he is faithful and just to forgive us our sins, and to cleanse us from all unrighteousness" (1 John 1:9). Lord, I now want to hear You when You say to me, "You are forgiven." I believe You have forgiven me for my actions and faulty thoughts. Help me to leave my burdens with You, my compassionate God. You love me. You paid my debt in full. Let me no longer live ashamed and defeated. Let me live in Your peace and forgiveness. I give myself to You, Jesus. I love You.

In the name of Jesus, Amen.

12
.....

Seeking Grace in Service

"Each of you should use whatever gift you have received to serve others, as faithful stewards of God's grace in its various forms." (1 Peter 4:10 NIV)

"You and Me, Us Never Part"[1]

Renee and I are best friends. We've been friends since childhood. I won't mention how long that's been. Let's just say more than a decade has passed in our friendship. Though we are not blood sisters, I think you would recreate the Celie and Nettie separation scene from the movie, *The Color Purple* if you tried to tear our friendship apart. Over the years we have shared many life events. We're so close that some of those events have tracked in time and type, including losing our fathers and losing a close sibling. It may not surprise you that we were even pregnant at the same time—though it surprised us. During our pregnancies, our daily conversations centered around the births and lives of our future children, whom we decided would also be best friends.

At about six months farther along than me and as expected, Renee went into labor first. She gave birth to a beautiful baby girl. I could not wait to see her. When I held that little angel close, I realized she was the most perfect, little Renee mini-me imaginable. Once Renee's baby, Malaika, my goddaughter, was born we anticipated my baby's birth in just a few months all the more. But when I went into premature labor and lost my son thirteen days after my goddaughter's birth, it was anything but joyful.

Renee was devastated at my loss. I didn't anticipate how my loss would affect her. Frankly, I only thought about my own pain and how I longed for my baby. For months, I avoided my friend because she had her baby and I did not have mine. Jealously ruled my heart and overtook my interactions with everyone. Renee and I talked often on the telephone, but I alluded seeing her and holding Malaika again. I couldn't bear the thought of seeing Renee's child when I knew I'd never again see or hold my goddaughter's little best friend, my own child. Every time Renee and I discussed getting together with her little one, I found something else more pressing to do. That went on month after month, until Renee insisted my recovery must include getting to know little Malaika.

At about the time of my Daniel's original due date, Renee reunited me with Malaika. Seeing this little angel in a sundress and matching hat brought tears to my eyes. Her playful inquisitiveness tugged at my heart. She noticed everything, even me. Neither Malaika nor I reached for each other, to Renee's displeasure.

"Here, hold her," Renee said to me.

"No," I resisted.

"You are going to hold your goddaughter. She is going to be in your life. It's time, Kim."

With those words, Renee placed her in my arms. Before this moment, my Daniel was the last baby I held for the few minutes I spent with him in the hospital. I then told myself I would never hold another baby again. Now Renee's little angel wiggled in my arms as uncomfortable with me as I was with her. When she looked up at me, I was unbelievably smitten.

Looking back on that summer day, I'm grateful Renee didn't allow me to wallow in my sadness and shrink away from my life and responsibilities. She instinctively came to my house, armed with Malaika and a plan. She had to draw me out and bring together two people who matter to her into a lifelong relationship. Renee understood that my angel needed me and I needed my little angel. The strength of the extended family we cultivated over the years depended on this moment.

My best friend's determination held power beyond her daughter in my arms. In that one act, she obediently used the gift that did not discourage her. It propelled her into action.

It's All About Love

If you can't already tell, Renee is endowed with the gift of service. She naturally goes into action when situations seem dire, times are tough and someone is in need, especially if children are involved. It's normal to visit Renee's home and find it full of young people. They love her because they find refuge and protection under her care. She ensures they eat well and have a chance in life. Whether she's mom, godmom, grandmom, auntie, or simply Ms. Renee, her special way of tending to their individuality not only helps the child but also provides indispensable support to their mothers.

Of course, she doesn't stop there. She is equally prone to help the sick and vulnerable. Though she works the graveyard shift, she frequently spends her days taking others to doctor's appointments and running errands for them. If you ask her why she does these things, Renee will tell you that it's how she demonstrates the love in her heart. She does what she believes she is supposed to do to meet the needs of those in her life. She serves them faithfully and daily. But the one day that made the most significant impact on my recovery is the day Renee sensed her best friend's need to be delivered from depression and united with Renee's baby girl. My presence in her daughter's life could not be denied.[2]

Renee obeys her calling. She does it wisely, cunningly, and effectively. In so doing, she follows a history of spiritual women who by serving at-risk mothers, serve their community and their God.

The Wrong Ones

Do you know these two women, Shiphrah and Puah? They may be unfamiliar to you now, but in the next few pages, we'll take a first person walk with them. By the end, these two women will inspire you.

Shiphrah and Puah are women who live in or around Egypt during the days of the Hebrew enslavement there. Though they're not depicted in Cecil B. Demille's movie, *The Ten Commandments*,[3] their story is dramatic. As working women, they loyally serve the community as midwives, planning, ushering in, and caring for life,[4] until a meeting with Pharaoh, the king of Egypt, tests their professional, communal, and spiritual lives. You see, Pharaoh orders these two midwives to do an unthinkable act. Shiphrah and Puah bravely disobey his command. They honor God by continuing to serve the Hebrew women. When the king realizes what they did, he asks these two why they disregarded his order. They reply artfully and bravely. As a result, the entire Hebrew community grows in numbers and Shiphrah and Puah are specially blessed.

Now about those odd-sounding names. Such distinctive names must reveal more information about these women. It turns out that the name Shiphrah means, "that does good"[5] in Hebrew. The name Puah means, "splendid".[6] Putting this all together, the Bible indicates that Pharaoh foolishly asked two midwives who represent the righteousness and goodness of God to kill His chosen people. What a colossal mistake!

> *"And the king of Egypt spake to the Hebrew midwives, of which the name of the one was Shiphrah, and the name of the other Puah: And he said, When ye do the office of a midwife to the Hebrew women, and see them upon the stools; if it be a son, then ye shall kill him: but if it be a daughter, then she shall live." (Exodus 1:15-16)*

This is the order Pharaoh gives the midwives—kill the Hebrew baby boys.

Sounds frightening and barbaric.

Pharaoh's order is the first Bible story to discuss a plan to prematurely kill babies. It is key to note the obvious. It's Pharaoh, not God, who orders the slayings. Some equate Pharaoh's command to modern-day, so-called partial-birth abortion.[7] We may not want to go that far in interpreting this passage, though the command is enormously controversial. By its nature, it's somewhat understandable why this story is not discussed much in church services or in Bible studies. For women like you and me however, it is vital to understand what this story communicates. Our freedom from the shame we harbor about past events shouts for it. This biblical account reminds us that God's all-encompassing love even reaches to the mothers of the babies who die because of a murderous trend in an unholy society.

As we study this story, we'll start with this question: Why does the king want to kill Hebrew baby boys? The verses prior to this passage expose Pharaoh's insecurity about the growth of the Hebrew people under his captivity. He fears that if this foreign community continues to grow in size, they will outnumber and possibly overthrow Egypt as their oppressors, and Pharaoh as king. In his depraved, sinful mind, killing the Hebrew boys would halt their growth while stroking his greed and pride.

You may be thinking, "Wait, I thought we were past this sort of thing in this book. Why this unpredictable turn? I thought by now we would be more focused on how grace helps us to live and have hope. Why does she keep talking about sin? And why is she now adding a tale about intentionally killing babies?"

Good question. I know talking about killing babies is hard to digest, but as we help each other, we have to deal with this issue as the Bible does. Our liberty in Christ depends upon our knowledge and acceptance of the truth. If we never accept what is true from God's perspective, then we will never be free from the guilt of the loss of a baby, especially loss by abortion, termination, or murder. If we never acknowledge and believe the truth about the origins of the intentional or premature killing of babies, then we won't be free to come to God boldly, and seek His love, comfort, and peace in our own lives.

So, how do I know that baby killing is not from the mind of God? After all, there are scriptures where God orders the killing of entire nations, including the women and children. To deal with this question, we must remember that in Genesis 3:16, God gave Eve the ability to bear children. Add to this the principle given to us in Exodus 20:13 which simply says, "Thou shalt not kill."

This is the sixth of the Ten Commandments. Many people say that the Bible is contradictory because here, God says do not kill, yet He later orders Joshua, Saul, David, and others to kill men, women, children, and cattle. You however, must believe God and know He does not contradict Himself and endeavor to search out an authentic understanding of these verses and the Bible as a whole. While many English translations of the Bible seem to state this commandment as a prohibition on killing, the Hebrew word, *ratsach*, which is used in this verse does not mean to kill but means to murder.[8] Murder is a type of killing that is hateful, premeditated and unlawful.[9] The sixth commandment therefore is a prohibition on murder.

There is a lesson we must grasp here. If we agree by faith that the God who gave women the ability to bear children did not then order the murder of their babies, those of us who have lost our babies will be in a better position to receive His comfort as we seek His peace and grace in our own lives. But there are still questions to ask. If it's true that God's mercy is displayed in Genesis 3:16 and God prohibits murder in Exodus 20, why does God allow this murderous command in Exodus 1?

God uses Pharaoh's order to show the tremendous capacity that we women have to trust Him and overcome the oppressiveness of societal whims. To fully understand this, we turn back to Shiphrah and Puah and how they are willingly used by God in the tension of this diabolical command. As is typical of ungodly rulers, Pharaoh tries to use people he deems weak to carry out his plot. It seems a failsafe plan, but let's dig into it more.

First, notice that rather than perform his hateful scheme himself, the king of Egypt seeks the assistance of Shiphrah and Puah. It's a preposterous idea from the beginning. As the commander-in-chief of the Egyptian military, Pharaoh doesn't order his soldiers to go into the homes of Hebrews families to kill their babies. That could be reasonable in an evil kind of way, because killing by a soldier in response to a commander's order may be justifiable, not murder. On the other hand, the killing of a newborn baby by a midwife is not the same. Even in response to a king's command. It's unimaginable. What's Pharaoh thinking?

Second, how does Pharaoh know Shiphrah and Puah? Why does he pick them out from the local midwives? Were they the only midwives in Egypt and the surrounding area? The short answer to these questions is we do not know, because the Bible does not say directly. Maybe Shiphrah and Puah are the only midwives serving in Egypt and its territories or maybe they're the head midwives of all the midwives in the area. Nonetheless, for Pharaoh to know them, they have to be reputably good at what they do. They're likely pillars in their community who are unquestionably trusted by women throughout the land. But Pharaoh's request amounts to a total disregard for the midwives' work and status in the community. That further sets up the failure of his plan. His wickedness prevents him from seeing that the only reason he knows of Shiphrah and Puah is because of the fame of their skill.

Another thing is not clear about why Pharaoh approached Shiphrah and Puah. The Bible says that they're "Hebrew midwives." Does this mean that they're midwives who are Hebrew, or does it mean that they're the midwives who serve the Hebrew women? The latter is more plausible. Think about it—would Pharaoh make a direct, secret command to a Hebrew? And to two Hebrew women on top of that? Highly unlikely. Though evil doesn't think logically when directing a sinister plan. The fact that we know these two women's names and that their names have Hebrew meanings might indicate that they're Hebrew. It could just as well indicate that the Hebrew people so closely identify with them that their names became meaningful among the people.

Whether these women are Hebrew or not, it is curious still that Pharaoh goes to them directly instead of sending a messenger to speak to them. Not only that, but Pharaoh refers to their work as an "office." That sounds noteworthy despite biblical commentaries mentioning this merely means that he is referring to the duty and work of midwifery. Nonetheless, it gives their work significance. So much so that Pharaoh designs his plan around this office, only asking Shiphrah and Puah to carry it out against only the Hebrew women, at the specific exclusion of Egyptian or any other women the midwives may attend to. Thus, no matter their ethnicity, Shiphrah and Puah are the central characters in this story. But Pharaoh doesn't count on how crucial they are. And of course, he has no idea what God is up to.

Third, the command is explicit as to when the baby boys are to be murdered. Not before birth, but as soon as they are born, at the point when the midwives personally observe the Hebrew women on the birth stool, or in the act of giving birth. Sounds like an odd specification to make, right? Not only would a midwife certainly see the mother on the birthing stool, she would actively attend to the mother and child at that time. Only a person who's ignorant of the actions of a midwife could devise such a plan. It makes sense here, because Pharaoh's self-centered, power-fed arrogance prevents him from researching or respecting the honored work of the midwife. How else could he ask these women to perform such a heinous task?

Service to the Community

"But the midwives feared God, and did not as the king of Egypt commanded them, but saved the men children alive."
(Exodus 1:17)

Hooray for Shiphrah and Puah!

Unquestionably, the fact that they fear God is the point of this verse, but before we get to that, there is a vital message here. Shiphrah and Puah do not agree to carry out Pharaoh's plan. They neither verbally respond to him nor condone his command. Perhaps they simply look at him, in respect for his office, in keen, feminine silence. They also don't repeat this brutal plan to anyone. Instead, they secretly choose to let their actions speak for them, and not their words.

They do respond however. They do so by obeying God.

Not to belabor the point but notice this passage states that these women obeyed God. It does not state they obeyed their God, but God. This further suggests to me that Shiphrah and Puah may not have been Hebrew women but at least women who know about the Hebrew God from being in the presence of the Hebrew people. Even though the Ten Commandments have not yet been given, these women exhibit knowledge of Hebrew standards, such as God's prohibition on murder. Perhaps they even know what happened to Cain for murdering his brother Abel.[10] For Shiphrah and Puah, the king's request is unthinkable, despicable, and inhuman. Not just because it would violate their fiduciary position with expectant mothers, but because it violates what they know about God. Weighing the costs, Shiphrah and Puah obey the principles of God, and disobey the pressures of the king.

And they "saved the men children alive." What a bold act! They do something in order to specifically rescue the baby boys and not murder them. What do they do? Once again, we don't know. Whatever it is, it directly opposes the evil command.

> *"And the king of Egypt called for the midwives, and said unto them, Why have ye done this thing, and have saved the men children alive? And the midwives said unto Pharaoh, Because the Hebrew women are not as the Egyptian women; for they are lively, and are delivered ere the midwives come in unto them." (Exodus 1:18-19)*

Pharaoh's plan fails at the hand of these midwives and he knows it. What he can't understand is why they did this. He thought he had it all figured out. Two women couldn't possibly outthink him. The collapse of his plan is so upsetting that he calls for the midwives to speak with them a second time. This time instead of barking out a required task, he must concede by asking a defeated request—why did you do this?

The genius of Shiphrah and Puah's simple reverence to God astounds here. Like my friend Renee, the midwives are wise, cunning, and effective. Unlike their previous encounter, this time, Shiphrah and Puah respond to this "why" question. Though they speak, they don't exactly answer what he asks. Instead, they tell him what happened. Playing upon Pharaoh's irrational anxieties, they compare the Hebrew women to the Egyptian women. In what could be considered stereotypical language, they call the Hebrew women "lively." This may suggest that the Hebrew women are like animals who give birth without the aid of or need for a human midwife.[11] It's a shrewd retort aimed to tickle Pharaoh's ears. At the same time, they subtly underlie their response by inferring that the "hard bondage" and rigorous work that Pharaoh maliciously inflicts on the Hebrew people has only served to make all of them, even the women, more resilient than the Egyptians.[12]

I have to stop here and turn to you for a minute to tell you that you are like these Hebrew women! As a mother, you have endured great pain. As a believer in Christ, you are chosen as the elect of God, just as the Hebrew women who were helped by Shiphrah and Puah. Though your child may not have been "saved alive," it doesn't take away from the fact that you are still standing and you're a force to be reckoned with. No one expected you to survive. They saw how distraught you've been and counted you out. Some may have even told people to stay away from you, to not associate with you, that you are not their kind of people and made you suffer the stereotypical misinformation about women who lose children the way you did. God says otherwise. He loves you! And He has an alternative plan of deliverance for you. Hold on, my sister. There is joy coming.

Back to our activists, Shiphrah and Puah. We cannot forget that they are professional women and nurturers who protect babies and mothers. In their response to Pharaoh, they do not say that the baby boys came too fast. Instead Shiphrah and Puah turn the attention to the unsuspecting threat of the Hebrew mothers, saying the mothers deliver too fast. Playing on Pharaoh's disregard for the fight of a mother, they obtain victory over him. When he issues the command, Pharaoh's focus is on the Hebrew boys who would grow up to fight against Egypt. In fact, referring to the Hebrews, he told his assistants, "Come, we must deal shrewdly with them or they will become even more numerous and, if war breaks out, will join our enemies, fight against us and leave the country" (Exodus 1:10 NIV). Since women aren't warriors, he's not concerned about a women's uprising against him. Though he should have. Shiphrah and Puah turned the tables on him by using the weapon of motherhood against the enemy. What a mighty weapon it is!

We learn in this verse that in fear of God, Shiphrah and Puah tell Pharaoh that they arrive after the Hebrew women give birth. How could this be? A good midwife doesn't let this happen. She's more exacting than that. Unless we're missing something. Perhaps Shiphrah and Puah miss the births because they were late, but could they have missed every birth? The commonsensical next question is how could they possibly attend to every birth in the Egyptian territories? Wouldn't there have to be other midwives? Maybe upon this command, Shiphrah and Puah trained midwife apprentices to deliver the babies of the Hebrew women so Shiprhah and Puah wouldn't be in the room when the Hebrew births occurred. It's possible.

Or maybe they lied to Pharaoh. We don't want to think of God-fearing people lying, but we've seen this before in the Bible. Remember Rahab, the prostitute of Jericho who lied in response to the command of the king of Jericho in order to protect the lives of the Hebrew spies?[13] Rahab and her family were saved because of her faith in the Hebrew God and her actions in reverence to Him. In much the same way, if we allow that Shiphrah and Puah may not be Hebrew, then maybe they too lie to the king, in favor of saving God's people. After all, our God is mighty to forgive and save all sinners from their sin. If Rahab, why not Shiphrah and Puah? Whatever the case, Shiphrah and Puah honored God, and God honored them.

Families of Their Own

"Therefore God dealt well with the midwives: and the people multiplied, and waxed very mighty. And it came to pass, because the midwives feared God, that he made them houses."
(Exodus 1:20-21)

Upon the brave convictions of these two women, two things happen: God's grace is manifested, and the entire Hebrew community grows in numbers and strength. The Bible does not state that only the Hebrew households where the baby boys are saved grows mighty, but every Hebrew household gains. In addition to the households of Shiphrah and Puah, which before this incredible act are childless. As the TLB version of the Bible states in verse twenty-one, "And because the midwives revered God, he gave them children of their own."

Can you imagine being a motherless woman who's in the business of blessing expectant mothers, but told to murder their babies just because they're male and born to a Hebrew woman? We don't know if Shiphrah and Puah are previously without their own children because they lost them, or because they're barren, but we learn that their faithful service while without make them ripe recipients of the gift of motherhood.

Maybe as a mother who lost her child you cannot immediately appreciate the service and sacrifice of Shiphrah and Puah. Maybe you cannot see your own strength or deliverance in their story. After all, Shiphrah and Puah said women of God's chosen people, the Hebrews, are strong. All of them! They didn't limit their statement to the pregnant women. They included women like them in that statement. Women like you and me are included in that statement, too. In spite of the state of their own "houses," Shiphrah and Puah served the community with might and influence. We could venture to say that Shiphrah and Puah's grasp of God's compassion showed itself in the most fundamental form of motherhood—the support of children at their most vulnerable moments in life.

Notwithstanding any residual grief, us mothers who have lost children can be blessed by the faithfulness of these two women. You see, their faithful service must motivate us into service to save children in our communities. We don't have to become midwives to serve. We can be like Renee and host children in our homes. We can become foster parents. We can mentor young people in our churches or in youth-oriented associations. The loss of our own children doesn't diminish the essence of our motherhood, or our intrinsic capacity to nurture, feed, teach, coach, direct, and love the numerous children in our communities. Who knows, maybe God will give you "houses," too.

Faithful Stewards Of God's Grace

I don't know why God allows some of us to be affected by child loss when other women can experience the pleasing fulfillment of childbirth. Why my Daniel died while Renee's daughter lived remains a mystery to me. On the other hand, I do understand that the Lord always has a greater plan. I know that if Shiphrah and Puah had not risked their lives and disobeyed Pharaoh, then God's plan to save His precious babies would not have succeeded, and years later, in Egypt, Moses would have never been born, the Red Sea would have never parted, and we would not know that God's power is greater than the power of His creation. As the scripture tells us, Shiphrah and Puah's obedience to God results in them having their own children. What is clear to my heart is that they became mothers, because they faithfully cherished children.

Shiphrah and Puah remind me that though I don't have my own living children to love and hold today, I am a strong woman who matters in my community. I know that if my best friend's little girl had died when my little boy died, then I would not have that angel in my life. I would not have the pleasure of observing her many talents and beauty, or the chance to advise and help her. I also know that if I fail to act as a Shiphrah and Puah in my community, then I forfeit that chance to experience the pleasure of mentoring and serving as a "second mother" to young men and women around me to have my own "houses." See, God's greater plan always includes loving His humanity. Through our hurt and pain, we cannot always see it. It's at those times that we must remember that He knows the future. We must just be like those lowly midwives who feared God, served His people, and received His favor.

Reflection

Whom have you mothered since the loss of your baby?

How can you give your time and talents to the young people in your community?

Prayer

Dear Lord,

I do not understand You. Your ways are higher than my ways. Your thoughts are higher than my thoughts. You are beyond finding out. Yet, God, You reveal Yourself to me in mysterious ways. I'm in awe of You and amazed that despite my disbelief, You still love me. You still care for me. You still mature me. Give me strength to go on, in the midst of my misunderstanding and lack of comprehension. Give me the ability and strength to look beyond my circumstances to help others in my community. Remind me that I didn't suffer loss in order to wallow in my pain alone. I bless You, Father, for Paul tells me in 2 Corinthians 1:3-4 that You are "the God of all comfort; Who comforteth us in all our tribulation, that we may be able to comfort them which are in any trouble, by the comfort wherewith we ourselves are comforted of God." Help me to trust that I can serve others and my community. Teach me to allow You Father to direct my paths.

In the name of Jesus, Amen.

13
····

Seeking Grace in Ministry

"For the Lord God is our sun and our shield. He gives us
grace and glory. The Lord will withhold no good thing
from those who do what is right."
(Psalm 84:11 NLT)

The Greatest Miracle

Losing a child arouses a myriad of emotions.

One that engulfs me is the uselessness of my mothering inclinations. In my mind, there's no need for me to continue to expect that I'll ever experience the joy of watching a child graduate or get married or excel in their career. Since first steps, bike rides, preschool graduations, first day of school, plays, tournaments, and the like were all but ripped from my future, it's safe to assume that the rest necessarily follows. Which is not all together a bad thing, especially when I see little children crying and acting out in the grocery store. At those moments, I'm glad they're not mine.

"Lord, you knew what you were doing, I guess. I could not deal with that."

Mostly though, I convince myself that not being a mother is best for me since I have nothing to offer. Besides, no child would want me as their mom anyway. It's better if I submerge myself into my career.

Here and there, the desire to be a mother rears its head as I watch my friends' kids experience major moments and achievements. That little ache in my heart says, "Wonder if my child would be able to do that?" Smiling, I pretend that the nurturer in me doesn't care as I learn to suppress those feelings. Life has dealt me a different path. No sense crying over spilled milk.

Those Other Mother's Kids

Quite unexpectedly, I'm appointed the youth choir advisor at church. It's not anything I want. More importantly, the young people don't want it either. I've successfully developed a stand-off, mean Sister Kim persona with them. They don't talk to me and I don't talk to them. They can't know the reason for my resistance. Instead, they just think I hate them. Until the Lord, through the pastor, decides my time is up.

I've been in this position before, and it wasn't a good experiment. I have no reason to think it will work out better this time, yet the youth and I oblige our spiritual leader. Knowing it's my responsibility to break the ice, I develop a three-fold strategy to build a relationship with them. I figure, since we have to do this, let me at least try to like them. It's not their fault that I'm childless.

The first thing I do is create rules. Young people need to know that they have limits and responsibilities. For the choir, our rules include things like no cell phones in rehearsal. Or combs, brushes, gum, or anything that will be a distraction. If they're caught with any of these, the item will be confiscated, and the child will have to pay one dollar to get it back at the end of rehearsal. These kids will have to be responsible and abide by the rules.

Secondly, the youth have to try to sing the songs. Nothing beats a failure but a try. No one will be reprimanded for trying. If you fail, then just try again. No one is perfect and we all fail sometimes. My final rule is the trust rule. I know I have to get them trust me. The best way to do that is to take us all, myself included, out of our comfort zones by requiring hugs at the end of each rehearsal. Each child will have to give me a hug to leave the choir room. Along with that, each child will have to get on the church van or have a ride home at the end of rehearsal. Otherwise, they have to ride with me in my car. They have no idea this final rule is going to be more uncomfortable for me than them, but it's what the Lord is guiding me to do.

To my surprise, they do it. Of course, there are those who challenge each rule, but by and large, they do it. Who knew what kinds of stuff teenagers carry to church choir rehearsal? Removing their items becomes a chore and a tussle. They watch me to see if I mean what I say and how I'll enforce the rules. I'm tough, and consistent. Always there and always available. Overtime, they come to realize that they can count on Sister Kim to be there. Some wish I would go away, I'm sure.

Nevertheless, at the end of each rehearsal, the kids hug me. Sure, there are a few who require some coaxing and a few who require me to physically grab them, but the rest voluntarily hug me. It becomes a joke between us where I run to the door before we finish our closing prayers and I yell, "I want my hugs. I want my hugs before you leave. Hey Shaleesa, did you give me a hug? Tony, don't leave without giving me my hug. You know I'll steal one!"

Week after week, they become more comfortable with me and with the hugging. I insist on getting my hugs because I know many of them don't get this one-on-one attention at home or in school. In my mind, it doesn't seem right for a child to live a whole week around adults and never feel nurturing love from an elder. When they come to church, they can't fail to be loved there, too.

The biggest surprise in all of this is the impact these hugs and these young people have on me. I'm only supposed to be doing this because of a pastoral appointment. I'm finding myself looking forward to youth choir rehearsal night and seeing these young lives blossom before me. Hearing their stories. Watching the shy ones gain confidence. Seeing the strong ones help the weaker ones. Proudly guiding them as they recognize the voice inside of them. My prayers at night are full of their names, addresses, schools, and gifts. Speaking of them one at a time. Asking God to guide, protect, and help them. Praying for hours. They are becoming my babies. Leaving the rehearsals each week, and Sunday after church services, my heart is beginning to beat to a different rhythm.

God directs me to make sure they all know my phone number and that they can call me anytime about anything. I'm not sure about this. What can I say to them? Besides the words of the songs, what do I have to offer them? Nevertheless, I'm obedient to the heavenly directive.

Interestingly, I feel the Lord impressing upon me the need to ensure a good relationship with their parents and guardians. Especially their mothers. I don't want any of them to think that I am overstepping my bounds. My goal is to be a supplement and support to them. Family rules and relationships come first to my choir rules and hugs. It's important that everyone know this as my love for these children grows.

Mom

"Tony, sit down, please. We're about to start rehearsal," I announce one rehearsal.

"Okay, Mom," Tony replies.

What did he say? Who's he talking to?

"Tony, what are you talking about? Sit down, boy."

"You're my second mom, Sister Kim. I'm going to start calling you, Mom."

The words echo in my head. I can't focus on it because we have to rehearse for this coming Sunday. It's Youth Weekend. This is a big deal. They've prepared for months and this is their big day. We decide on our theme and our outfits. We coordinate. One of the girls, Shaleesa, tells me that I can't embarrass them by wearing something corny. She'll have to inspect my clothes before we go out to sit in the choir stand. Because their choir "Mom" can't look all messed up on Youth Day.

After I get my hugs and drop the last child off at his home, I'm left to recall the events of the night.

Mom.

A word that has never been directed towards me before that day. A word that would certainly never be uttered by a child who'd lived in my womb. Today, this word addressed *me*. It gave me a title I've coveted since I held my first *It's Alive* baby doll. I'd only ever heard it in the make-believe voices of my dream children. Today, a real human being said it. He meant it specifically for me. She matter-of-factly said it during a lovingly juvenile chastisement. Tonight, I cry for my motherhood. The motherhood that found me through the voice of another mother's son. Solidified by a different mother's daughter's expression of embarrassment at the thought of me wearing mom-jeans and grocery store sneakers on their big day. That sealed it. I somehow became a mother while I wasn't looking.

Gradually more of the youth begin to refer to me as Mom.

I love it. I can't get enough of it. Each week, the young people confide in me more. They share parts of their lives that call on the caring, supportive, understanding, encouraging, comforting, and loving parts of me. The more they share, the more I love them. They are becoming mine. This inkling is solidified when, a couple months after Youth Day, the young people are reprimanded for the unruliness they displayed at a birthday celebration of one of their friends, our pastor refers to them as belonging to me.

"They are your children," he says. "It's up to you to teach them how to take responsibility for this. They will not be allowed to sing this month." Having to break the news to them, it occurs to me that we have to endure this together. I express my disappointment and love in the same breath, telling them that they must share accountability for this together. Simultaneously, I show them that through this ordeal, I'll remain Sister Kim and their Mom. Nothing will change our relationship. They proudly rise to the occasion. They display the unified resolve of siblings. They are mine. We're one big happy family.

Before long, as the older ones enter the last year of high school, the advice they seek turns to more adult themes like dating, coping with heartbreak, choosing where to go to college, and deciding whether to enter the military. Emails and text messages invite me to prom send-off celebrations and graduation parties. Suddenly, the life events I thought would elude me are my reality. Before long, college graduations, weddings, and baby showers follow. It's staggering to think of how God has regarded my life and all that has occurred to give me this privilege of having young people around me in this way. I am a contemporary display of the reality of Psalm 113. In praise to the Lord, I proclaim as the psalmist, "Who can be compared with the Lord our God, who is enthroned on high? He stoops to look down on heaven and on earth. He gives the childless woman a family, making her a happy mother. Praise the Lord!" (Psalm 113:5-6, 9 NLT).

When my husband and I believe it's time to move our membership to another church, I fear losing my babies. Suspecting the relationships we've built will survive, there's nonetheless some concern. To my great delight, every Christmas, my kids conspire with my husband to surprise me by visiting us for the holiday. A homecoming of sorts. Our house is filled with family. My family. The doorbell rings hour after hour with my children coming in and out through the evening. We reminisce, laugh, eat, and celebrate each other. They individually share intimate details of their lives, seek advice, and there are, of course, hugs. I can't image God could give me anything more than this.

Oh, but He has more.

As we settle in to our new congregation, God directs me to join the choir. There I find more incredible young people. They are already leaders in the ministry. This is not a place for me to become mother hen of the youth choir. I'm believing my service is not needed. Until one night I'm overwhelmingly directed to pray for a young woman.

In my spirit, I sense she needs to know that I'm praying for her. I'd never spoken to her before, thus I'm not really sure how to approach her. Simply, I put my arm around her and say, "I'm praying for you."

Each time I see her, I tell her the same thing. We begin to talk often. She helps me to understand youthful sayings and how to use social media. As much as I think I'm hip and with it, I'm not. Thank God for her help. In return, I continue to pray. When needed, I'm available to listen. Weekly conversations evolve into career, relation-ship, and life advice. All of which further fuels my prayers.

One night, in choir rehearsal, she and I buddy up for prayer. She shares that her birthday is coming soon. Knowing the year, I ask the month. Innocently, she informs me that she was born the same month and year that I lost my Sunshine. To say that I'm flabbergasted is a terrible understatement. Coincidence? You can say that. You can even believe that if you'd like. As for me, I believe this is an expression of divine providence.

You see, this is how it all happened. Back in the mid-1980s, when my naivety led me to succumb to the pressure to abort my child, God, in His infinite wisdom, allowed another mother to continue her pregnancy and give birth to a beautiful little girl. He navigated the path of that little girl to grow up and leave her hometown to seek a graduate degree in a particular northern city. She would join a church there, become a leader, and meet a woman whose life simultaneously twists and turns in the stories shared in this book. The two share a type of mentor-mentee relationship that they both appreciate, until "in the fullness of time" God reveals the supernatural connection they couldn't concoct.

Without speaking it out loud, I'm convinced the Lord has granted me another special, surrogate daughter of sorts. Then she seals it. She thanks me, "Momma Kim" for telling her I would care for her and meaning it. When her mother comes to town for a visit, she thanks me, too.

"It's never easy for your child to be away from you. I just want to thank you for taking her in as your own. I'm grateful," my *daughter's* mother says to me. Then her mother looks me in the eye. A sufficiently long enough look that I recognize. It's the same look I gave the funeral home director at Daniel's grave site. The look a mother gives to the woman who has cared for her child when, for some reason, she could not. Then, she hugs me.

The Restored Mother

Words cannot adequately convey the feeling of knowing that for over thirty years, God has been guiding my footsteps. All the time I thought He'd forgotten or was too busy to care about my aching heart, He was orchestrating the terms of a great miracle. Because it's my story, I think it is uniquely remarkable. Perhaps you have a similar story to share. I don't doubt it. You see the Lord has been restoring lost motherhood for centuries.

There's one more biblical woman we must bring along on this journey. You may have forgotten you know her story. Maybe it's because you didn't realize how much she's like us. So, let's look at her story again for the first time.

"Now there stood by the cross of Jesus his mother, and his mother's sister, Mary the wife of Cleophas, and Mary Magdalene." (John 19:25)

Imagine the scene by the cross where Jesus is being crucified. He's been beaten. There's blood everywhere. A crown with big, pointed thorns dig into His skull. Ripped skin along His back slides across the rugged splinters of the wooden crucifix. Wind, dirt, and the staleness of the changing atmospheric pressure graze against the gapping puncture wound in His side. Tasteless insults are hurled at Him. He hangs by the nails forced through His hands and feet. His agony drenches the air, confusing the order of nature. All eyes are on Him. Every ear listens to hear what He might say. For those who watch Him, standing on this dark hill is difficult. His death is inevitable.

His mother is there, witnessing it all.

Amid the soldiers and antagonists are some of His closest follow-ers. Not the apostles, or disciples as they are also known. You would think that these men would be here since they jointly strode with Him along His earthly ministry. The Bible does not note the eleven who now remain as standing by. The followers identified are these women. Depending on how you read this verse, there are either three wom-en, all named Mary, or four women standing by; three of whom are named Mary. A clue to solving this conundrum might be provided in the Amplified Bible rendering of this text which states, "But standing by the cross of Jesus were His mother, His mother's sister [Salome], Mary the wife of Clopas, and Mary Magdalene."

We'll prefer this rendering to the KJV. Hence, there are four wom-en standing by the cross. These women are significant. That's why they're specifically mentioned. We should probably spend some time to get to know them.

The non-Mary in the group is Salome, Jesus' aunt. His mother's sister. She's the mother of two of the apostles, James and John. Yes, she's the mother who asked Jesus to give her two sons prominent seats on either side of Jesus when He takes His throne. In kind response, Jesus informs her of the suffering of this day she now wit-nesses. (Mark 20:20-23)

Of the three Marys, there is Mary the wife of Clopas or Cleophas, the man who unknowingly spoke to Jesus after His resurrection on the road to Emmaus. (Luke 24:18) This same man, Clopas is also called Alpheus in Matthew 10:3. We see that he and his wife, Mary have a son named James who is a disciple of Jesus. By standing at the cross, Clopas' wife, Mary is also a follower of Christ. There's also the Mary from the city of Magdala in Galilee, a region where Jesus taught. (Matthew 15:39) Hence, we refer to her as Mary Magdalene. This Mary is the one Jesus healed of seven demons. (Luke 8:2) Undoubtedly, this Mary believes Jesus is the Christ and has no desire to leave His side.

Then there's the Lord's mother. The Mary known as the Virgin Mary. She is the mother who, as an unwed, teenaged girl, became pregnant by the Holy Spirit, giving birth to her first son. An illegitimate holy baby boy. Even as a young girl, she perceived the things of God, and "kept all these things in her heart and thought about them often" (Luke 2:9 NLT). On this day, those things bring her to this moment when she witnesses the death of her holy Son.

In the Company of Friends

Jesus' mother is watching it all with her female companions. They are there to hold her up. They are like my four friends who rushed to my side when my mother died. One by one, on that warm Saturday night in 2009, my friends came to the house to sit outside on the front stoop with me. They held me, cried with me, and suffered the pain of death with me. My girls. The women with whom I didn't need to say anything, yet they knew every emotion I felt.

These women are the same for Mary as she watches her son's brutal and undeserved death. As she's unable to fully comprehend it all, they are her understanding. When she feels the urge to rescue Him, they keep her from taking her boy down from that cross. They share her tears, literally, and emotionally supporting her. Alas, for all their effort, they cannot feel the connection being ripped from her slowly over those excruciating six hours.[1]

As her Son takes on the iniquities of the world, she withstands the pain of her ancestors. Eve's anguish. Bathsheba's discomfort. Rachel's resolve. Tamar's astonishment. Naomi's gloom. Lady Job's devastation. Rizpah's steadfastness. Hannah's aching. The Adulteress' denunciation. The Syrophencian's demoralization. The Disabled's separation. The Sinner's disgrace. Shiphrah and Puah's resistance.

This Mary, Jesus' mother can feel it all.

> *"When Jesus therefore saw his mother, and the disciple standing by, whom he loved, he saith unto his mother, Woman, behold thy son!" (John 19:26)*

And Jesus feels it all. "For since he himself has now been through suffering and temptation, he knows what it is like when we suffer and are tempted, and he is wonderfully able to help us" (Hebrews 2:18 TLB). He knows His mother and her ancestors suffering. He knows our travail, too. On the cross, in the midst of His own pain, He continues to care for others, especially His mother. Hearing Him address His mother's pain confirms that He's able to see our pain. The sting of child loss. To which He responds by giving another child to love.

Please don't be offended that Jesus calls His mother, "woman." He's not disrespecting her. Quite the opposite. This is a term of esteem and honor. It's also a term of affection. He is carefully letting His mother know that she must begin to accept what is about to happen. Consider if He'd called her "Mommy" at this moment. Isn't that a more heart-wrenching sentiment? Rather, the Lord attentively forces her attention towards the man standing next to her. Not on the man hanging up above her.

Jesus is repurposing her motherhood. He's giving her a new love commitment. Though she will no longer be able to mother Him, her motherhood is not dying with Him. It continues to live. He's introducing Mary to her new son. The man she can begin to care for and cherish as she's done for Jesus. In exactly the same way, the Lord has said similar words to me over and over again with the young people I have been blessed to care for and love.

"Then saith he to the disciple, Behold thy mother! And from that hour that disciple took her unto his own home."
(John 19:27)

A mother needs a child. A child needs a mother. Mary gets John. And John gets Mary. But doesn't John already have Salome? Isn't she standing right there? Yes, and yes. Jesus never tells John that Mary is to replace his own mother. He just tells him to look upon Mary differently than he has in the past. From this moment forward, John is to observe Mary as his mother. Appears odd? Not at all. Remember the story I just shared about the young lady whose mother thanked me for caring for her child? This woman remains my *daughter's* mother. My presence in this young lady's life is not instead of her mother. My role is as much a supplement of a mother for this young lady as it is a relief to the mother of this young lady. As it is with Mary, John and Salome.

Jesus appoints them to each other. They immediately accept the assignment.

Did you notice something strange about this story? There's a group of people who are noticeably missing from the tale—Jesus' siblings. Mary's other biological children. Mark 6:3 tells us her sons are named James, Joses, Juda, and Simon and she has at least two daughters. If this is the case, why does Jesus speak as if His death will leave Mary childless?

Actually, He doesn't. Not in the natural, biological sense. His brothers and sisters remain Mary's children. She remains their mother. But Jesus is not talking about genetic mother-child relationships. He's speaking of a different kind of relationship. The one termed in Mark 3: 34-35: "And looking at those who were sitting around him in a circle, he said, 'Here are my mother and my brothers! For whoever does the will of God is my brother and sister and mother'" (NET).

At the cross stands those who are determined to do God's will by believing and following Jesus. His biological siblings are not among those people "For even his own brothers did not believe in him" (John 7:5 NIV). Jesus knows that His followers will need each other as they face the world without His physical presence. They will need to rely on each other as family. The family of God. Thus, He leaves His mother in the care of a man whose character and commitment He knows and trusts. The man who will attentively serve her will receive parental comforting from her.

This is the essence of ministry. In ministry, we receive those good things that God reserves for those who obey Him. What's better than His family? For the childless mother who's surrendered her life to

Jesus, He gives a household of children if she's willing to answer the opportunities to mother again. God always provides. He restores what has been lost in order to serve Him and His people.

Exceeding Abundantly

I love what Jesus does for Mary. I imagine this scene vividly, because I am Mary. I'm a spiritual mother to someone else's child. I know the pain of losing a child, but I also know the extreme joy of rising through the ashes of my mourning to bless where God says bless by loving the young people in my community.

As a second and spiritual mom, I'm blessed to be mother-figure to children of varied ages, races, ethnicities, professions, sexual preferences, and economic statuses. The one thing they all have in common is the need to be accepted, encouraged, embraced, celebrated, admonished, and most of all, loved. For who they are, what they do, how they express themselves and their unique gifts to the world, they need the ministering compassion of a mother figure. No one but a mother, biological and certainly spiritual, can give a child the reassurance that makes them feel they can try again, stand up, be counted and soar.

The other day, one of my spiritual daughters sent me a video in a text message. Its sentiment stopped me in my tracks. The video was of a young man who described a recent encounter at the airport. He experienced delays at the customer service counter to which he responded rudely. An older woman he did not know pulled him aside to gently convince him that his behavior was unacceptable. She told him that she was sure he had been raised to conduct himself more suitably than he had. She impressed upon him the need to always put his best foot forward. In respect, he obliged, knowing this woman to be veracious. He corrected himself, regaining his composure and dignity. The moral of his story, he taught, is that non-biological mothers are a necessary blessing to the universal human community. His heartfelt message warmed my heart. I asked this spiritual daughter why she sent the video to me. Had this been a mistake?

"Am I one of the mothers described in the video?"

"YES, YOU ARE!!!!" she replied.

All I can do in response is bless God! The God who uses the offering of my two babies to bless my life with more spiritual children than I could ask for or count. The God who says in the spirit of each mother's child that has ever been in my life, whether for a moment, a season or a lifetime, "Behold, thy mother!"

He Gives Us Grace and Glory

Sought grace is found only one way. By faith. "But without faith it is impossible to [walk with God and] please Him, for whoever comes [near] to God must [necessarily] believe that God exists and that He rewards those who [earnestly and diligently] seek Him" (Hebrews 11:6 AMP).

Seek Him ladies, while He may be found.

Speaking of that, there's someone new in this chapter you may have noticed. My husband. Where did he come from? Well, if you'll recall, in chapter 10 of this book, I had to make a choice between mother and wife. I chose wife, even though I wasn't dating or interested in anyone. All along, it turns out God had a man standing by. My now husband had been trying to get my attention for two years. Singing in the choir and participating in the Single Adult's Sunday School class, this man patiently prayed for me. Once the Lord opened my eyes, we were married sixteen months after we started dating. God gave me what He promised. And He did something else exceedingly magnificent.

You see, the day I became a wife to my husband, I simultaneously became a stepmother to his children. My husband's son even walked in our wedding as a groomsman. That day, when he agreed to participate in our wedding, he also accepted me as his stepmom. When he called me for the first time for advice, he confirmed it. When he brought his girlfriend over to meet us, it was sealed. He is my son. I certainly didn't see a stepmother ministry in my future and never thought to ask for this blessing. God has generously given me this honor. I guess that's what you get when you submit to God by faith.

In my life, the Lord continues to say, "Woman, behold thy children!"

What a gracious God we serve!

Reflection

What steps will you take to reclaim your motherhood?

As a minister of motherhood, take time to thank God for motherhood found.

Prayer

Dear Lord,

It never occurred to me that my motherhood has not been lost. I am grateful that it lives in me and that there are opportunities to express that part of me. Please direct me where You would have me to offer myself. It is a bit scary, I'll admit, but I'm ready to love again. I'm ready to live again. Direct me, God. Show me where my brand of love is needed. I refuse to allow my motherhood to remain dormant and silent anymore. Let Your love express itself through me as I care for and encourage the growth and maturity in another mother's child. Even now I pray for the one I will help. I pray for my child, God. Thank You in advance for him, her or them. Bless them.

In the name of Jesus, Amen.

AFTERWORD

Celebrating Grace Found

"And he said unto me, 'My grace is sufficient for thee: for my strength is made perfect in weakness.' Most gladly therefore will I rather glory in my infirmities, that the power of Christ may rest upon me. Therefore I take pleasure in infirmities, in reproaches, in necessities, in persecutions, in distresses for Christ's sake: for when I am weak, then am I strong." (2 Corinthians 12:9,10)

Today is Mother's Day. A day I've hated for many years. Initially, I hated it because I was not a mother. I hated watching my friends and other women being treated like queens while I was ignored and overlooked. After I admitted to myself how much I had wanted my Sunshine, I began to hate Mother's Day, because I was not with my child. He had been taken from me. He had been sacrificed and killed.

After losing Daniel, I hated Mother's Day because it just seemed a cruel joke. I wanted to have another chance to be his mother, or someone's mother, yet I could find no one to get me pregnant. I asked a couple friends to consider fathering my child, and their responses told me that this was not a good idea. But, I wanted to be a mother. Desperately.

Once I found out that I could not be a mother, I hated Mother's Day because it reminded me not just that I was not a mother, but that I would never be a mother. Each year, Mother's Day came. Each

KIM PARIS UPSHAW | 231

year, I hated it because it became a day when people said the stupidest things to me.

"You're a cat mommy."

"Godmothers are mothers, too."

"Well, I am going to say Happy Mother's Day to you, anyway."

"You have been like a mother to so many."

And on and on. Sure. These people meant well, but their words only reignited the despair in my heart. Their words reminded me that I was not worthy to be called, mother. Most people had no idea about my story or the children who had been in my womb. They did not know that I was a mother of two children who did not make it to live birth. They didn't know about the despair and desperation I experienced year after year. They didn't know about the ridiculous things I tried with the most inappropriate and undesirable men just for the chance to be called, mother.

They didn't know about the days I cried, begging God to please let me get pregnant and allow my pregnancy to succeed to birth. The times I prayed that I was no longer the misfit who had a prolapsed uterus, prone to fibroids, that couldn't carry a baby to term. I felt like people could see all of this when I entered a room. As if I carried the *Scarlet Letter*[1] on my chest. Only instead of the letter "A" for adulteress, I carried the letter "F" for failure. I failed at pregnancy. I failed at carrying to term. I failed at protecting my babies. I failed at fertility. A big fat failure.

In 2009, my selfish Mother's Day pity parties took another dramatic turn when my own mother passed away. For years, I took my mother for granted. Like most, I celebrated her on Mother's Day, and I made sure she knew she was loved, but I spent so much time living in my pain that I neglected her. I should have been living in the presence of my mom. The presence of the motherhood that existed in my life.

The Mother's Day that followed her death was suffocating. I hated Mother's Day all the more. That day, a dear friend invited me to come celebrate with her family. It was a great time, but when I got home I was reflective, realizing how blessed I'd been to have gone through the loss of my Sunshine and Daniel with my own mom. I wanted to tell her that now. I wanted to tell her that I understood what she had done for me. I wished to say thank you for mothering as best she knew how.

Reflecting on her, I recalled how she shined when I learned I was pregnant with Daniel. I was unsure what to do this being the second time I would have to tell her that I am pregnant. I made the call expecting the disappointment of about twenty years prior.

"I'm pregnant."

She said, "I know."

"You know?"

"Yes, I know," she said.

"How do you know?" I was mesmerized by her words. Had Timothy called and told her? Why would he have done that?

"Mothers know things about their children. You will see when you become a mother. You will see. Kim, you will be a good mother."

I could not speak. My mom just said something that in my wildest dreams I didn't think I'd ever hear her say. She said she believed I would be a good mother. Tears streamed down my face with ease. I was proud, relieved, and encouraged. I thought I could be a good mother. I wanted to be. And now, with my mom's pledge, I truly believed I could be.

That's why when it was announced that Daniel was coming four months too early, my mother's disappointment hung in the delivery room air like a cloud of doom. I watched her walk out of the room just before the delivery. She couldn't bear to see me go through the pain. She couldn't bear to watch her grandchild die. She had already seen her mother, husband, and son die. This little baby that I wanted, and I believe she wanted, would not pass by her eyes when he would never pass through her arms. She never saw him. She never saw Daniel.

But what she did one night less than a week later, showed me what the power of a mother's love could do. How a mother could give her child to God in only her most nurturing and compassionate way. After I begged Timothy to stay with me, my mother took over when he left. She planted a chair in my bedroom right at the foot of my bed. She sat there and watched me until I cried myself to sleep. She didn't let me run back to the hospital to retrieve my son's body. She didn't let me cut my wrists. She didn't let me cover my face to suffocate under my tear-soaked pillow. She didn't let me drown in my tears. My mom just let me talk and ask those unanswerable questions, and cry into the wee hours of the night until I finally slept. All night, and much of the next two days, she sat in that chair and stayed with me. There wasn't much for her to say during those days. Her job was to kept watch. Making sure I bathed and ate. Making sure visitors stayed away right now.

She let me let go.

My mother was what I needed. She knew it. I knew it. Timothy too, I guess. My mother loved me as only a mother who knows the needs of her daughter could do or would do. And, at the right time, she went home. She loved me through it. She loved me through it.

"You don't look like what you've been through."

This is the statement I heard today, on Mother's Day, after I shared a little information about my Sunshine and my Daniel. This one statement startles me. Partly, because when I look in the mirror, I see the stains on my cheeks of every tear I've cried for my two little ones. I see every heartache that wished to hold them, feed them, burp them, change them, and comfort them. I see the teenager who naively yielded to abortion. I see the young woman who wanted to cross her legs hard and long enough to keep that little boy in her womb for just eight more weeks. I see the woman who cried for hours on end when she realized that any chance of ever having her own child was gone, forever. I remember the hurtful, judgmental looks of older women who, knowing nothing of my story, believed I did not have children, because I was "chasing my career." I recall the neighbor who asked me if I was too good to stop succeeding in my career to have a child, or was I going to order a baby like that local television news anchor who had artificial insemination.

"You don't look like what you've been through."

Praise God! I'm so grateful. If I don't look like I have been through this, or that being a mother was one thing I wanted my whole life, then I cannot claim any responsibility for the fact that I don't look like the things I have shared in this book. If it's true that I don't look like I've been through what's been described, then there is one reason for that.

His name is Jesus Christ.

He is my healer and comforter. He is my refuge and rock. He is the receiver of my babies and all my hopes and dreams. It was to Him I ran each time I lost a child. Each time I tried to get pregnant. Each time I learned that I was not, again. And when I learned that I would never, again. It was to Him I turned to ask, "Why?" It was to Him I demanded to know, "Why?" It was to Him I aimed my indictments. I yelled at Him. I begged Him. I accused Him. I cursed Him. I argued at Him. I hated Him.

I went through periods of studying every mother in the Bible. I believed I was each of them. I did all I could to learn from them. I closed my eyes tight to see them and to ascribe their lives onto mine. I tried to have their attitudes. Their faith. I tried, and I tried. Honestly, I gave up more often than that. Throwing things was normal. Refusing to believe it would get better was the looming default of my mind. I wrestled with the Bible and wondered how it could possibly speak to my heart and my life. Being a childless mother on Mother's Day, and gentle and patient with people who made those ridiculous statements was farthest from my mind. Believing that God loved me was as inconceivable as my empty womb.

Until it was not anymore. When I stopped trying to understand and stopped trying to reconcile my circumstances with what should have been, according to my life plans, I started living again. I started loving children who were not mine. I started opening my heart and my home to other mother's children. I started hugging people. I started smiling at people. And, I started to let God be right.

When He asked me that question, even then, He was right. Of course, He had always been right about everything. It took some time however for my faith to catch up with His righteousness. When I stopped trying to rationalize what happened in my life I was open to just be loved by Him.

Logic was not in control anymore. Reason didn't matter. My plans were abolished. Other women's motherhood was of no consequence to me. It was just me and Him. Him and me. His love and my growing need for it. That's when I heard Him say, "I love you." Sure, He'd said it before. It had always been there in the Bible. In each of the stories of the women there. My own life told me many times He loved me. His sacrifice on Calvary told me He loved me. This me and Him time, however, told me He loved me like none had before. Yet, He didn't just say He loved me, He also said deep into my spirit, "My grace is sufficient for your life, Kim. My strength is at its perfect best when you are a weak mess" (My version of 2 Corinthians 12:9).

I cannot find the words to explain how I knew this scripture was for me at this time in my life, but it seemed there was no other Word that mattered. The words came off the page of that old Bible and gripped, and massaged, and soothed my wounded, aching, dysfunctional heart in its hand. It said in my ears, mouth, blood, fingers, toes, and tears that God's love, joy, and favor were right there with me to give me the strength I needed to keep going. I didn't need to give up. I just needed to give it all over to Him. To no longer hold on to the anger, jealousy, and confusion that had been my three best friends since Daniel died, and had turned up their influence on me when my mom died. I could stop meeting them at my bedside most nights. I could stop carrying them on my back throughout the day. I could stop listening for them for guidance and direction. I could instead drop them off on the nearest curb, because God's Grace had reintroduced herself to me and showed me what a true friend does. She'd always been there, but she was now taking a lead in my life, because I was finally willing to let her.

Grace was a gentle woman. She waited on me. She had always been around in every situation, standing out of the way, while close enough to step forward at the first sign of me stepping backward. She was not presumptuous, but proper and decent. She was like Anna, the old prophetess who waited at the Temple for years just to see the Messiah. She didn't step in to the spotlight until Jesus was born. "And she coming in that instant gave thanks likewise unto the Lord, and spake of him to all them that looked for redemption in Jerusalem" (Luke 2:38).

That is how Grace was in my life, and she has not stopped being that way for me. She waited for years for the right time to instantaneously make herself known to me. She was there when I was raped and scared. She was there when I was eighteen and learned I was pregnant. She was there when my Sunshine's light was dimmed. She was there in the waiting room at the doctor's office as I observed pregnant woman after pregnant woman walk by with their thirty-eight-week full bellies while I knew in my heart something was wrong with my pregnancy and my Daniel. She held my tongue when the doctor lacked compassion and I was sure the treatment I received was substandard. Grace spoke for me when I sat next to Timothy at the grave site, over a month after Daniel died. She selected silence for me when I could only think of exactly the wrong words to say.

Though it was too many weeks too late to just now bury him, Grace kept me in that chair during the service, hushed though demur. She was there when I returned to work guiding my words when coworkers asked how I was doing. She was there when I returned to church, standing in the sanctuary for me as I lifted my hands, clapped, and shouted in triumph.

I had always felt Grace in my life, but one day, I understood who she was and why she was there. She held my hand when it shook with the uncertainty of whether I could make it or not. She breathed for me. She smiled for me. She held me up. She sat at the end of the bed after my mother left to return home. Years later, when my mom died, Grace laid in the bed beside me and held me close. Grace kept my mind on God and not on depression. She was that miraculous guardian who drove me home from the doctor's office when I learned I would never, ever be a mother.

Over time, Grace has uncovered joy, peace, and the beauty of life. Throughout my life, with all its hurts, pains, and disappointments, Grace has shown me the blessings in my losses. Because I had no strength to undo or redo any of it, Grace has changed the lens through which I view my life. She's shown me how God has been there all the time in her work, but I never noticed the two of them before. She showed me how He'd caught me over and over again, but I had wiggled my way back to negative thinking and a warped accounting of events. Grace has shown me a better way of seeing. A better way of doing. A better way of being.

You see, the way of Grace is to let Grace have her way.

Let her handle it when I cannot. Let her take the helm when I don't understand. Give her the steering wheel when my tires are churning out of control. She's stood before me so often that one day, I let her stay there. She has been in front of me ever since.

Grace stood tall for me today, on Mother's Day. And today, again, I let her have her way. She gave me a wonderfully, joyous day today.

She is amazing, that Grace.

Endnotes

Chapter 1 Notes

1   "Geraldine Ferraro in 1984 'Hounded' with 'Intensity' by Sexist Anti-Abortion Conservatives," *Media Research Center: https://www.mrc.org/articles/geraldine-ferraro-1984-hounded-intensity-sexist-anti-abortion-conservatives.*

2   Cameron Crowe, Tom Cruise, *Jerry Maguire,* (Culver City: TriStar Pictures, 1996), Motion Picture, 139 mins.

3   James Strong, *Strong's Exhaustive Concordance of the Bible,* (Iowa Falls: World Bible, 1986), s.v. "Cain."

4   Ibid., s.v. "Abel"

Chapter 2 Notes

1   "Cardiomyopathy", *Health Topics. NIH National Heart Lung and Blood Institute: https://www.nhlbi.nih.gov/health-topics/cardiomyopathy#Causes.*

2   "Hypertrophic Cardiomyopathy." Last reviewed March 2016. *American Heart Association: http://www.heart.org/HEARTORG/Conditions/More/Cardiomyopathy/Hypertrophic-Cardiomyopathy_UCM_444317_Article.jsp#.Wx2dTNPwbox.*

3   Christian Burt and Jacqueline Durbridge, "Management of cardiac disease in pregnancy," *Continuing Education in Anaesthesia Critical Care & Pain,* Volume 9, Issue 2, 1 (April 2009), 44–47.

4   Genesis 35:16-19.

5   James Strong, *Strong's Exhaustive Concordance of the Bible,* (Iowa Falls: World Bible, 1986), s.v. "possessed."

Chapter 3 Notes

1   Yan Yu Yip and Mei Yuen, "Rape Trauma Syndrome," *Student Projects. Cornell University Law School, Social Science and Law: https://courses2.cit.cornell.edu/sociallaw/student_projects/RapeTraumaSyndrome.html.*

2   James W. Hopper, "Why many rape victims don't fight or yell," *Grade Point.* June 23, 2015. *The Washington Post: https://www.washingtonpost.com/news/grade-point/wp/2015/06/23/why-many-rape-victims-dont-fight-or-yell/?noredirect=on&utm_term=.77671c2536f4.*

3   "Date Rape," *PsychPedia A-G.* Last updated May 16, 2018. *GoodTherapy.org: https://www.goodtherapy.org/blog/psychpedia/a-g.*

4   Pennsylvania Abortion Control Act, 18 Pa.C.S. § 3203, Definitions, "Abortion."

5   Nivin Todd, "D and C (Dilation and Curettage)," *Women's Health, Guide.* Last reviewed October 17, 2016. *WebMD: https://www.webmd.com/women/guide/d-and-c-dilation-and-curettage#2.*

6   David Guzik, "Amnon, Tamar and Absolom," *David Guzik, Study Guide for 2 Samuel 13. https://www.blueletterbible.org/Comm/guzik_david/StudyGuide_2Sa/ 2Sa_13.cfm?a=280010.*

7   W. Clarkson, "The Significance of the Palm Trees," *Sermons, Ezekiel 41:18-20, 25.* Bible Hub: *http://biblehub.com/sermons/auth/clarkson/the_significance_of_the_ palm_trees.htm.*

8   1 Chronicles 3:1

9   1 Samuel 13:14 and Acts 13:22.

10   John Gill, "2 Samuel 13:17," *John Gill's Exposition of the Bible. Bible Study Tools: https://www.biblestudytools.com/commentaries/gills-exposition-of-the-bible/2-samu- el-13-17.html.*

Chapter 4 Notes

1   Frances Grandy Taylor, "Huge Pool Of Money Funds Anti-abortion Commer- cials," *Collections, Abortion Rights.* August 15, 1994. *Hartford Courant: http:// articles.courant.com/1994-08-15/features/9408130043_1_abortion-rights-life-com- mittee-ads.*

2   Marc Peyser, "Death in a Dumpster," *News.* December 1, 1996. *Newsweek: http://www.newsweek.com/death-dumpster-175278.*

3   Robert Hanley, "New Jersey Charges Woman, 18, With Killing Baby Born at Prom," *N.Y., Region.* June 25, 1997. *The New York Times: https://www.nytimes. com/1997/06/25/nyregion/new-jersey-charges-woman-18-with-killing-baby-born-at- prom.html.*

4   Peyser, *Death in a Dumpster.*

5   Ibid.

6   Hanley, *Baby Born at Prom.*

7   Ibid.

8   Ibid.

9   James Strong, Strong's Exhaustive Concordance of the Bible, (Iowa Falls Madi- son: World Bible, 1986), s.v. "Bethlehem."

10   Ibid., s.v. "Judah."

11   Ibid., s.v. "Elimelech."

12   Ibid., s.v. "Naomi."

Chapter 5 Notes

1   *Griswold v. Connecticut*, 381 U.S. 479 (1965).

2   Pennsylvania Abortion Control Act, 18 Pa.C.S. § 3203, Definitions, "Viability."

3   See *Griswold.*

4   James Strong, *Strong's Exhaustive Concordance of the Bible*, (Iowa Falls Madison: World Bible, 1986), s.v. "Daniel."

5   PA Abortion Control Act, at §3216 (b)(1), Fetal Experimentation.

6   Zondervan, "Job's Wife: The Woman Who Urged Her Husband to Commit

Suicide," *Resources, All the Women of the Bible, Chapter 3. Nameless Bible Women.* 1988. *Biblegateway: https://www.biblegateway.com/resources/all-women-bible/Job-8217-s-Wife.*

7   Chris Thurman, *The Lies We Believe*, (Carmel: Guideposts, 1989), 146 -148.

8   Walt Latimore, *His Brain, Her Brain: How Divinely Designed Differences Can Strengthen Your Marriage*, (Grand Rapids: Zondervan, 2009), Kindle Edition, 70.

Chapter 6 Notes

1   H.R. 4292 - Born-Alive Infants Protection Act of 2000, Report 106-835, September 11, 2000.

2   Ibid.

3   Ibid.

4   J. Kowaleski, "State definitions and reporting requirements for live births, fetal deaths, and induced terminations of pregnancy." October 1997. *U.S. Department of Health and Human Services, Centers for Disease Control and Prevention, National Centers for Health Statistics, National Center for Health Statistics: https://www.cdc.gov/nchs/data/misc/itop97.pdf56.*

5   Ibid.

6   Pennsylvania SB 326, "Certification of Birth Reaulting (sic) in Stillbirth," July 7, 2011.

7   William Cullen Bryant, "Rizpah - Poem by William Cullen Bryant." *PoemHunter.com: https://www.poemhunter.com/poem/rizpah/.*

8   Joseph L. Chester, "Rizpah," *The Ark, and Odd Fellows' Western Monthly Magazine: A Monthly Periodical Devoted to the Cause of Odd Fellowship*, Volume 8, No. 1 (January 1851), 19. *https://books.google.com/books?id=U5geAQAAMAAJ&printsec=frontcover&source=gbs_ge_summary_r&cad=0#v=onepage&q&f=false.*

9   Alfred Lord Tennyson, "647. Rizpah," *English Poetry III: From Tennyson to Whitman. The Harvard Classics.* 1909-14. *Bartleby.com: http://www.bartleby.com/42/647.html.*

10 Menella Bute Smedley, "Rizpah," *All Poetry: https://allpoetry.com/poem/8569157-Rizpah-by-Menella-Bute-Smedley*

11 Ibid.

12 Enis Dake, *The Dake Annotated Reference Bible*, (Lawrenceville: Dake Publishing, 2003), Old Testament, 2 Samuel 3, 565.

13 Bryant, *Rizpah*.

14 Zondervan, "Rizpah: The Woman Who Guarded Her Dead," *Resources, All the Women of the Bible, Chapter 2, Alphabetical Exposition of Named Bible Women, R, Rizpah.* 1988. *Biblegateway: https://www.biblegateway.com/resources/all-women-bible/Rizpah.*

15 Claude Mariottini, "The Sons of Rizpah: Reflections on a Mother's Love," Posted on May 9, 2008. Dr. Claude Mariottini – Professor of Old Testament: https://claudemariottini.com/2008/05/09/the-sons-of-rizpah-reflections-on-a-mother%E2%80%99s-love/.

Chapter 7 Notes

1   Lawrence Morton, "12 Myths About Birth Mothers." *Scary Mommy: http://www. scarymommy.com/myths-about-birth-mothers/.*

2   Tamar Kadri, "Peninnah: Midrash and Aggadah," *Encyclopedia. Jewish Women's Archive: https://jwa.org/encyclopedia/article/peninnah-midrash-and-aggadah.*

3   *See* 1 Samuel 1:5.

4   *See* Genesis 15-16.

5   *"Barrenness and Fertility," Encyclopedia Judaica: http://www.jewishvirtuallibrary. org/barrenness-and-fertility.*

6   Judith R. Baskin, "Infertile Wife in Rabbinic Judaism," *Encyclopedia. Jewish Women's Archive: https://jwa.org/encyclopedia/article/infertile-wife-in-rabbinic-judaism.*

7   James Strong, *Strong's Exhaustive Concordance of the Bible,* (Iowa Falls: World Bible, 1986), s.v. "Lord."

8   *See* 1 Samuel 1:3.

9   Strong, s.v. "Shiloh."

10 Robert Jamieson, A.R. Fausset, and David Brown, *Jamieson, Fausset & Brown's Commentary,* (Grand Rapids: Zondervan 1961), 206.

11 "What was the significance of weaning a child in the Bible (Genesis 21:8*)*?" *Got Questions: https://www.gotquestions.org/weaning-child-Bible.html.*

12 Strong, s.v. "offering."

13 Anonymous, *Life Application Study Bible, Mark 7:26,* (Grand Rapids: Zondervan Publishing Company, 2009), 529.

Chapter 8 Notes

1   Matthew Henry, *Unabridged Matthew Henry's Commentary on the Whole Bible* (Kindle Edition, 2010), OSNOVA, 35314-35315.

2   Ibid.

3   Ibid., 35321-35322

4   Romans 3: 24-25.

Chapter 9 Notes

1   James Strong, *Strong's Exhaustive Concordance of the Bible,* (Iowa Falls: World Bible, 1986), s.v. "certain."

2   Anonymous, *Life Application Study Bible,* (Grand Rapids: Zondervan Publishing Company, 2009), 2071.

3   Enis Dake, *The Dake Annotated Reference Bible,* (Lawrenceville: Dake Publishng, Inc., 2003), New Testament, 75.

4   David Guzik, "Declaring Food and People Clean," *David Guzik: Study Guide for Mark 7. Blue Letter Bible: https://www.blueletterbible.org/Comm/guzik_david/ StudyGuide2017-Mar/Mar-7.cfm?a=964027.*

5   Strong, s.v. "dogs."

6 Matthew Henry, *Commentary of the Whole Bible*, (Grand Rapids: Zondervan, 1963), 1381.

7 Ibid.

8 Ibid.

9 *See* Mark 6:34-44.

Chapter 10 Notes

1 Robert Jamieson, A.R. Fausset, and David Brown, *Jamieson, Fausset & Brown's Commentary*, (Grand Rapids: Zondervan 1961), 959.

2 *Life Application Study Bible*, (Grand Rapids: Zondervan Publishing Company, 2009), 204.

3 Mayo Clinic Staff, "Anemia," *Patient Care & Health Information, Diseases & Conditions. Mayo Clinic:* https://www.mayoclinic.org/diseases-conditions/anemia/symptoms-causes/syc-20351360.

4 Mark A. Hall, and Carl E. Schneider, "Patients as Consumers: Courts, Contracts, and the New Medical Marketplace," *Michigan Law Review*, Vol. 106, No. 643 (February 8, 2008).

5 Ibid.

6 Enis Dake, *The Dake Annotated Reference Bible*, (Lawrenceville: Dake Publishing, Inc., 2003), 70.

7 *See* Matthew 14:36, Mark 6:56, and Luke 8:44.

8 David Guzik, "Jesus Demonstrates His Authority," *David Guzik: Study Guide for Mark 5. Blue Letter Bible: https://www.blueletterbible.org/Comm/guzik_david/StudyGuide2017-Mar/Mar-5.cfm?a=962034.*

Chapter 11 Notes

1 Melissa Willet, "Mom Whose Baby Died at Daycare Is Making a Difference—And You Can Help," *All About Babies. Parents: https://www.parents.com/baby/all-about-babies/mom-whose-baby-died-at-daycare-is-making-a-difference-and-you-can-help.*

2 Elisabeth Rosenthal, "Parents Find Solace In Donating Organs." May 1993. *The New York Times: https://www.nytimes.com/1993/05/11/science/parents-find-solace-in-donating-organs.html.*

3 Mighty Clouds of Joy, *Live in Charleston*, Intersound Records, 1996.

4 Matthew Easton, *Easton's Bible Dictionary*, (Kindle Edition, 2012), 20491.

5 Ibid., 7187-7188.

6 *Webster's New World Dictionary and Thesaurus*, 2nd ed., s.v. "ointment."

7 Robert Jamieson, A.R. Fausset, and David Brown, *Jamieson, Fausset and Brown's Commentary on the Whole Bible*, (Grand Rapids: Zondervan, 1961), 999.

8 *Lexicon: Strong's G4228 – pous. Blue Letter Bible: https://www.blueletterbible.org/lang/lexicon/lexicon.cfm?Strongs=G4228&t=KJV.*

9 Matthew 13:10-17.

10 Stephen Jones, "The Pharisee's bad manners," *Daily WebLogs*. February 13, 2014. *God Kingdom Ministries: https://gods-kingdom-ministries.net/daily-we-blogs/2014/02-2014/the-pharisees-bad-manners/.*

Chapter 12 Notes

1   Stephen Spielberg, Alice Walker, and Menno Meyjes, *The Color Purple*, (Mentryville, CA: Warner Brothers,1985), Motion Picture, 154 min.

2   Charles F. Stanley, "The Gift of Service" November 3. 2014. *In Touch Ministries: https://www.intouch.org/read/the-gift-of-service.*

3   Cecil B. DeMille, *The Ten Commandments*, (Hollywood, CA: Paramount Pictures, 1956), Motion Picture, 3h 40min.

4   "What is a Midwife" *About Midwives. Midwives Alliance North America: http://mana.org/about-midwives/what-is-a-midwife.*

5   Roswell Hitchcock, *Hitchcock's Dictionary of Bible Names*, Shirphah, *Bible Study Tools: https://www.biblestudytools.com/dictionaries/hitchcocks-bible-names/shiphrah.html.*

6   William Smith, *Smith's Bible Dictionary*, s.v. Puah, *Bible Study Tools, http://www.biblestudytools.com/dictionaries/smiths-bible-dictionary/puah.html.*

7   David Roach, "*ANALYSIS: Does Scripture address abortion?*" January 16, 2015. *Baptist Press: http://bpnews.net/44054/analysis-does-scripture-address-abortion.*

8   James Strong, *Strong's Exhaustive Concordance of the Bible*, (Iowa Falls: World Bible, 1986), s.v. "kill."

9   *Webster's New World Dictionary and Thesaurus*, 2nd ed., s.v. "murder."

10 *See* Genesis 4:11-15.

11 John Gill, "Exodus 1:19," *John Gill's Exposition of the Bible. Bible Study Tools: https://www.biblestudytools.com/commentaries/gills-exposition-of-the-bible/exodus-1-19.html.*

12 *See* Exodus 1:14.

13 *See* Joshua 2.

Chapter 13 Notes

1   *See* Mark 15:25 and Matthew 27:45. According to these verses, the crucifixion of Jesus started at 9:00 am and ended at 3:00 pm.

Afterword Notes

1   A. Nathaniel Hawthorne, *The Scarlet Letter*, 1850.

The Silent Women's Club

Silent Women's Club

Out of our love for you, our readers, our mothers, and our sisters, we created The Silent Women's Club. We know it's not easy to talk about your loss. Friends and family mean well, but they don't always know what to say to us, and they can't quite understand our struggles. On the other hand, finding mothers who share our experiences is challenging. You can't really walk up to a woman and ask, "Have you ever lost a child?" It's not a proper question.

So, we've created The Silent Women's Club. An online support group where mothers can read stories, share experiences, continue to study, and help each other to live and love again. Whether you stop by to read an inspirational message, share a comment, or request a personal Note Card with a message for a mom in need, at The Silent Women's Club, "our love speaks for us."

For more information and support, visit the Silent Women's Club at www.SilentWomensClub.com. While there, be sure to sign up for e-mail alerts to stay connected.

Colleen,

Be blessed
& Brave,

Kim
Upshaw

ABOUT THE AUTHOR

Kim Paris Upshaw

Kim lives in greater Philadelphia, Pennsylvania with her husband, Michael. Once weakened with the grief and shame of past choices, Kim desperately searched for answers and help after the loss of her children. During her quest for relief, she discovered great purpose from her pain. Passionately, Kim now shares how God's favor strengthens lives. After all, it restored hers! Using fresh perspectives on Biblical characters and stories, Kim inspires readers to live life more abundantly.

Although she's a lawyer from 9 to 5, Kim makes up for it as an author, gospel recording artist and songwriter the rest of the day. Through her words, lyrics, and voice, Kim motivates readers and listeners to courageously love better and live better.

CPSIA information can be obtained
at www.ICGtesting.com
Printed in the USA
BVHW03s1751050918
526585BV00011B/484/P

9 780999 268308